BADGES AND BATTLE HONOURS OF H.M. SHIPS

BADGES

AND

BATTLE HONOURS

OF H.M. SHIPS

———————•———————

Lt. Cdr. K. V. BURNS D.S.M., R.N.

MARITIME
BOOKS

First published 1986
Maritime Books, Lodge Hill,
Liskeard, Cornwall, U.K.

ISBN 0 907771 26 2

© *Maritime Books 1986*

Design by Evan Jones

Typeset and printed in Great Britain
by Penwell Ltd., Callington, Cornwall

Colour separations
by Peninsular Repro Service Ltd, Exeter, Devon.

Bound by R. Booth Bookbinder Ltd., Mabe,
Penryn, Cornwall.

ACKNOWLEDGEMENTS

The author was in touch with a large number of official organisations during the lengthy preparation of this book. Invaluable help was given by C. Boase Esq., (Secretary of the Ships' Name Committee): The staff of the Naval Historical Branch MOD: Naval History Library, City of Plymouth: Design Dept. H.M. Dockyard Devonport.

No doubt other individuals, unknown to the publishers after the author's death, were also of help in compiling this book. We are indeed grateful for their assistance.

PHOTOGRAPH ACKNOWLEDGEMENTS

The publishers would like to express their thanks to the following organisations and individuals for allowing photographs to be reproduced in this publication.

Ministry of Defence, Official Photographs
11, 20, 27, 32, 50, 54, 55, 56, 60, 63, 68, 69, 75, 76, 80, 83, 86, 89, 95, 97, 98, 99, 101, 117, 118, 122, 123, 128, 131, 132, 139, 147, 152, 162, 165, 166, 167, 168, 173, 177, 180, 185 (bottom), 187 (bottom), 197, 201, 206.

Imperial War Museum
22, 29, 37, 107, 138, 185 (top), 203, 204.

Vosper Thornycroft (U.K.) Ltd.
46, 77.

Cammel Laird Ltd.
28, 41, 111.

Maritime Photo Library
130, 187 (top).

S. Goodman Collection
30, 40, 78, 124, 136, 153, 163.

Scotts' (Shipbuilders), Greenock
62.

Wright & Logan
16, 31, 34, 38, 39, 51, 52, 91, 92, 94, 100, 106 (bottom), 108, 116, 119, 121, 133, 134, 135, 137, 141, 142, 144, 145, 146, 154, 161, 164, 171, 182, 189, 192, 195 (top & bottom), 200.

M. Lennon
85.

Robin Walker
93.

Gary Davies
104.

Cowes Branch Library & Maritime Museum
112.

RN Submarine Museum
170, 190, 191, 193, 198.

National Maritime Museum
106 (top).

It is with great regret that on publication of this book, we have to announce the death of its author—Lieutenant Commander K.V. Burns D.S.M., R.N.

As readers will appreciate, there are many years of research packed between the pages of this book. He was able to complete the manuscript just weeks before passing away. We trust you will agree the book is a fitting tribute to him.

We at Maritime Books have lost a fine editor—I have lost a good friend.

Publisher

We would like to record our thanks to Lt. Cdr. B. Warlow R.N., Sid Goodman, Messrs Wright & Logan, Bob Todd at the National Maritime Museum and Paul Kemp at the Imperial War Museum—all of whom stepped in at the last minute to help complete the book.

INTRODUCTION

Badges

The badge of the Royal Navy is the Naval Crown which consists of a circlet surmounted by four sterns of men-of-war (each with three poop lanterns) and four square sails each spread on a mast and yard, fully fitted and sheeted home; the ships and sails being positioned alternately. This badge, or the Royal Crown, is often displayed on the trucks of Ensign and Jack staffs. The whole of the crown is gold and the sails and pennants should on no account be painted white. The centre stone is a red ruby; the stones on either side are green emeralds; the stones at the extremities are blue sapphires; and the studs either side of the emeralds are white pearls.

When were individual badges first worn by HM Ships? The search for the answer to this question has occupied the minds of naval historians for many years. It is known when badges became official—1918—but they had appeared on naval vessels for many years previous to that date.

From earliest times ships carried decorative shields and banners, and later the most popular emblem of all—figureheads. Eventually though, the last named became so massive that their weight, placed high in the bows, made the ships nose-heavy and unwieldy to manoeuvre. Carvings in soft wood were tried but the savings in weight had little effect and the figures suffered in their ability to withstand the weather.

Early in the 19th century the rounded bow became the normal ship-building practice, a shape which did not lend itself to the incorporation of a figurehead. The Admiralty thereupon decreed that its use should be curtailed and the decorative bow, with elaborate scroll work—often surmounted by a crest or coat of arms—became fashionable. From 1860 this form of decoration became more rare and ships began using unofficial badges, usually on boats and often on note-paper.

The ideas of individual Commanders and their ships' companies resulted in many ingenious designs. If the Commander was of noble lineage his coat of arms formed the basis of the ship's badge, or if the ship was named after a character in mythology, then the appropriate classical figure was utilised. Town and County crests also played their part. Although the procedure of adopting badges assumed alarming proportions, no official notice was taken of this practice.

Towards the end of World War I—when the designs of badges were as varied as the large number of ships—the system came under Admiralty review. It was found that every ship sported a badge of some description—some simple, others elaborate and occasionally humorous.

However, the form of present ships' badges must be attributed to an army officer—one Major Charles ffoulkes, CB, OBE, once Master of the Tower Armouries and then Director of the Imperial War Museum. He became involved when the Commanding Officer of a new destroyer, HMS Tower, requested his assistance and advice with the design of a badge appropriate to his ship. The completed design, representing the White Tower, part of the Tower of London, set him on the way to making badges official.

Allocating suitable badges involved Major ffoulkes in an enormous amount of research, some of it based on a collection of crests from note-paper which he received in response to an advertisement. His offer to supply them was accepted by the Admiralty on 10 December, 1918, and a Ships' Badges Committee was set up with the Major appointed as the Admiralty Adviser on Heraldry.

When the designs were approved they were sent to Messrs. Martyns of Cheltenham, who produced the carvings. This work later passed to a Mr H. L. Maschek of Wembley, London, who once worked for Martyns but then, for 30 years, worked on his own. His carvings in yellow pine, when approved by the Committee, were sent to HM Dockyard, Chatham, for casting in brass. In more recent times though, they have been manufactured in epoxy resin and fibreglass.

Major ffoulkes, during his 17 years in the job, was credited with the designs of more than 550 badges. In 1935 his place was taken by a representative from the College of Arms, but the initial design remained—and still does—the responsibility of the Ships' Badges Committee. Every endeavour is made to select a design suitable for the name, tradition or association of the ship and each one is heraldically perfect.

Until 1976, design shapes varied according to the type of ship concerned. A circular ground was used for capital ships (battleships and battlecruisers); pentagonal for cruisers; shield for destroyers and submarines; and diamond for aircraft carriers, depot ships, etc. In 1976, the variation in the shape and size of badges came to an end when the Ministry of Defence standardised them as follows:-

a)   the shape of the frame for HM Ships, Submarines and RN Air Squadrons, is to be circular; for shore establishments, diamond; for RFA, RMAS/PAS vessels, pentagonal;

b) the size is to be 30 cms inside diameter of frame for circular badges and in proportion for diamond shaped and pentagonal badges, except for conventional submarines, where the inside diameter is to be 14 cms. Boats' and presentation badges are to be 12 cms inside diameter.

However, permission was granted for existing badges which had been approved and issued in shapes and/or sizes other than the above, to continue to be used. Where an existing badge is to be re-issued for use by a new ship, HM Dockyard, Devonport (which assumed the duties on the closure of HM Dockyard, Chatham), is instructed to amend the shape of the master carving and endorse the sealed pattern accordingly. No departure from the approved design as shown in this sealed pattern can be undertaken, nor any badge displayed by a ship or establishment, unless it is first approved by the Ships' Names and Badges Committee.

The present Committee meet about three times a year, and consists of representatives from the Naval Historical Branch, the Naval Staff, DGST(N), Naval Signals, and the Secretariat. Commodore Naval Ship Acceptance is the Chairman and the Admiralty Adviser on Heraldry also attends. Not all new ships inherit a badge from a previous ship of the same name and the new badges are designed by the Admiralty Adviser on Heraldry and approved by the Committee.

Mottoes

Only official mottoes have been included in the text.

Battle Honours

The award of Battle Honours to HM Ships is intended to foster 'esprit de corps' among their officers and ships' companies, who are thereby encouraged to take a personal interest in the war-time exploits not only of their present ship but also those of the same name which distinguished themselves in the past.

On 1 October, 1954, the Admiralty published an official list of Fleet Actions, Campaigns, etc., for which a Battle Honour was awarded. Before that date, Battle Honours had been displayed in ships solely on the authority of Commanding Officers. There had inevitably been a tendency to regard them in terms of general naval history and to include many actions and incidents which, meritorious in themselves, were not of sufficient importance to be ranked as Battle Honours.

Battle Honours are awarded for successful war service rather than as a record of service. Successful war service implies not only the actual sinking or capture of an enemy warship, but also the sinking of enemy merchant ships in escorted convoy; engagements with enemy light forces, when both sides often incurred losses; or operations which resulted in the more or less complete frustration of the enemy's intention at the time, although no warship may have been sunk.

In deciding which actions are to rank as Battle Honours, the Admiralty set out the following guidelines:-

A Battle Honour will be awarded for those actions which resulted in the defeat of the enemy, or when the action was inconclusive but well fought, and in exceptional cases where outstanding efforts were made against overwhelming odds. One will not be awarded for a British defeat, or when the action was inconclusive and badly fought.

Certain fleet action Battle Honours which had sometimes been displayed in the past, were now omitted from this official list, which, with recent additions, appears below.

ARMADA 1588	BARFLEUR 1692	LAKE CHAMPLAIN 1776
AZORES 1591	VIGO 1702	ST LUCIA 1778
CADIZ 1596	GIBRALTAR 1704	ST VINCENT 1780
DOVER 1652	VELEZ MALAGA 1704	CHESAPEAKE 1781
MONTECRISTO 1652	MARBELLA 1705	DOGGER BANK 1781
KENTISH KNOCK 1652	PASSERO 1718	USHANT 1781
PORTLAND 1653	PUERTO BELLO 1739	ST KITTS 1782
GABBARD 1653	FINISTERRE 1747	SADRAS 1782
SCHEVENINGEN 1653	USHANT 1747	THE SAINTS 1782
PORTO FARINA 1655	CAPE FRANCOIS 1757	PROVIDIEN 1782
SANTA CRUZ 1657	SADRAS 1758	NEGAPATAM 1782
LOWESTOFT 1665	LOUISBURG 1758	TRINCOMALEE 1782
FOUR DAYS' BATTLE 1666	NEGAPATAM 1758	MARTINIQUE 1794
ORFORDNESS 1666	LAGOS 1759	FIRST OF JUNE 1794
NORTH SEA 1667	PORTO NOVO 1759	GENOA 1795
BUGIA 1671	QUEBEC 1759	CORNWALLIS' RETREAT 1795
SOLE BAY 1672	QUIBERON BAY 1759	GROIX ISLAND 1795
SCHOONEVELD 1673	BELLE ILE 1761	CAPE OF GOOD HOPE 1795
TEXEL 1673	MARTINIQUE 1762	ST LUCIA 1796
SARDINIA 1681	HAVANA 1762	ST VINCENT 1797

CAMPERDOWN 1797	CRIMEA 1854-5	SFAX 1941
NILE 1798	CHINA 1856-60	GREECE 1941
DONEGAL 1798	LUCKNOW 1857-8	CRETE 1941
MINORCA 1798	AMORHA 1858	Bismarck 1941
ACRE 1799	NEW ZEALAND 1860-6	CAPE BON 1941
COPENHAGEN 1801	ABYSSINIA 1868	MALTA CONVOYS 1941-2
GUT OF GIBRALTAR 1801	ASHANTEE 1873-4	ARCTIC 1941-5
EGYPT 1801	ALEXANDRIA 1882	SIRTE 1942
CAPE TENEZ 1805	BENIN 1897	ST NAZAIRE 1942
TRAFALGAR 1805	SOUTH AFRICA 1899-1900	SUNDA STRAIT 1942
BAY OF BISCAY 1805	CHINA 1900	DIEGO SUAREZ 1942
CAPE OF GOOD HOPE 1806	HELIGOLAND 1914	CORAL SEA 1942
SAN DOMINGO 1806	FALKLAND ISLANDS 1914	SAVO ISLAND 1942
CURACOA 1807	CAMEROONS 1914	DIEPPE 1942
CAYENNE 1809	MESOPOTAMIA 1914-7	BARENTS SEA 1942
MARTINIQUE 1809	BELGIAN COAST 1914-8	GUADALCANAL 1942-3
BASQUE ROADS 1809	DOGGER BANK 1915	NORTH AFRICA 1942-3
GUADELOUPE 1810	SUEZ CANAL 1915	NEW GUINEA 1942-4
AMBOINA 1810	DARDANELLES 1915-6	MALAYA 1942-5
BANDA NEIRA 1810	JUTLAND 1916	PACIFIC 1942-5
TERNATE 1810	DOVER 1917	SICILY 1943
LISSA 1811	SCANDINAVIAN CONVOYS 1917	KULA GULF 1943
TAMATAVE 1811	ZEEBRUGGE 1918	SALERNO 1943
JAVA 1811	OSTEND 1918	NORTH CAPE 1943
PELAGOSA 1811	BELGIAN COAST 1914-8	AEGEAN 1943-4
GROIX ISLAND 1812	RIVER PLATE 1939	ADRIATIC 1944
BOSCALINE BAY 1813	ATLANTIC 1939-45	ANZIO 1944
SAN SEBASTIAN 1813	ENGLISH CHANNEL 1939-45	NORMANDY 1944
GLÜCKSTADT 1814	NORTH SEA 1939-45	SABANG 1944
CATTARO 1814	NARVIK 1940	SOUTH FRANCE 1944
ALGIERS 1816	DUNKIRK 1940	LEYTE GULF 1944
BURMA 1824-6	CALABRIA 1940	WALCHEREN 1944
NAVARINO 1827	SPADA 1940	BURMA 1944-5
ADEN 1839	TARANTO 1940	LINGAYEN GULF 1945
SYRIA 1840	SPARTIVENTO 1940	PALEMBANG 1945
CHINA 1841-2	LIBYA 1940-2	OKINAWA 1945
NEW ZEALAND 1845-7	NORWAY 1940-5	JAPAN 1945
KUA KAM 1849	BISCAY 1940-5	KOREA 1950-3
BURMA 1852-3	MEDITERRANEAN 1940-5	FALKLAND ISLANDS 1982
BALTIC 1854-5	MATAPAN 1941	

Single Ship and Boat Service actions

The more outstanding of these actions, when the enemy was of equal or superior force, were considered to be worthy of a Battle Honour and are usually shown by quoting the name of the ship captured, or sunk, with the year date.

Achille 1761	*Foudroyant* 1758	*Pégase* 1782
Admiral Hipper 1940	*Frederikscoarn* 1807	*Piémontaise* 1808
Admiral Jawl 1808	*Furieuse* 1809	*Pique* 1795
Admiral Scheer 1940	*Gamo* 1801	*President* 1815
Africaine 1801	*Gelderland* 1808	*Prévoyante* 1795
Aquilon 1757	*Gloire* 1795	*Proserpine* 1796
Argus 1813	*Golden Horse* 1681	*Psyche* 1805
Athalante 1804	*Guillaume Tell* 1800	*Raison* 1795
Auguste 1746	*Havik* 1810	*Raisonnable* 1758
Badere Zaffer 1808	*Hercule* 1798	*Résistance* 1797
Belle Poule 1806	*Hermione* 1799	*Réunion* 1793
Bellone 1759	*Hirondelle* 1799	*Révolutionnaire* 1794
Bonhomme Richard 1779	*Hokoku Maru* 1942	*Rivoli* 1812
Bouffonne 1761	*Immortalité* 1798	*Santa Dorotea* 1798
Cap Trafalgar 1914	*Königsberg* 1915	*Santa Monica* 1779
Cerbère 1800	*Kormoran* 1941	*Scharnhorst* 1940
Chesapeake 1813	*Leopard* 1917	*Sevolod* 1808
Chevrette 1801	*Lexington* 1777	*Sibylle* 1794
Cléopâtre 1793	*Ligurienne* 1800	*Sylphe* 1808
Clorinde 1814	*Lynx* 1807	*Takao* 1945
Constance 1797	*Magnanime* 1748	*Tamise* 1796
Courageux 1761	*Mahonesa* 1796	*The Seven Algerines* 1669
Curieux 1804	*Manly* 1809	*Thétis* 1808
Désirée 1800	*Marengo* 1806	*Tirpitz* 1943
Didon 1805	*Mercure* 1812	*Tourterelle* 1795
Droits de l'Homme 1797	*Minerve* 1795	*Tribune* 1796
Echo 1810	*Mutine* 1797	*Two Lions* 1681
Emden 1914	*Néréide* 1797	*Vengeance* 1800
Émeraude 1757	*Niémen* 1809	*Vestale* 1761
Essex 1814	*NS de Covadonga* 1743	*Virginie* 1796
Essex Junior 1814	*Oreste* 1810	*Weser* 1813
Étoile 1814	*Orphée* 1758	*Zefier* 1809
Forte 1799	*Pallas* 1779	

NILE   1798
ALGIERS   1816
CRIMEA   1854~5
KULA GULF   1943

ABDIEL

Designed as a Headquarters and Support Ship for Mine Countermeasure Forces and an Exercise Minelayer; 1,375 tons (standard); 1,500 tons (full load). Built by Thornycroft, Woolston, Southampton. Launched 27.1.1967. Carries 44 mines; 1 x 40mm gun.

Description of Badge

Field:- Green.
Badge:- A mine (NS) silver, winged gold, over two wavelets silver.

(Abdiel was one of the Archangels who remained faithful when Lucifer fell from heaven. *Paradise Lost*).

Motto

Semper Fidelis — Always faithful.

Battle Honours

Jutland	1916	Biscay	1941
Libya	1941	Sicily	1943
Crete	1941		

Previous ships of the name

1. Destroyer minelayer, 1,687 tons, 3 x 4" guns, 70 mines. Built by Cammell Laird, Birkenhead. Launched 12.10.1915. Distinguished herself at Battle of Jutland, laying a field of 80 mines in Horns Reef Channel through which the German Admiral Scheer's High Seas Fleet was to pass. 24.8.1920 Reduced to Reserve at the Nore. 14.9.1925 Paid off into Dockyard Control. 30.9.1926 Commissioned at Sheerness for the Atlantic Fleet. 25.1.1927 Again reduced to Reserve at the Nore. 7.1936 Sold to Rees, Llanelly for breaking up.

2. Minelayer, 2,650 tons, 6 x 4.7" guns, 160 mines. Built by J. S. White, Cowes. Launched 23.4.1940. Brilliant career in English Channel, Mediterranean and Far East. On day of announcement of Italian armistice, she was amongst the force intending to seize the important base at Taranto. While at anchor in the harbour, early on 10.9.1943, she detonated a magnetic mine, broke in two and sank. Suffered heavy casualties amongst the 400 troops on board. Six of her own officers and 42 ratings were killed. The ship's bell was recovered and this, and the bell from the first *Abdiel*, are carried in the present ship.

HMS *Abdiel*

ACHILLES

A Batch Three "Leander" class (broad-beamed) frigate, 2,500 tons (standard). Built by Yarrow, Scotstoun, Glasgow. Launched 21.11.1968. Sea Cat SAM System; A/S mortars; 2 x 4.5" and 2 x 20mm guns; 1 helicopter.

Description of Badge

Field:- Red.
Badge:- The head of Achilles helmeted, all gold.

(Achilles, the son of Peleus and Thetis, was a Greek chieftain in the Trojan War).

Motto

Fortiter in Re — Bravely in action.

Battle Honours

Belle Ile	1761	River Plate	1939
*Trafalgar	1805	Guadalcanal	1942-3
Leopard	1917	Okinawa	1945

*The Trafalgar battle honour was awarded to *Achille*.

Previous ships of the name

1. An 8 guns vessel, whose origin is unknown. Probably hired. 1744 On West Indies Station. 14.11.1745 Captured by 2 Spanish ships near Jamaica.

2. Fourth rate, 1,234 bm, 60 guns. Built by Barnard, Harwich. Launched 16.7.1757. 29.5.1758 With *Dorsetshire*, captured French *Raisonnable*, 64 guns. 1761 At capture of Belle Ile; carried home despatches. 1780 Reduced to a hulk. 1.6.1784 Sold out of the service.

3. French third rate, *Achille*, 1,801 bm, 78 guns. Captured by *Ramillies*, 1.6.1794, At Battle of the Glorious First of June. 2.1796 Broken up at Plymouth.

4. Third rate, 1,930 bm, 74 guns; sometimes called *Achille*. Built by Cleverley, Gravesend. Launched 16.4.1798. 1805 At Trafalgar. 1823 Rebuilt. 11.1865 Sold to Messrs Castle and Beech for breaking up.

5. Iron steam ship, 9,820 tons, 4 x 110 pdr and 16 x 100 pdr guns. Built in Chatham Dockyard. First iron warship built in a Royal Dockyard. Launched 23.12.1863. Stepped 4 masts, reduced to 3 in 1865. 1868 Re-armed with 22 x 7" and 4 x 8". 1874 Re-armed with 14 x 9" and 2 x 7" MLR guns. 1902 Became Base Ship at Malta and renamed *Hibernia*. 3.1904 Renamed *Egmont*. 1914-25 Base Ship at Chatham. 19.6.1916 *Egremont*; and 6.6.1919 *Pembroke*. 26.1.1923 Sold to Granton Shipbreaking Company.

6. "Warrior" Class Armoured Cruiser, 13,550 tons, 6 x 9.2" and 4 x 7.5" guns; 3 x 18" TT. Built by Armstrong, Elswick. Launched 17.6.1905. 1907 Home Fleet. 1908 In the Baltic. 1909 In Reserve. 1910-4 Home Fleet. 30.11.1914 Gun explosion on board. 16.3.1917 With *Dundee* sank German raider *Leopard* north of the Shetlands. 1917-8 North America and West Indies Station. 1918-9 Stokers' Training Ship. 9.5.1921 Sold to T. W. Ward, Briton Ferry.

7. "Leander" class cruiser, 7,030 tons, 8 x 6" and 4 x 4" AA guns; 8 x 21" TT. Built by Cammell Laird, Birkenhead. Launched 1.9.1932. 1936-43 Loaned to RNZN. 12.1939 With *Ajax* and *Exeter*, at Battle of River Plate. 1941 Convoy escort in South Pacific and around New Zealand. 1942 Served with distinction at Guadalcanal. 4.1.1943 Bomb hit, and exploded, on 'X' turret. 22.3.1943 Arrived Portsmouth for long refit. Completion was delayed by an explosion in an empty fuel tank which killed several Dockyard staff. 23.5.1944 Re-commissioned but delayed by machinery defects. 16.8.1944 To Mediterranean. 22.11.1944 Part of British Pacific Fleet on its formation. 1945 At Okinawa. 6.10.1945 Arrived Tokyo to relieve *Gambia* as guardship. 10.9.1946 Arrived Sheerness for refit. 5.7.1948 Sold to the Royal Indian Navy; renamed *Delhi*. 1958 Refitted for use as a Training Ship. 5.1978 Deleted.

Footnote

a) French 64 guns *Achille* was captured by *Thunderer* off Cadiz, 17.7.1761.
b) Storeship *Achille* 420 bm, 14 guns. Purchased 1781. 8.1.1784 Sold out of the service.
c) Trawler *Achille II* was hired in 1914. Sunk 26.6.1918 by mine off the Shipwash.

ACTIVE

A Type 21 "Amazon" class General Purpose frigate, 2,750 tons (standard), 3,250 tons (full load). Built by Vosper Thornycroft, Woolston, Southampton. Launched 23.11.1972. Exocet SSM and Sea Cat SAM systems; 6 TT; helicopter launched torpedoes; 1 x 4.5"; 4 x 20mm Oerlikons; 1 helicopter.

Description of Badge
Field:- Blue.
Badge:- A chamois saliant gold.

Motto
Festina lente — Hasten slowly.

Battle Honours

Lagos	1759	Jutland	1916
Trincomalee	1782	Atlantic	1939-44
Camperdown	1797	*Bismarck*	1941
Egypt	1801	Diego Suarez	1942
Lissa	1811	Arctic	1944
Pelagosa	1811	Falkland Islands	1982
Ashantee	1873-4		

Previous ships of the name

1. Sixth rate, 594 bm, 28 guns. Built by Stanton, Deptford. Launched 11.1.1758. 1767-77 Laid up at Plymouth. 1.8.1778 Captured off San Domingo by the French.

2. Brig-sloop, 109 bm, 14 guns. Purchased in 1776. 1780 Captured by the Americans off New York.

3. Cutter, 12 guns. In service 1779. 18.8.1779 Captured by the French cutter *Le Mutin* in the Channel.

4. Fifth rate, 697 bm, 32 guns. Built by Raymond, Northam. Launched 30.8.1780. 7.1796 Wrecked in the St Lawrence river.

5. Brig-sloop, 14 guns. In service in 1782.

6. Fifth rate, 1,058 bm, 38 guns. Built in Chatham Dockyard. Launched 14.12.1799. 2.1826 Reduced to Harbour Service at Plymouth. 15.11.1833 Renamed *Argo*. 10.1860 Broken up at Plymouth.

7. Fifth rate, 1,627 bm, 36 guns. Originally ordered from Pembroke Dock but built in Chatham Dockyard. Launched 19.7.1845. Never commissioned. 30.7.1867 Renamed *Tyne* for RNR Drill Ship. 18.11.1867 Renamed *Durham*. 12.5.1908 Sold out of the service.

8. Iron steam corvette, 3,980 tons, 18 x 64 pdrs. Built on the Thames at Blackwall. Launched 13.3.1869. Served with distinction during the Colonial Wars of the latter part of the 19th century. 10.7.1906 Sold out of the service.

9. Name ship of class of Scout cruisers, 3,360 tons, 10 x 4" and 4 x 3 pdr guns; 2 x 21" TT. Built at Pembroke Dock. Launched 14.3.1911. 1911-4 2nd DF, Home Fleet. 1914-5 At Harwich. 1915 Grand Fleet. 1915-6 Refit. 31.5.1916 Battle of Jutland. 1916-7 4th DF, Portsmouth. 1917-8 Queenstown Patrol Flotilla. 1918 Atlantic Patrols. 21.4.1920 Sold out of the service.

10. "Acasta" class destroyer, 1,350 tons; 4 x 4.7" guns; 8 x 21" TT. Built by Hawthorn Leslie, Hebburn-on-Tyne. Launched 9.7.1929. 1941 *Bismarck* action. 8.5.1942 With *Panther*, sank French submarine *Monge*. 23.5.1943 With *Ness*, sank Italian submarine *Leonardo da Vinci*. 1.11.1943 With other ships sank *U 340* off Tangiers. 1.1947 Ship Target Trials in Loch Striven. 20.5.1947 Arrived Troon to be broken up by West of Scotland Shipbreaking Company.

Footnote
a) Other ships named *Active* were 3 small Cutters hired for service 1794-1803; 1803-14; and 1804-8; and a Tug hired for Harbour Service 1915-8.
b) *Active II* was a drifter hired 1915-9.
c) *Active III* another drifter hired in 1915 and sunk by a mine off Milford Haven 15.10.1917.
d) *Active IV* was a trawler hired 1916-8.

AJAX

A Batch One "Leander" class frigate, ex-*Fowey*, 2,450 tons (standard). Built by Cammell Laird, Birkenhead. Launched 16.8.1962. 1970-3 Ikara conversion at Devonport. New armament:-Ikara A/S missiles (forward); Sea Cat SAM System; 2 x 40mm guns; Limbo A/S mortars (aft); 1 helicopter. 1985, Static Training ship for HMS Raleigh trainees on the River Tamar.

Description of Badge

Field:- Black.
Badge:- A Greek helmet gold, crested red.

(The name is derived from Greek mythology. There were two Chieftains of the name—Ajax the Greater, son of Telamon, and Ajax the Lesser, son of Oileus, King of Locris).

Motto

Nec quisquam nisi Ajax — No one but Ajax can overcome Ajax.

Battle Honours

St Vincent	1780	Mediterranean	1940-1
St Kitts	1782	Malta Convoys	1941
The Saints	1782	Matapan	1941
Egypt	1801	Greece	1941
Trafalgar	1805	Crete	1941
San Sebastian	1813	Aegean	1944
Baltic	1854-5	Normandy	1944
Jutland	1916	South France	1944
River Plate	1939		

Previous ships of the name

1. Third rate, 1,615 bm, 74 guns. Built in Portsmouth Dockyard. Launched 23.12.1767. 10.2.1785 Sold out of the service.

2. Third rate, 1,953 bm, 74 guns. Built by Randall, Rotherhithe. Launched 3.3.1798. 14.2.1807 Caught fire; burned all night; drifted onto the Island of Tenedos and blew up at 5 o'clock the next morning.

3. Third rate, 1,761 bm, 74 guns. Built by Perry, Blackwall. Launched 2.5.1809. 1846 Undocked as a steam ship. 1860 Became a Blockship (C9). 1864-5 Broken up.

4. Third rate, "Vanguard", 2,609 bm, 78 guns. Built at Pembroke Dock. Launched 25.8.1835. Not commissioned after 1850. Lay at Devonport until 1859 then at Sheerness. 20.10.1867 Renamed *Ajax*. 6.1875 Broken up at Chatham.

5. Turret ship, 8,660 tons, 4 x 12.5" and 2 x 6" guns. Built at Pembroke Dock. Launched 10.3.1880. With *Agamemnon* were the last RN capital ships fitted with muzzle-loading main armament. 1887 Collided with *Devastation* off Portland. 3.1904 Sold to Castle on the Thames for breaking up.

6. "King George V" class battleship, 23,000 tons, 10 x 13.5" and 16 x 4" guns. Built by Scotts, Greenock. Launched 21.3.1912. 1916 At Jutland. 1919-24 In the Mediterranean. 1924-6 Nore Reserve. 11.1926 Sold to Alloa Shipbreaking Company.

7. "Leander" class cruiser, 6,985 tons, 8 x 6" and 8 x 4" guns; 8 x 21" TT. Built by Vickers Armstrong, Barrow. Launched 1.3.1934. 1935-8 South American Division but in 6.1935 was in the Mediterranean for Abyssinian crisis. 12.1939 With *Achilles* and *Exeter* in Battle of River Plate. 1940 Repaired at Chatham. 3.1941 Battle of Matapan. 1.1.1943 Hit by bomb from a Ju 87 during air attack on Bone Harbour. 2.1.1943 Again hit by a bomb. Towed to Gibraltar for temporary repairs; then to Norfolk, Virginia, USA. 6.1944 Normandy landings. 19.10.1944 German garrison of Island of Santorin, north of Crete, surrendered to *Ajax*. 1946-8 In the Mediterranean. 2.1948 Reduced to Reserve at Chatham; afterwards laid up in River Fal. 3.1949 Proposed sale to Chile cancelled. 18.11.1949 Arrived Newport to be broken up by J. Cashmore.

Footnote
Drifter *Ajax II*, 81 tons, built in 1909, was hired in 1914. 27.10.1916 Sunk by German torpedo boats in North Sea.

ALACRITY

A Type 21 "Amazon" class, General Purpose frigate, 2,750 tons (standard), 3,250 tons (full load). Built by Yarrow, Scotstoun, Glasgow. Launched 18.9.1974. Exocet SSM and Sea Cat SAM systems; 6 TT; helicopter launched torpedoes; 1 x 4.5"; and 4 x 20mm Oerlikons; 1 helicopter.

Description of Badge

Field:- Silver.
Badge:- A heart red, winged gold.

(Alacrity is defined as "cheerful readiness").

Motto

Adjuvare propero — I hasten to help.

Battle Honours

China	1900	Falkland Islands	1982
Korea	1950-52		

Previous ships of the name

1. "Cruizer" class brig-sloop, 384 bm, 18 guns. Built at Newcastle. Launched 13.11.1806. 26.5.1811 Captured off Corsica by the French *Abeille*. In French service until 1822.

2. "Cherokee" class brig-sloop, 236 bm, 10 guns. Built in Deptford Dockyard. Launched 29.12.1818. 1826 Destroyed 3 Greek pirate ships off Psara. 28.8.1835 Sold out of the service.

3. "Vigilant" class wood steam gun vessel, 675 bm, 1 x 110 pdr, 1 x 68 pdr, and 2 x 20 pdr guns. Built by Mare, Blackwall. Launched 20.3.1856. 7.10.1864 Sold for breaking up by Castle on the Thames.

4. Despatch vessel, 1,700 tons, 4 x 5" guns. Built by Palmer, Jarrow-on-Tyne. Launched 28.2.1885. Took part in Third China War. 9.1913 Sold at Hong Kong.

5. Despatch vessel *Surprise*, 1,650 tons, 4 x 5" guns. Built by Palmer, Jarrow-on-Tyne. Launched 17.1.1885. 22.6.1886 Commissioned at Portsmouth for China. Served as C in C's yacht. Took part in Boxer Wars of 1900. Recommissioned at Hong Kong, about every three years until 1906. 28.9.1908 Recommissioned at Shanghai. 8.10.1910 Recommissioned at Hong Kong. 1.3.1913 Recommissioned at Chatham. 1913 Renamed *Alacrity*. Paid off in 1915. No further war service. 1919 Sold out of the service.

6. Yacht *Margarita*; renamed *Semiramis*; sold to a Russian Princess who renamed her *Mlada*. 1918 Taken over by the Admiralty. 7.8.1919 Commissioned at Devonport. 1919-22 In China as HMS *Alacrity*, afterwards handed back to her original owners.

7. Modified "Black Swan" class anti-aircraft sloop, 1,350 tons; 6 x 4" and 10 x 20mm guns. Built by Wm Denny, Dumbarton. Launched 1.9.1944. 4.1945 to 1952 Third Frigate Flotilla, Far East. Saw much action during Korean War. 1952 Reduced to Reserve at Portsmouth. 1953-6 Reserve at Lisahally, Londonderry. 15.9.1956 Arrived Dalmuir to be broken up by W. H. Arnott Young. 3.11.1956 Hull arrived Troon to complete breaking up.

Footnote

Ex-*Ethel*, 85 bm, 1 x 12 pdr gun. Purchased at Sydney 4.11.1872. 1882 Sold at Sydney.

ALDERNEY

An "Island" class Offshore Patrol Vessel, 925 tons (standard), 1,260 tons (full load). Built by Hall Russell, Aberdeen. Launched 27.2.1979. 1 x 40mm gun. Able to carry a small RM Detachment.

Description of Badge

Field:- Green.
Badge:- A lion rampant gold, holding in his dexter fore paw a sprig of oak, proper, and crowned with a Royal Crown, red.

Motto

Battle Honours

None.

Previous ships of the name

1. Bomb, 263 bm, 8 guns. Built in Woolwich Dockyard. Launched 29.3.1735. 2.1741 Reduced to a hulk at Jamaica.

2. Sixth rate, 504 bm, 24 guns. Laid down as *Squirrel* by Reed, Hull. 11.2.1742 Renamed *Alderney*. Launched 18.3.1743. 26.6.1749 Sold out of the service.

3. Sloop, 235 bm, 12 guns. Built by J. Snook, Saltash, Cornwall. Launched 5.2.1757. 1758 Employed on cruising and convoy duties. 1759 Blockade of the port of Dunkirk. 1761 At capture of Belle Ile. 1762 Off Madagascar. 1764-7 In Ordinary. 1.5.1783 Sold at Deptford.

4. "A" class submarine, 1,120 tons (surface), 1,620 tons (submerged), 1 x 4" guns; 10 x 21" TT. Built by Vickers Armstrong, Barrow. Launched 25.6.1945. Designed for service in the Far East theatre of war but the war ended before she became available. 8.1972 Arrived Cairn Ryan to be broken up by Shipbreaking (Queensborough) Ltd.

HMS *Alderney* (July 1950).

AMAZON

Name ship of the class of Type 21 General Purpose frigates, 2,750 tons (standard) 3,250 tons (full load). Built by Vosper Thornycroft, Woolston, Southampton. Launched 26.4.1971. Exocet SSM and Sea Cat SAM systems; 6 TT; helicopter launched torpedoes; 1 x 4.5"; 4 x 20mm Oerlikons; 1 helicopter.

Description of Badge

Field:- Red.

Badge:- An Amazon's head gold.

(In Greek mythology the Amazons were a fierce tribe of female warriors. No men were permitted to live among them but once a year, in order to propagate their race, the Amazons visited a neighbouring tribe. However, all male children were quickly banished or killed.

The name Amazon was probably derived from the Greek word "A-mazos", meaning "breastless". It is said that the Amazon women removed their right breast for greater ease in using their hunting bows).

Motto

Audaciter — Boldly.

Battle Honours

Martinique	1762	Atlantic	1939-43
Droits de l'Homme	1797	Norway	1940
Copenhagen	1801	Arctic	1942
Belle Poule	1806	Malta Convoys	1942
Belgian Coast	1914-6	North Africa	1942-3

Previous ships of the name

1. French sixth rate *Panthere*, 471 bm, 26 guns. Captured in 1745 by *Monmouth* in the Channel. Took part in attack on Martinique and capture of Guadaloupe. 6.10.1763 Sold out of the service.

2. Fifth rate, 687 bm, 32 guns. Built by Wells, Rotherhithe. Launched 24.5.1773. 6.1794 Broken up at Plymouth.

3. Fifth rate, 934 bm, 36 guns. Built by Wells, Rotherhithe. Launched 4.7.1795. 14.1.1797 Wrecked on Ile de Bas, French coast, during action with French *Droits de l'Homme*.

4. Fifth rate, 1,038 bm, 38 guns. Built in Woolwich Dockyard. Launched 18.5.1799. Distinguished herself at Battle of Copenhagen in 1801. 5.1817 Broken up at Plymouth.

5. Fifth rate, 1,078 bm, 46 guns. Built in Deptford Dockyard. Launched 15.8.1821. Engaged in suppression of Chinese piracy. 12.1844 Reduced to sixth rate, 24 guns. 9.1863 Sold to Lethbridge for breaking up at Plymouth.

6. "Vestal" class wood steam sloop, 1,040 bm, 2 x 6" and 2 x 64 pdrs guns. Built at Pembroke Dock. Launched 23.5.1865. 10.7.1866 On passage from Spithead to Halifax, Nova Scotia, was in collision with SS *Osprey* in the Channel near Torquay. She was cut in two and sank within a few minutes.

7. Destroyer, 970 tons, 2 x 4" guns; 2 TT. Built by Thornycroft, Woolston, Southampton. Launched 29.7.1908. 1909-12 1st Destroyer Flotilla, Home Fleet. 1913 4th DF, then 3rd DF. In WW1, served in the Channel from Dover. Saw action off coast of Belgium. 22.10.1919 Sold to T. W. Ward, Preston, for breaking up.

8. Destroyer, 1,352 tons, 4 x 4.7" guns; 6 x 21" TT. Built by Thornycroft, Woolston, Southampton. Named 18.1.1926 but owing to bad weather was not launched until 27.1.1926. 29.4.1940 With *Witherington* sank *U 50* north of Shetlands. 4.1942 Damaged in action, Russian convoy 'QP II'. 8.1942 Operation 'Pedestal'. 10.1942 Operation 'Torch'. 8.1944 Flying Target Trials ship at Rosyth. 1947 Damage Control tests. 25.10.1948 Sold to Arnott Young. 4.1949 Arrived Troon to be broken up by West of Scotland Shipbreaking Co.

AMBUSCADE

A Type 21 ''Amazon'' class General Purpose frigate, 2,750 tons (standard), 3,250 tons (full load). Built by Yarrow, Scotstoun, Glasgow. Launched 18.1.1973. Exocet SSM and Sea Cat SAM systems; 6 TT; helicopter-launched torpedoes; 1 x 4.5″; 4 x 20mm Oerlikons; 1 helicopter.

Description of Badge

Field:- Black.
Badge:- A blunderbus, red, with barrel and mounts, gold.

Motto

Tempori insidior — I bide my time.

Battle Honours

Finisterre	1747	Atlantic	1940-4
Lagos	1759	Arctic	1942
Jutland	1916	Falkland Islands	1982

Previous ships of the name

1. French fifth rate *Embuscade*, 740 bm, 40 guns. Captured 21.4.1746. Following year was in action off Finisterre under Admiral Anson. 1759 Off Lagos with Admiral Boscawen. 9.2.1762 Sold out of the service.

2. Fifth rate, 684 bm, 32 guns. Built by H. Adams, Deptford. Launched 17.9.1773. 14.12.1798 Captured by the French *Bayonnaise* in Bay of Biscay. 28.5.1803 Recaptured as *Embuscade*. 6.1810 Broken up at Deptford.

3. French fifth rate *Embuscade*, 906 bm, 40 guns. Captured 12.10.1798 off the Donegal coast. 16.1.1804 Renamed *Seine*. 8.1813 Broken up.

4. French fifth rate *Pomone*, 1,085 bm, 38 guns. Captured 29.11.1811 by *Active* and *Alceste*. 11.1812 Broken up at Woolwich.

5. Destroyer, 935 tons, 3 x 4″ guns; 2 TT. Built by J. Brown, Clydebank. Launched 25.1.1913. In WW1 saw action at Jutland; against the German raid on Scarborough; Dover Patrol; and in the Humber Squadron. 6.9.1921 Sold to Petersen and Albeck.

6. Destroyer, 1,170 tons, 4 x 4.7″ guns; 6 x 21″ TT. Built by Yarrow, Scotstoun, Glasgow. Launched 15.1.1926. 10.1928 In 4th Destroyer Flotilla in Mediterranean. 1933-9 Attached to HMS *Vernon*. 6.1940 Off north coast of France supporting the withdrawal of 51st Highland Division. Damaged by a German field battery. 1941-3 Iceland and Greenock. 1943-4 Fleet Air Arm target ship based at Greenock. 1944-5 A/S Training ship, also based at Greenock. 1.1946 Shock trials in Loch Striven. 23.11.1946 Sold, and broken up at Troon by West of Scotland Shipbreaking Company.

Footnote
Fifth rate, 1,285 bm, 36 guns, was laid down in Woolwich Dockyard as *Ambuscade* on 15.4.1830 but was renamed *Amphion* before her launching in 1831.

ANDROMEDA

A Batch Three "Leander" class (broad-beamed) frigate; 2,500 tons (standard). Built in Portsmouth Dockyard. Launched 24.5.1967. 1977-80 Exocet conversion at Devonport. New armament:- Exocet SSM and Sea Wolf SAM systems; A/S torpedo tubes; 2 x 20mm guns; 1 helicopter.

Description of Badge

Field:- Blue.

Badge:- A six-pointed star above six bars wavy barry, three argent, three azure. Sinister, a rock from which hangs a broken chain or.

(In Greek mythology, Andromeda was the daughter of Capheus, King of Ethiopia, who was forced by tradition to chain her to a rock as a sacrifice to a sea monster, a fate from which she was saved at the last minute by Perseus. As a reward, she jilted her fiance and married Perseus. When she died Perseus turned her into a brilliant star in the heavens).

Motto

Unfettered.

Battle Honours

St Vincent   1780   Falkland Islands   1982

Previous ships of the name

1. Sixth rate, 609 bm, 28 guns. Built by Fabian, East Cowes. Launched 18.11.1777. 1778 Took part in the indecisive action off Ushant. 11.10.1780 Lost, with all hands, in a hurricane off Martinique in the West Indies.

2. Fifth rate, 721 bm, 32 guns. Built by Sutton, Liverpool. Launched 21.4.1784. 1796 With *Ranger* and *Kite*, captured in Firth of Forth, the Dutch frigate, 36 guns, *Zefir*. 1808 Reduced to Harbour Service. 1811 Broken up.

3. American sixth rate, *Hannibal*, 812 bm, 24 guns. Captured in 1812. 18.4.1816 Sold out of the service.

4. Fifth rate, 1,215 bm, 46 guns. Built in Bombay Dockyard. Launched 6.1.1829. 24.12.1863 Sold to Barnett and Wake.

5. Cruiser, 11,000 tons, 16 x 6" guns. Built at Pembroke Dock. Launched 30.4.1897. Saw service in the Mediterranean and Indian Ocean and on the China Station. 23.9.1913 Renamed *Powerful II*, Training ship; 11.1919 *Impregnable II*; 20.1.1931 *Defiance*. 14.8.1956 Arrived Burgt in Belgium to be broken up.

Footnote

a) Sixth rate was laid down in Deptford Dockyard but was renamed *Nimrod* 10.5.1827 before launching 26.8.1828. The Admiralty had received news of the fifth rate being built at Bombay, so changed the Deptford ship's name.
b) Trawler, 149 tons, built in 1898, was hired 1917-9.
c) Tug, 134 tons, built in 1933, was in service from 1942-5.
d) Tug, 658 tons, built in 1910, was requisitioned in 1941 for minesweeping duties. 18.4.1942 Sunk by air attack at Malta.

ANGLESEY

An "Island" class Offshore Patrol Vessel, 925 tons (standard), 1,260 tons (full load). Built by Hall Russell, Aberdeen. Launched 18.10.1978. 1 x 40mm gun. Able to carry a small RM Detachment.

Description of Badge

Field:- White.
Badge:- A demi-heraldic tiger sable and tufted argent, supporting a branch of oak, flexed over the head, leaved and fructed proper.

Motto

Battle Honours

None.

Previous ships of the name

1. Fourth rate *Anglesea*, 620 bm, 44 guns. Built in private yard at Plymouth but probably by Dockyard labour. Added to the Navy 17.4.1694. 10.1694 Took the privateer *St Louis*, 38 guns, after an hour's action. 6.1697 With *Plymouth* brought in to Kinsale, the French 18 guns privateer *Gaillarde*. After a commission in the West Indies, Admiralty Order dated 30.6.1719 directed she be reduced to a Fifth rate. Taken to pieces at Chatham in 1720; rebuilt and launched 19.5.1725. 8.1741 Surveyed at Woolwich; needed great repair. Employed as a hulk. 31.5.1742 Sailed from Woolwich to be sunk as a breakwater at Sheerness.

2. Fifth rate, 711 bm, 44 guns. Built by Blaydes, Hull, in 1742. 28.3.1745 Captured by the French *Apollon*. In their service until 1753.

3. Fifth rate, 714 bm, 44 guns. Built by Gorrill and Parks, Liverpool. Launched 3.12.1746. 1759 Became a storeship. 8.1764 Sunk as a breakwater in Mount's Cove.

HMS *Anglesey*

APOLLO

A Batch Three "Leander" class (broad-beamed) frigate; 2,500 tons (standard). Built by Yarrow, Scotstoun, Glasgow. Launched 15.10.1970. Sea Cat SAM system; A/S mortars; 2 x 4.5" and 2 x 20mm guns; 1 helicopter.

Description of Badge

Field:- Blue.
Badge:- A sun in splendour, gold.

(Derived from Greek mythology, in which the sun is represented by Apollo, one of the principal Gods of the Greek Pantheon. The source of inspiration, art, poetry and medicine).

Motto

Fortis et benignus — Strong and kindly

Battle Honours

St Vincent	1780	Crimea	1854
China	1842	Normandy	1944

Previous ships of the name

1. French storeship *Apollon*, 744 bm, 20 guns. Captured by Lord Anson off Finisterre on 3.5.1747. Served briefly as Hospital Ship in the East Indies. 12.4.1749 Wrecked in a hurricane off Madras.

2. Fifth rate, 679 bm, 32 guns. Built by Blaydes and T. Hodgson, Hull. Launched 24.10.1763 as *Glory*. 30.8.1774 Renamed *Apollo* 31.1.1779 Captured French 32 guns *Oiseau*. 1.1786 Broken up at Woolwich.

3. Fifth rate, 984 bm, 38 guns. Built by Perry and Sons, Blackwall. Launched 18.3.1794. 7.1.1799 Wrecked on Haak Sands on Dutch coast.

4. Fifth rate, 956 bm, 36 guns. Built by Dudman, Deptford. Launched 16.8.1799. 2.4.1804 Wrecked on coast of Portugal whilst escorting an outward bound convoy.

5. Fifth rate, 1,086 bm, 28 guns. Built by Parsons, Bursledon. Launched 27.6.1805. 1822-30 Used as a Royal Yacht. 1838 Converted to Troopship. 1839-42 China Station. 1853 Converted to Storeship. 1854 Served in Black Sea. 9.1856 Broken up at Portsmouth.

6. Name ship of class of cruiser, 3,400 tons, 2 x 6" and 6 x 4.7" guns. Built in Chatham Dockyard. Launched 10.2.1891. 1892-9 Not in commission, but took part in annual manoeuvres. 1901-5 RNR Drillship at Southampton. 1905-8 Laid up at Portsmouth. 1908 Fitted for service as Minelayer. Outbreak of WW1 was acting as Home Fleet Minelayer based at Dover. 1917 Depot Ship for 4th Flotilla at Devonport. 8.1920 Arrived S. Castle, Plymouth, to be broken up.

7. *Amphion*, modified "Leander" class cruiser, 7,105 tons, 8 x 6" and 8 x 4" guns. Built in Devonport Dockyard. Launched 9.10.1934. 1936-8 America and West Indies Station. 29.9.1938 Transferred and commissioned into RAN as *Hobart*. 1942 Heavily bombed in Malayan waters; slightly damaged. 20.7.1943 Torpedoed by Japanese submarine; considerable damage. 31.8.1945 In Tokyo Bay for Japanese surrender. 8.1947 Reserve at Sydney. 1953 Conversion to Training Ship commenced, but abandoned in 1956. 22.2.1962 Sold to Mitsui and Company. 3.3.1962 Left Sydney for Japan to be broken up. 2.4.1962 Arrived Miyachi Shipyard, Saki, Osaka, Japan.

8. Fast minelayer, 2,650 tons; 4 x 4" guns; 160 mines. Built by Hawthorn Leslie, Hebburn-on-Tyne. Launched 5.4.1943. 1944 Laid mines to protect Normandy beachhead. 7.6.1944 Ran aground off Normandy. Post-war served in Pacific, Mediterranean and West Indies. 1951-61 Served as Despatch Vessel, frequently wearing the flag of C in C. 28.11.1962 Arrived Blyth to be broken up by Hughes Bolckow.

ARCHER

Coastal Training Craft of 43 tons, for the RNR. Built of GRP by Watercraft Ltd., Shoreham-by-Sea. Launched 25.6.1985. Delivered 9.8.1985. Allocated to Tay Division, RNR, at Dundee.

Description of Badge

Field:- White.
Badge:- A demi archer to the sinister, clad in green, and drawing a bow, proper.

Motto

Battle Honours

Baltic	1854-5	Atlantic	1943-4
Heligoland	1914	Biscay	1943

Previous ships of the name

1. Gun-brig, 179 bm, 12 guns. Built by Perry, Blackwall. Launched 2.4.1801. 14.12.1815 Sold out of the service.

2. Wood steam sloop, 973 bm, 2 x 68 pdr and 12 x 32 pdr guns. Built in Deptford Dockyard. Launched 27.3.1849. 15.3.1866 Arrived Castle's at Charlton to be broken up.

3. Torpedo cruiser, 1,630 tons, 6 x 6" guns, 8 TT. Built by J. & G. Thomson, Glasgow. Launched 23.12.1885. 1889-91 Cape of Good Hope and West Coast of Africa. 1892 To China Station. 1900-4 Australian Station. 4.4.1905 Sold to Forrester, Swansea.

4. Destroyer, 775 tons, 2 x 4" and 2 x 12 pdr guns; 2 TT. Built by Yarrow, Scotstoun, Glasgow. Launched 21.10.1911. 1914-6 With the Grand Fleet. 10.1916 to 8.1917 At Devonport. 9.1917 to end of War, in Mediterranean. 9.5.1921 Sold to T. W. Ward, Rainham, for breaking up.

5. Escort Carrier, 9,000 tons, 3 x 4" guns; 15 aircraft. Ex-mercantile *Mormacland*. Built by Sun S.B. & D.D. Co., Chester, Pennsylvania, USA. Launched 14.12.1939. Acquired by USN 6.3.1941. Hull converted by Newport News S.B. & D.D. Co., Va. 17.11.1941 Transferred to RN on Lend-Lease. First of the 39 Escort Carriers which US shipyards provided for the RN. Employed on convoy escort duties. 23.5.1943 A rocket-equipped Swordfish from *Archer* sank *U 752*, 750 miles west of Ireland. 1945 To Ministry of War Transport as *Empire Lagan*. 8.1.1946 Returned to USN. 30.8.1947 Sold as *Anna Salen*; 1955 *Tasmania*; 1961 *Union Reliance*. 7.11.1961 In collision with the Norwegian ship *Berean* in Houston Ship Channel. 3.1962 Broken up at New Orleans.

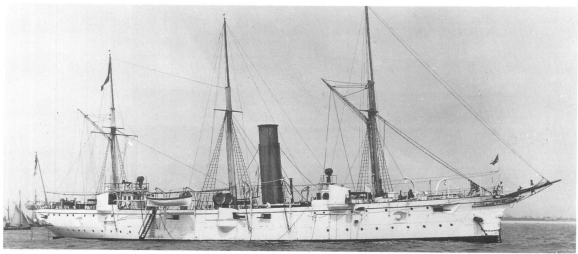

HMS Archer

22

ARETHUSA

A Batch One "Leander" class frigate, 2,450 tons (standard). Built by J. S. White, Cowes. Launched 5.11.1963. 1974-7 Ikara conversion at Portsmouth. New armament:- Ikara A/S missile (forward); Sea Cat SAM system; Limbo A/S mortars (aft); 2 x 40mm guns; 1 helicopter.

Description of Badge

Field:- Green.
Badge:- A crescent moon gold, over wavelets, silver and blue.

Motto

Celeriter audax — Swiftly daring.

Battle Honours

Ushant	1781	Dogger Bank	1915
St Lucia	1796	Norway	1940-1
Curacoa	1807	Malta Convoy	1941-2
Crimea	1854	Normandy	1944
Heligoland	1914		

Previous ships of the name

1. French fifth rate *Arethuse*, 700 bm, 32 guns. Captured by *Venus*, 36 guns, on 18.5.1759. Renamed *Arethusa*. Later fought famous action with French frigate *Belle Poule* after which the ballad of the "Saucy Arethusa" was composed. 19.3.1779 Wrecked on Molene Island near Ushant.

2. Fifth rate, 948 bm, 38 guns. Built by J. H. Hillhouse, Bristol. Launched 10.4.1781. Played active part in Second Napoleonic War. 5.1814 Broken up at Sheerness.

3. French fifth rate, 1,064 bm, 38 guns. Captured at Toulon on 29.8.1793. 1795 Renamed *Undaunted*. 27.8.1796 Wrecked on Morant Keys in the West Indies.

4. Fifth rate, 1,085 bm, 46 guns. Built at Pembroke Dock. Launched 29.7.1817. 6.1836 Reduced to Harbour Service. Allocated as Lazaretto at Liverpool. 12.3.1844 Renamed *Bacchus*. 8.1883 Broken up by Castle on the Thames.

5. Fourth rate, 2,132 bm, 50 guns. Built at Pembroke Dock. Launched 20.6.1849. Saw action in Crimea. Her seamen went ashore and fought at Battle of Inkerman. Was the last sailing vessel to go into action under sail alone. 9.8.1861 Undocked after conversion to steam. 1874 Converted to Boys' Training Ship in the Thames at Greenhithe. 1934 Broken up by Castle on the Thames.

6. Cruiser, 4,300 tons, 10 x 6" guns. Built by Napier, Dalmuir. Launched 23.12.1882. 1893-6 Mediterranean Station. Experimented with new explosive, Lyddite. 1900 On China Station; her seamen fought on shore in Boxer Rebellion. 4.4.1905 Sold to Garnham for breaking up.

7. Name ship of class of cruiser, 3,500 tons, 2 x 6", 6 x 4" and 1 x 4" AA guns; 4 x 21" TT. Built in Chatham Dockyard. Launched 25.10.1913. At outbreak of war was Flotilla Leader of Harwich Destroyer Force. 28.8.1914 In Battle of Heligoland Bight; suffered such damage that she had to be towed home. 24.1.1915 Battle of Dogger Bank. 9.8.1915 In chase and sinking of German minelayer *Meteor*. 9 & 10.1915 Captured 6 German trawlers. 11.2.1916 Struck a mine laid by *UC 7*, drifted on shore near Harwich, broke her back and was wrecked.

8. Name ship of class of cruiser, 5,220 tons; 6 x 6" and 8 x 4" AA guns; 6 x 21" TT. Built in Chatham Dockyard. Launched 6.3.1934. 1935-40 In Mediterranean. 27.10.1940 Collided with merchantman; repaired on the Tyne. 11.1940 Moored close to Tower Bridge as part of London's AA defences. 11.1942 Hit by aerial torpedo off North Africa. Towed to Alexandria. Extensively repaired in USA. 6.1944 Again damaged by bombs. 10.1945 Paid off into Reserve at Chatham. 1.1948 Laid up at Falmouth. 8.1948 Used as a Target. 9.5.1950 Arrived Newport to be broken up by J. Cashmore.

Footnote

Coaster, 480 tons, built in 1906, named *Arethusa II*, was hired as a Fleet Messenger and Store Carrier from 29.5.1915 to 26.4.1920.

ARGONAUT

A Batch Two "Leander" class frigate, 2,450 tons (standard). Built by Hawthorn Leslie, Hebburn-on-Tyne. Launched 8.2.1966. 1976-80 Exocet conversion at Devonport. New armament:- Exocet SSM and Sea Cat SAM systems; 2 x 40mm guns; 6 TT; 1 helicopter. Towed Array Sonar system.

Description of Badge

Field:- Red.

Badge:- Upon water in base barry wavy white and blue, a Lymphad gold, therein a demi Greek warrior in armour gold, holding in the dexter hand a fleece, also gold, and in the sinister hand his shield, also gold.

(The Argonauts were Greek heroes who sailed in the *Argo* in search of the "Golden Fleece" under the command of Jason).

Motto

Audax omnia perpeti — Bold to endure.

Battle Honours

Arctic	1942	Aegean	1944
Mediterranean	1942	South France	1944
North Africa	1942	Okinawa	1945
Normandy	1944	Falkland Islands	1982

Previous ships of the name

1. French third rate *Jason*, 1,452 bm, 64 guns. Captured off Puerto Rico in the West Indies on 19.4.1782 by a squadron under Rear Admiral Sir Samuel Hood. 20.1.1783 Renamed *Argonaut*. 8.1.1795 Assisted by *Oiseau*, captured off Chesapeake, the French 22 gun sloop *Espérance*. 1797 Reduced to Harbour Service and used as a Hospital Ship in the Medway. 1822 Similar role at Chatham. 2.1831 Broken up at Chatham.

2. "Diadem" class cruiser, 11,000 tons, 16 x 6" and 14 x 12 pdr guns. Built by Fairfield, Govan, Glasgow. Launched 24.1.1898. 1900-4 Far East. 1904 Reduced to Reserve at Chatham. 1907-11 Home Fleet at Portsmouth. 1912 Training Ship for stokers at Portsmouth. 8.1914 Joined 9th Cruiser Squadron patrolling Western Approaches. 1916-9 Accommodation Ship at Portsmouth. 18.5.1920 Sold to T. W. Ward, Milford Haven, for breaking up.

3. "Dido" class cruiser, 5,972 tons, 10 x 5.25" and 8 x 2 pdr AA guns; 6 x 21" TT. Built by Cammell Laird, Birkenhead. Launched 6.9.1941. 10.1942 Russian convoy duties. 6.11.1942 Supported Allied landings in North Africa. 14.12.1942 Badly damaged when hit on starboard side by 2 torpedoes from Italian submarine *Mocenigo*, west of Galita Island. Temporary repairs at Gibraltar; then to Philadelphia, USA. 2.12.1943 Arrived in the Clyde. 31.12.1943 to 1.4.1944 Refit completed on the Tyne. 6.1944 Normandy landings. 30.6.1944 Hit on quarterdeck by 155mm shell. 8.1944 In Mediterranean. 22.11.1944 Allocated to British Pacific Fleet on its foundation. 1.10.1945 At Shanghai. 6.6.1946 Returned to Portsmouth; reduced to Reserve. 16.11.1955 Sold, and broken up by J. Cashmore at Newport.

Footnote

The Spanish *Argonaut*, 74 guns, was captured at the Battle of Trafalgar. She was reduced to a state of surrender by *Achille* and taken possession of by *Belleisle*. Nine days later *Argonaut* was scuttled, too damaged to be of further service.

ARIADNE

A Batch Three "Leander" class (broad-beamed) frigate; 2,500 tons (standard). Built by Yarrow, Scotstoun, Glasgow. Launched 10.9.1971. Sea Cat SAM system; A/S mortars; 2 x 4.5" and 2 x 20mm guns; 1 helicopter.

Description of Badge

Field:- Blue.
Badge:- Within a wreath of vine, gold, a celestial crown, also gold, with silver stars.

(Ariadne, in Greek mythology, is a personification of the return of spring—the season when Ariadne married Dionysos (Bacchus)).

Motto

Swift and fearless.

Battle Honours

St Lucia   1778   Leyte Gulf   1944

Previous ships of the name

1. Sixth rate, 430 bm, 20 guns. Built in Chatham Dockyard. Launched 27.12.1776. 1778 Supported invasion and seizure from the French of St Lucia. 1792 Rebuilt at Northam as 24 guns sixth rate. 17.7.1805 With others engaged a division of Napoleon's invasion flotilla off Ostend. 7.8.1814 Sold out of the service.

2. Advice boat, 187 bm. Purchased 7.1805. Renamed *Dove* in 1805 and *Flight* in 1806. 9.1806 Foundered.

3. Sixth rate, 511 bm, 20 guns. Built at Pembroke Dock. Launched 10.2.1816. 1822-8 At Cape of Good Hope and in Mediterranean. 1828-30 Commanded by Captain Frederick Marryat, the novelist. 1830-4 In West Indies, 1837 Became a Coal Hulk at Alexandria. 23.7.1841 Sold out of the service.

4. Wood paddlewheel sloop, 432 bm. Built by Wm Laird, Birkenhead. Launched 12.1839. 23.6.1842 Foundered off Chusan.

5. Wood steam frigate, 3,214 bm, 24 x 10" guns. Built in Deptford Dockyard. Launched 4.6.1859. 1871-3 Training Ship for Cadets. 1876 Tender to *Vernon* Torpedo School. 1884 Reduced to Harbour Service. 6.6.1905 Renamed *Actaeon.* 11.12.1922 Sold out of the service.

6. Cruiser, 11,000 tons, 16 x 6" guns. Built by J. & G. Thomson, Glasgow. Launched 22.4.1898. 1902-3 Controlled the blockade of the Venezuelan coast, though remaining mostly at Trinidad. 3.1917 Converted to minelayer with 4 x 6" and 1 x 4" guns and 400 mines. 26.7.1917 Torpedoed and sunk by *UC 65* off Beachy Head whilst on passage from the Humber to Portsmouth.

7. Fast minelayer, 2,650 tons, 4 x 4" guns; 160 mines. Built by Alex Stephen, Linthouse, Glasgow. Launched 16.2.1943. 1944 In action at Leyte Gulf. 15.11.1944 Her Commanding Officer, Captain Lord Ashbourne, controlled the landing of Allied forces on Pegun Island, north of Dutch New Guinea. 4.1946 Returned to UK for refit; but spent the rest of her career in Reserve at Devonport. 1963 Disposal List. 6.1965 Broken up at Dalmuir and Troon.

Footnote
Trawler, 225 tons, built in 1906, armed with 1 x 6 pdr, was hired 1914-9.

ARK ROYAL

An ''Invincible'' class, anti-submarine warfare, aircraft carrier; 20,000 tons, ex-''Indomitable''. Built by Swan Hunter, Wallsend-on-Tyne. Launched 2.6.1981. Primary role, to act as Command Ship of A/S Warfare Forces. Armament:- Sea Harriers, Sea King helicopters; Sea Dart missiles; Sea Gnat; Phalanx anti-aircraft/anti-missile automatic gun system.

Description of Badge

Field:- Blue.
Badge:- An Ark, silver, crowned gold upon three wavelets gold.

Motto

Desire n'a pas repos — Desire has no rest.
(The motto of Lord Howard of Effingham who, in *Ark Raleigh,* commanded the fleet against the Spanish Armada).

Battle Honours

Armada	1588	Spartivento	1940
Cadiz	1596	Mediterranean	1940-1
Dardanelles	1915	*Bismarck*	1941
Norway	1940	Malta Convoys	1941

Previous ships of the name

1. *Ark Raleigh* galleon, 694 bm, 55 guns. Built for Sir Walter Raleigh by Chapman, Deptford, in 1587. 1588 Led the English Fleet in its rout of the Spanish Armada. 1603 Renamed *Anne Royal.* 1608 Rebuilt at Woolwich. 4.1636 Bilged on her own anchor in the Medway and sank. Later refloated and broken up.

2. Steam collier, building at Blyth Shipbuilding Company's yard, was purchased in 5.1914. Launched 5.9.1914. Converted to Seaplane Carrier, 7,080 tons. Served in the Dardanelles and the Gallipoli landings. 1918 In Russian operations in Black Sea. Became a Trials Ship to evaluate the catapult. 12.1934 Renamed *Pegasus.* Early days of WW2 acted as a Fighter Catapult Ship on Atlantic convoy duties. Later became an accommodation ship. 18.10.1946 Sold as *Anita I.* Registered in Panama. 1949 Purchased by a Dutch Company, Boomse Sheepss Boujen. 4.1950 Sold to B.I. and S. Co. Broken up at Grays, Essex.

3. Aircraft Carrier, 22,000 tons, 16 x 4.5" guns; 72 aircraft. Built by Cammell Laird, Birkenhead. Launched 13.4.1937. One of her Skua aircraft shot down a German aircraft, the first German aircraft to fall to the British. From then onwards she was the centre of German attacks and propaganda. 5.1941 Her Swordfish torpedo bombers scored a direct hit which crippled the German battleship *Bismarck,* allowing other ships to move in and sink her. She provided cover for troop landings and evacuations off Norway; and in the Mediterranean joined Force 'H' to provide air cover for the hard-pressed Malta Convoys. Her end came when torpedoed by the German submarine *U 81,* 150 miles east of Gibraltar. Foundered whilst being towed on 14.11.1941. Only one rating lost his life.

4. Aircraft Carrier, 50,590 tons (deep condition). Ex-''Irresistible''. Built by Cammell Laird, Birkenhead. Launched 3.5.1950. 2.1955 Accepted into the RN in the Firth of Clyde. She was the first RN carrier to feature all the new British developments which made intensive jet operations possible—the angled deck, steam catapult, and mirror landing aids. Costly refits enabled her to operate first the swept-wing Scimitar and Sea Vixen aircraft and the powerful Phantom fighters. After 23 years and 900,000 miles of valuable service, she returned to Devonport to de-store. 13.2.1979 Paid off for the last time. 22.9.1980 Left Devonport in tow for breaking up at Cairn Ryan, Wigtownshire.

ARROW

A Type 21 "Amazon" class General Purpose frigate; 2,750 tons (standard); 3,250 tons (full load). Built by Yarrow, Scotstoun, Glasgow. Launched 5.2.1974. Exocet SSM and Sea Cat SAM systems; 6 TT; helicopter-launched torpedoes; 1 x 4.5"; 4 x 20mm Oerlikons; 1 helicopter.

Description of Badge

Field:- Green.
Badge:- Two arrows, gold, feathered red.

Motto

Celeriter certus — Swiftly sure.

Battle Honours

Copenhagen	1801	Libya	1942
Cape Tenez	1805	North Sea	1942
San Sebastian	1813	Malta Convoys	1942
Crimea	1854-5	Sicily	1943
Norway	1940	Falkland Islands	1982
Atlantic	1940-3		

Previous ships of the name

1. Sloop, 386 bm, 20 guns. Built by Hobbs, Redbridge in 1796, and purchased for the RN. 4.2.1805 Captured by two French frigates off Gibraltar.

2. Cutter, 152 bm, 14 guns. Built in Deptford Dockyard. Launched 7.9.1805. From 5.1814 Used as a breakwater. 5.1828 Broken up.

3. Cutter, 157 bm, 10 guns. Built in Portsmouth Dockyard in 1823. 1.1852 Broken up.

4. Name ship of class of wood steam gun vessels, 477 bm, 2 x 68 pdr ML guns. Built by Mare, Blackwall. Launched 26.6.1854. 1855 Crimean War, operated in Black Sea and Sea of Azov. 17.10.1855 In bombardment of the fortress of Kinburn. 19.5.1862 Sold to Marshall, Plymouth, for breaking up.

5. "Ant" class, iron, steam gunboat, 254 tons, 1 x 10" gun. Built by Rennie, Greenwich. Launched 22.4.1871. At Portsmouth, except 1873-80 when attached to RN College, Greenwich. 1.3.1922 Sold to W. H. Webber.

6. "Acasta" class destroyer, 1,350 tons, 4 x 4.7" guns; 8 x 21" TT. Built by Vickers Armstrong, Barrow. Launched 22.8.1929. 1936 Spanish Civil War. 1938 Gunnery Training Tender at Portsmouth. 4.1940 Rammed by German trawler. 1942 Mediterranean and Eastern Fleets. 1.1943 Special Escort Division at Liverpool. 7.1943 13th Destroyer Flotilla, Gibraltar. 4.8.1943 Damaged beyond repair in Algiers harbour by explosion of ammunition ship *Fort La Montee*. 1944 Stripped at Taranto. Broken up c.1949, probably in Italy.

HMS *Arrow*

ARUN

A ''River'' class Fleet Minesweeper, 890 tons (full load); 1 x 40mm gun. Built by Richards, Lowestoft. Launched 20.8.1985. Allocated to Sussex Division, RNR.

Description of Badge

Field:- Argent.
Badge:- In front of a roundel barry wavy sinister bendwise argent and azure, a martlet or.

Motto

Battle Honours

None.

Previous ships of the name

1. Torpedo boat destroyer, 550 tons, 4 x 12 pdr guns; 2 TT. Built by Laird Bros., Birkenhead. Launched 30.4.1903. 13.8.1904 Whilst engaged in night manoeuvres off Isles of Scilly, collided with, and sank, the TBD *Decoy*. 1905-6 Served for a short time on China Station. 1906 Tender to *Sapphire,* Flagship at Portland. 1907-8 Channel Fleet. 1909-11 Home Fleet, Second Division. 1911 Home Fleet, Third Division. 1912-4 9th Patrol Flotilla at Chatham. 1917 Escort Flotilla, Portsmouth. 30.6.1920 Sold to T.W. Ward, Hayle, for breaking up.

HMS *Arun*

ATHERSTONE

A "Hunt" class Mine Countermeasures Vessel, 615 tons (standard) 725 tons (full load); 1 x 40mm gun. Built (of GRP) by Vosper Thornycroft, Woolston, Southampton. Launched 1.3.1986.

Description of Badge

Field:- Red.

Badge:- Upon a white roundel, a fox's mask, red, within a mascle, also red.

(The mascle is from the Arms of Osbaldeston, a Master of the Pack).

Motto

Battle Honours

English Ch	1940-2	Salerno	1943
St Nazaire	1942	Mediterranean	1943
North Sea	1942-3	South France	1944
Atlantic	1943	Adriatic	1944
Sicily	1943		

Previous ships of the name

1. "Ascot"—or "Racecourse"—class paddle minesweeper, 810 tons, 2 x 6 pdr guns. Built by Ailsa S.B. Co., Troon. Launched 4.4.1916. 1920 Laid up. 1927 Purchased by New Medway Steam Packet Co. for service across the Channel; renamed *Queen of Kent*. 1930 Excursions to Dover from the Thames. 1938 Laid up. 11.1939 Fitted out at Sheerness to join 9th Minesweeping Flotilla. 1.1940 AA ship at Sheerness. 9.1940 7th MS Flotilla at Granton. 1.1944 Accommodation Ship at Granton. 1.1945 Anti-mine laying duty at Antwerp. 1946 Returned to owners. 1.1949 Bought by Red Funnel steamers, renamed *Lorna Doone*, for excursions from Bournemouth. 13.3.1953 Towed away for breaking up.

2. "Hunt" class Type 1 destroyer—name ship of the type—907 tons; 4 x 4" guns and 1 x 4 barrelled pom-pom. Built by Cammell Laird, Birkenhead. Launched 12.12.1939. 1942 For the raid on St Nazaire by *Campbeltown*, the HQ Staff were embarked in *Atherstone*, who acted as escort. 1943 To the Mediterranean. 25.9.1945 Sailed from Mediterranean for Portsmouth to pay off into Reserve. 1953 Laid up at Cardiff. 23.11.1957 Sold; broken up by Smith and Houston, Port Glasgow.

HMS *Atherstone*

ATTACKER

Name ship of the class of Seamanship and Navigational Training Vessels of 34 tons for the RNR and University RN Units. Built by Fairey Allday Marine, Cowes. Delivered 1.3.1983. Allocated to Strathclyde University.

Description of Badge
Field:- Blue.
Badge:- A ram in the act of butting, proper.

Motto

Battle Honours

Salerno	1943	South France	1944
Atlantic	1943-4	Aegean	1944

Previous ships of the name

1. Escort Carrier, 11,420 tons, 18 aircraft. A converted merchant hull. Built by Western Pipe and Steel Co., San Francisco, California, USA. Ex-USS *Barnes*. Ex-mercantile *Steel Artisan*. Launched as *Barnes* 27.9.1941. 30.9.1942 Transferred to RN on Lend-Lease. Battle Honours indicate her areas of activity as a support carrier. 5.1.1946 Returned to USA. 1952 Sold as *Castel Forte*. 1957 *Sitmar*. 1958 *Fairsky*. 1977 Sold to Fuji Marden, Hong Kong. 1978 Converted to floating hotel.

2. LST(3) 3010; 2,256 tons, 10 x 20mm AA guns. Built by Harland and Wolff, Belfast. Launched 30.9.1944. 1947 Renamed *Attacker*. 1947-54 In Reserve. 1954 To Ministry of Transport as *Empire Cymric*.

HMS *Attacker* (1944).

AURORA

A Batch One "Leander" class frigate, 2,450 tons (standard). Built by John Brown, Clydebank. Launched 28.11.1962. 1973-6 Ikara conversion at Chatham. New armament:- Ikara A/S missiles (forward); Sea Cat SAM system; 2 x 40mm guns; Limbo A/S mortars (aft); 1 helicopter.

Description of Badge

Field:- In chief red, a rising sun, gold.
Badge:- Party per fesse barry of silver and black.

(Aurora was goddess of the dawn; daughter of Hyperion; whose work was to open the gates of the east for the sun).

Motto

Post tenebras lux — After darkness, light.

Battle Honours

St Lucia	1778	Malta Convoys	1941
Minorca	1798	Mediterranean	1941-3
Guadeloupe	1810	North Africa	1942-3
China	1900	Sicily	1943
Dogger Bank	1915	Salerno	1943
Norway	1940	Aegean	1943-4
Bismarck	1941	South France	1944

Previous ships of the name

1. French fifth rate *Abenakise*, 946 bm, 36 guns. Captured by the *Unicorn* on 23.1.1757. 4.1763 Broken up.

2. Fifth rate, 679 bm, 32 guns. Built in Chatham Dockyard. Launched 13.1.1766. 1770 Burned, and lost, when on passage from the Cape to the East Indies.

3. Sixth rate, 596 bm, 28 guns. Built by Perry, Blackwall. Launched 7.6.1777. 3.11.1814 Sold out of the service.

HMS *Aurora* (November 1937).

4. Fifth rate *Aurore*, 860 bm, 32 guns. Captured from the French at Toulon on 29.8.1793. From 1779 to 1803 she was used as a Prison Ship at Gibraltar.

5. Sloop, 247 bm, 14 guns. Built in Bombay Dockyard in 1809. c.1810 Captured by the French off Mauritius.

6. French fifth rate *Clorinde*, 1,083 bm, 38 guns. Captured 26.2.1814 in the Atlantic by *Dryad* and *Eurotus*. Broken up in 5.1851.

7. Wood steam frigate, 2,558 tons, 1 x 110 pdr, 8 x 8", 4 x 70 pdr, 8 x 40 pdr and 18 x 32 pdr guns. Built at Pembroke Dock. Launched 22.6.1861. 1865 West Indies. 1868-72 At Devonport. 1872 Training Ship for Ordinary Seamen with the Detached Squadron. 1874 Coastguard Service at Greenock. 1877 Returned to Devonport. 12.1881 Broken up.

8. "Orlando" class Armoured Cruiser, 5,600 tons, 2 x 9.2" and 10 x 6" guns. Built at Pembroke Dock. Launched 28.10.1887. 1890-3 Channel Squadron. 1893-5 Coastguard Ship at Bantry. 1895-8 Refit and Reserve. 1899-1902 China. 1900 Took part in Relief of Peking Legations, which were besieged during Boxer Rebellion. 1902-7 Reserve. 2.10.1907 Sold to Payton, Milford Haven, for breaking up.

9. "Arethusa" class light cruiser, 3,500 tons, 2 x 6", 6 x 4" and 1 x 4" AA guns; 4 x 21" TT. Built in Devonport Dockyard. Launched 30.9.1913. 24.1.1915 Damaged in Dogger Bank action by 3 hits from the German cruiser *Kolberg*. 9.8.1915 In chase and sinking of German minelayer *Meteor*. 25.3.1916 Seaplane raid on Hoyer. 2.1918 Acted as minelayer in first British minelaying operation in the Kattegat. 1918-9 7th LCS, Grand Fleet. 1919-20 In Reserve. 1.11.1920 Transferred as a gift and commissioned into the Royal Canadian Navy. 5.1923 Reduced to a Hulk. 8.1927 Sold to A.A. Lasseque of Sorel in the Province of Quebec.

10. "Arethusa" class cruiser, 5,270 tons, 6 x 6" and 8 x 4" guns; 6 x 21" TT. Built in Portsmouth Dockyard. Launched 20.8.1936. Home Waters until 10.1941. 3.6.1941 With *Kenya*, sank German supply ship *Belchen* in Denmark Strait. 19.12.1941 Damaged by mine off Libyan coast. 30.10.1943 Damaged by bomb in the Aegean. 17.4.1946 Arrived Portsmouth to pay off. 19.5.1948 Sold to Nationalist China. Renamed *Chungking*. 2.1949 Defected to Communist China; renamed *Tchounking*. 3.1949 Bombed and sunk in Taku Harbour. 1951 Salvaged and recommissioned. Renamed *Hsuang Ho*; then *Pei Ching*. 1955 Hulked, and renamed *Kuang Chou*.

Footnote
a) Trawler, 225 tons, built in 1906; 1 x 6 pdr gun; was hired as *Aurora II* from 1914-9.
b) The drifter *Aurora*, 74 tons, built in 1906, was hired as a Boom Tender from 5.1915 to 1919; and as the minesweeper *Aurora II* in 1940. 24.5.1941 Sunk by air attack at Tobruk.

HMS *Aurora*

AVENGER

A Type 21 "Amazon" class General Purpose frigate, 2,750 tons (standard), 3,250 tons (full load). Built by Yarrow, Scotstoun, Glasgow. Launched 20.11.1975. Exocet SSM and Sea Cat SAM systems; 6 TT; helicopter-launched torpedoes; 1 x 4.5"; 4 x 20mm Oerlikons; 1 helicopter.

Description of Badge

Field:- Argent.
Badge:- A pair of hands, gauntleted proper, grasping a double handed sword in bend sinister gold, enflamed proper.

Motto

Battle Honours

Martinique	1794	North Africa	1942
Arctic	1942	Falkland Islands	1982

Previous ships of the name

1. Sloop, 339 bm, 8 guns. Built by Randall, Rotherhithe. 9.10.1778 Purchased on the stocks. Originally commissioned as fireship *Lucifer*. 1779 Converted and renamed *Avenger*. Served on North American Station. 12.6.1783 Condemned and sold in New York.

2. French sloop *Vengeur*, 330 bm, 16 guns. Captured on 17.3.1794 at Martinique. Renamed *Avenger*. 9.9.1802 Sold out of the service.

3. Sloop, ex-mercantile *Elizabeth*, 264 bm. Purchased 8.1803. 5.12.1803 Foundered in the River Weser in Holland.

4. Collier *Thames* 390 bm. Converted and commissioned as 18 gun sloop in 5.1804. 8.10.1812 Wrecked on Chain Rock off St Johns, Newfoundland.

5. Steam paddle frigate, 1,444 bm. Built in Devonport Dockyard. Launched 5.8.1845. Engined at Deptford. 20.12.1847 Wrecked on Sorell Rocks off North African coast. Only 4 officers and 5 men from the 270 on board, were saved. Lt Marryat, son of Captain F. Marryat the famous novelist, was amongst those lost.

6. Liner, ex-*Aotearoa*, 15,000 tons, was being built for Union Steamship Company of New Zealand, by Fairfield, Govan, Glasgow. Taken over 1915 and armed with 8 x 6" guns. Served in 9th Cruiser Squadron. 14.6.1917 Torpedoed and sunk by *U 69* in North Atlantic. One man was killed by the explosion, but the rest of the ship's company were saved.

7. Liner *Rio Hudson*, 9,700 tons. Built by Sun S.B. & D.D. Co., Chester, Pennsylvania, USA. Launched 27.11.1940. Converted by Bethlehem Steel Corporation, Staten Island, New York. 2.3.1942 Transferred to RN under Lend-Lease. 30.4.1942 Sailed for UK. 9.9.1942 Joined Arctic Convoy 'PQ18'. 10.1942 Operation 'Torch'—invasion of North Africa. 15.11.1942 Blew up and sank west of the Straits of Gibraltar after being torpedoed by *U 155*. Only 12 survivors from over 500 on board. She was the largest ship sunk during the North African Landings.

8. LST (3) 3011, 2,256 tons, 10 x 20mm AA guns. Built by Harland and Wolff, Belfast. Launched 12.2.1945. 1947 Renamed *Avenger*. 1.3.1949 Sold to India. 1951 Renamed *Magar*. 1985 Still in service.

BATTLEAXE

A Batch One ''Broadsword'' class, Type 22 frigate; 3,500 tons (standard), 4,200 tons (full load). Built by Yarrow, Scotstoun, Glasgow. Launched 18.5.1977. Exocet SSM and Sea Wolf SAM systems; 2 x 40mm AA and 4 x 20mm AA guns; 6 TT; helicopter carried A/S torpedoes; 1 helicopter (ability to carry 2).

Description of Badge

Field:- Blue.
Badge:- A battle-axe gold.

Motto

Battle Honours

None.

Previous ships of the name

1. Minesweeping trawler (ex-Russian *T.16*), 292 tons. Built at Smith's Dock, South Bank-on-Tees. Launched 19.6.1916. Commissioned in 1918. 1920 Renamed *Dee*. 1946 Sold and renamed *Safir*.

2. Landing Ship Dock, 4,270 tons. Built at Newport News, USA. Launched 21.5.1943. Transferred to RN on Lend-Lease. 8.1943 Renamed *Eastway*. 5.1947 Returned to USA.

3. ''Weapon'' class destroyer, 1,980 tons, 4 x 4'' guns; 10 TT. Built by Yarrow, Scotstoun, Glasgow. Launched 12.6.1945. 1949-56 6th Destroyer Flotilla. 1959 Converted to Radar Picket ship. 2.8.1962 During night exercises in the Clyde, was badly damaged in a collision with *Ursa*. Found on survey to be beyond economical repair. Approved for scrapping. 1963 Moored alongside NCRE, Rosyth. 20.10.1964 Arrived Blyth to be broken up by Hughes Bolckow.

HMS *Battleaxe* (July 1951).

BEAGLE

A ''Bulldog'' class Coastal Survey Vessel, 800 tons (standard), 1,088 tons (full load). Built by Brooke Marine, Lowestoft. Launched 7.9.1967. Originally designed for service overseas. Built to commercial standards. Fitted for (but not with) 2 x 20mm guns.

Description of Badge

Field:- Green.
Badge:- A beagle proper.

Motto

To a finish.

Battle Honours

Basque Roads	1809	Atlantic	1940-5
San Sebastian	1813	North Africa	1942
Crimea	1854-5	Arctic	1942-4
China	1856-60	English Ch	1943
Dardanelles	1915-6	Normandy	1944
Norway	1940		

Previous ships of the name

1. ''Cruizer'' class brig-sloop, 384 bm, 16 x 32 pdr and 2 x 6 pdr guns. Built by Perry, Wells and Green, Blackwall. Launched 8.8.1804. 21.7.1814 Sold out of the service.

2. ''Cherokee'' class brig-sloop, 236 bm, 8 x 18 pdr and 2 x 6 pdr guns. Built in Woolwich Dockyard. Launched 11.5.1820. 1825 Survey ship. Surveyed Magellan Straits. 1831 Sailed on 10 year voyage of discovery round the world. 1846 Customs Watch Vessel at Southend. 5.1863 Renamed *W.V.7.* 13.5.1870 Sold to Murray and Trainer.

3. ''Arrow'' class wood steam gun vessel, 477 bm, 2 x 68 pdr ML guns. Built by Mare, Blackwall. Launched 20.7.1854. Landed naval brigade in Siege of Sebastopol. Later served on East Indies and China Stations; operated against Chinese pirates. 1863 Sold at Hong Kong. 1865 Became Japanese *Kanko.* 1889 Broken up.

4. Name ship of class of sloops, 1,170 tons, 8 x 5'' guns. Built in Portsmouth Dockyard. Launched 28.2.1889. 1889-1900 South East coast of America Station. 1900-1 Refit at home. 1901-4 Cape of Good Hope and West Coast of Africa Station. 11.7.1905 Sold out of the service.

5. Destroyer, 950 tons, 1 x 4'' and 3 x 12 pdr guns; 2 TT. Built by J. Brown, Clydebank. Launched 16.10.1909. 1915 In Dardanelles. 7.1918 Northern Anti-submarine patrol. 1.11.1921 Sold to Fryer, Sunderland.

6. ''Basilisk'' class destroyer, 1,360 tons, 4 x 4.7'' guns; 8 TT. Built by J. Brown, Clydebank. Launched 26.9.1930. 6.1940 Evacuation from St Nazaire. 20.6.1940 Landed demolition party for Bordeaux. 2.5.1942 In action with German destroyers. 3.1944 With aircraft from *Tracker* sank *U 355* while on Russian convoy escort duties. 9.5.1945 At St Peter Port when signing of surrender of German garrison in Channel Islands took place on board *Bulldog.* 15.1.1946 Sold to Metal Industries. Broken up at Rosyth.

Footnote
Schooner, 120 bm, 1 gun. Built by Cuthbert, Sydney, NSW, Australia. Launched 5.12.1872. 1883 Sold at Sydney.

BEAVER

A Batch Two ''stretched'' ''Broadsword'' class Type 22 frigate, 4,100 tons (standard), 4,800 tons (full load). Built by Yarrow, Scotstoun, Glasgow. Launched 8.5.1982. Exocet SSM and Sea Wolf SAM systems; 2 x 40mm and 4 x 20mm guns; 6 TT; 1 helicopter (ability to carry 2); helicopter-carried A/S torpedoes.

Description of Badge

Field:- Argent.
Badge:- A beaver, coloured proper, carrying a trident points downwards, or.

Motto

Battle Honours

Louisburg	1758	Heligoland	1914
Athalante	1804	Atlantic	1942

Previous ships of the name

1. Royalist ketch, 6 guns. Captured by Parliamentary forces in 1656. Broken up in 1658.

2. French privateer *Trudaine,* 338 bm, 18 guns. Captured 4.1757. At capture of Louisburg in Canada in 1758. 22.1.1761 Sold out of the service.

3. Sloop, 285 bm, 14 guns. Built by Inwood, Rotherhithe. Launched 3.2.1761. In War of American Independence. 18.5.1778 Captured American privateer *Oliver Cromwell*, 263 bm, 18 guns; became *Beaver Prize*. 17.7.1783 Sold out of the service.

4. Sloop, 269 bm, 14 guns. Built by Graham, Harwich. Launched 29.9.1795. 21.12.1808 Sold out of the service.

5. ''Cherokee'' class brig-sloop, 236 bm, 10 guns. Built by Bailey, Ipswich. Launched 16.2.1809. Served in Home, West Indies and South Atlantic waters. 24.6.1829 Sold to J. Cristall for breaking up.

6. ''Albacore'' class wood steam gunboat, 232 bm, 1 x 68 pdr, 1 x 32 pdr, and 2 x 20 pdr guns. Built by Wigram, Northam. Launched 28.11.1855. Never used in service. 1864 Broken up.

7. Destroyer—''I'' class special—810 tons, 2 x 4" guns; 2 TT. Built by Wm Denny, Dumbarton. Launched 6.10.1911. 21.12.1912 Stranded in fog near Great Yarmouth. Slight dent in bows. Refloated same day. In WW1 performed escort duty and A/S patrols. Was one of the Harwich Force destroyers which took part in Battle of Heligoland Bight. 1919 In Reserve Fleet at the Nore. 25.3.1920 Reduced to Care and Maintenance. 9.5.1921 Sold to T. W. Ward, Hayle, for breaking up.

Footnote
a) Gunvessel, was hired for just 3 months, 9-12.1801.
b) Wooden paddlewheel mail packet, GPO Vessel *Salamander* 114 bm. 1837 Transferred to RN and renamed *Beaver.* 1845 Became a Dockyard lighter.
c) War Department tender *Victor,* 125 tons. 1905 Transferred to RN and renamed *Beaver.* 7.7.1911 Sold to Laidler, Sunderland.

BERKELEY

A "Hunt" class Mine Countermeasures Vessel, 615 tons (standard), 725 tons (full load); 1 x 40mm gun. Built (of GRP) by Vosper Thornycroft, Woolston, Southampton.

Description of Badge

Field:- Gold.
Badge:- Upon a red roundel, in front of two hunting horns in saltire gold a cross patee white.

Motto

Dieu avec nous — God with us.

Battle Honours

None.

Previous ships of the name

1. "Hunt" class Type 1 "Atherstone" type, destroyer, 907 tons, 4 x 4" guns and 1 x 4 barrelled pom-pom. Built by Cammell Laird, Birkenhead. Launched 29.1.1940. 6.1940 During the withdrawal from Europe, she conveyed from England the Senior Naval Officers for the continental ports and distributed them along the coast. Proceeded up river to Bordeaux to act as wireless link. 19.6.1940 Many of the British Embassy and Consular staffs came down river from Bordeaux in *Berkeley* to embark in *Arethusa* for England. 19.8.1942 During the withdrawal of surviving ships from Dieppe, she was so badly damaged by German air attack that she had to be sunk by one of our own ships, the destroyer *Albrighton*.

HMS *Berkeley*

BICESTER

A ''Hunt'' class Mine Countermeasures Vessel, 615 tons (standard), 725 tons (full load); 1 x 40mm gun. Built of GRP by Vosper Thornycroft, Woolston, Southampton. Launched 4.6.1985.

Description of Badge

Field:- Red.
Badge:- A stirrup white and a key erect, ward upwards, gold, interlaced.

Motto

Battle Honours

Malta Convoys	1942	South France	1944
North Africa	1942-3	Adriatic	1944
Mediterranean	1943-4	Aegean	1944

Previous ships of the name

1. Early ''Hunt'' class Fleet Minesweeper, coal-fired 750 tons. Built by Ailsa S.B. Co., Troon. Launched 8.6.1917. 14.10.1919 Paid off at Grimsby. 1921 Placed in charge of ship-keepers at Harwich. 8.1.1923 Sold. 8.1923 Arrived Charlestown, Fife, to be broken up.

2. ''Hunt'' class destroyer, Type 2, ''Blankney'' type, 1,050 tons, 6 x 4" AA guns. Built by Hawthorn Leslie, Hebburn-on-Tyne. Launched 5.9.1941. Operated in the Mediterranean including (8.1942) 'Pedestal' convoy to Malta. 11.1942 Operation 'Torch'—invasion of North Africa. 23.2.1943 With *Lamerton* and *Wheatland*, sank *U 443* off Algiers. 7.1943 Operation 'Husky'—invasion of Sicily. 15.8.1944 Operation 'Dragoon'—landings in South France. 4.12.1945 Returned to UK after service in Indian Ocean. 1946-50 Leader of Nore Destroyer Flotilla; then to Reserve. 22.8.1956 Arrived Grays, Essex, to be broken up.

HMS *Bicester* (March 1949).

BIRMINGHAM

A Batch One "Town" class, Type 42, guided missile destroyer; 3,500 tons (standard), 4,100 tons (full load). Built by Cammell Laird, Birkenhead. Launched 30.7.1973. Sea Dart SAM system; 1 x 4.5" and 2 x 20mm Oerlikons; helicopter-launched Sea Skua missiles; 6 TT; 1 helicopter.

Description of Badge

Field:- White.
Badge:- An arm proper, holding a hammer proper, issuant from a mural crown gold.
(Derived from the Arms and Motto of the City of Birmingham).

Motto

Forward

Battle Honours

Heligoland	1914	Norway	1940
Dogger Bank	1915	Korea	1952-3
Jutland	1916		

Previous ships of the name

1. Name ship of class of light cruisers, 5,440 tons, 9 x 6" guns, 2 x 21" TT. Built by Armstrong Whitworth on the Tyne. Launched 7.5.1913. 1914-9 Grand Fleet. 9.8.1914 Rammed and sank *U 15* off Fair Island (first time a British ship had sunk a submarine). 28.8.1914 Action off Heligoland. 24.1.1915 Battle of Dogger Bank. 8/9.8.1915 In the hunt and destruction of the German minelayer *Meteor*. 31.5.1916 Battle of Jutland. Early 1917 Gibraltar convoys. Late 1917 Scandinavian convoys. 1919 Refit. 1919-20 Flagship 6th LCS, Africa Station. 1920-3 Reserve and Refit. 1923-6 Africa Station. 1926-8 Cape Station. 1928-9 Reserve. 1930 Used as a target. 5.2.1931 Sold to T. W. Ward. 12.3.1931 Arrived Pembroke Dock to be broken up.

2. "Southampton" class cruiser, 9,100 tons, 12 x 6" and 8 x 4" AA guns; 6 x 21" TT. Built in Devonport Dockyard. Launched 1.9.1936. China Station until 1.1940. Saw action off Norway. Flagship of C in C, South Atlantic until 2.1942. 6.1942 Operation 'Vigorous'—convoy to Malta. 28.11.1943 Torpedoed by *U 407* off Cyrenaica. 5.1945 Supervised German naval surrender at Copenhagen. 1946-7 Refit at Portsmouth; then to East Indies. 1950-2 Reconstructed at Portsmouth; then to Far East. During Korean War, patrolled the coast supporting Army units ashore. 6.1955 South Atlantic. 1956-9 Home and Mediterarnean Fleets. 7.9.1960 Arrived Inverkeithing to be broken up by T. W. Ward.

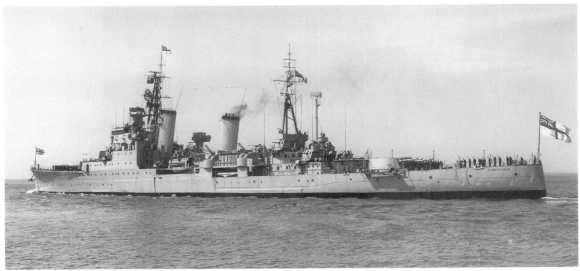

HMS *Birmingham* (June 1952).

BITER

A Coastal Training Craft, of 43 tonnes, for the RNR. Built of GRP by Watercraft Ltd., Shoreham-by-Sea. Launched 17.10.1985. Allocated to Mersey Division, RNR.

Description of Badge.

Field:- Blue
Badge:- A shark gold, in the mouth a trident, also gold.

Motto

Battle Honours

Baltic	1855	Atlantic	1943-4
North Africa	1942		

Previous ships of the name

1. Gunvessel (Gunboat No. 10), 169 bm, 12 guns. Built by Wells, Rotherhithe. Launched 13.4.1797. 5.1802 Sold out of the service.

2. Gun-brig, 177 bm, 12 guns. Built by Wallis, Blackwall. Launched 27.7.1804. 10.11.1805 Wrecked near Calais.

3. "Dapper" class wood steam gunboat, 232 bm, 1 x 68 pdr and 2 x 24 pdr guns. Built by Pitcher, Northfleet. Launched 5.5.1855. 9/10.8.1855 In bombardment of Sveaborg. 24.1.1865 Converted to Coal Hulk. Later named *C 16*. 3.1904 Sold to Castle, Woolwich for breaking up.

4. Escort Carrier, 8,200 tons, 15 aircraft. A converted merchant hull built by Sun S.B. & D.D. Co., Chester, Pennsylvania, USA. Ex-mercantile *Rio Parana*. Launched 18.12.1940. Converted at Atlantic Basin Iron Works, Brooklyn. 6.5.1942 Transferred to UK on Lend-Lease. 1942 Operation 'Torch'. At first light, 8.11.1942, sent planes over Oran to drop propaganda leaflets. End of 1942, refit at Dundee. 3.1943 Fifth Escort Group in North Atlantic. 23.4.1943 Swordfish aircraft from *Biter*, with *Pathfinder*, sank *U 203*. 8.1943 Refit at Belfast. 1944 Convoy escort. 24.8.1944 Serious fire on board; afterwards laid up in Reserve. 9.4.1945 Handed over to French Navy as *Dixmude*. 1945-6 Troop and Stores Carrier in the Mediterranean. 1947-8 In Far East. War in Indo-China. 1951 Re-rated an Aviation Transport. 10.6.1966 Returned to USA. End of 1966 sunk as a target in Gulf of Mexico.

Footnote

a) Wood paddlewheel gunvessel, 301 bm, was ordered from Chatham Dockyard in 1846, but cancelled 22.5.1849.
b) Tender, ex-War Department vessel *Sir William Reid*, 110 tons. Transferred to RN in 1905. 5.1923 Sold to Dover Ship-breaking Company.

HMS *Biter* (9th March 1943).

BLACKWATER

A ''River'' class Fleet Minesweeper, 890 tons (full load); 1 x 40mm gun. Built by Richards, Great Yarmouth. Launched 29.8.1984. Only ship of the Class to be RN manned. Completed 20.6.1985.

Description of Badge

Field:- Argent.
Badge:- In front of a roundel, barry wavy argent and sable, a seax palewise or.

Motto

Battle Honours

None.

Previous ships of the name

1. Destroyer, 550 tons, 1 x 12 pdr and 5 x 6 pdr guns; 2 single torpedo tubes, 2 x 18'' torpedoes. Built by Wm Laird, Birkenhead. Launched 25.7.1903. 1905 In Reserve at Devonport. 1906 At Portland, tender to *Sapphire*. 1907-8 Home Fleet. 1908-9 Channel Fleet. 6.4.1909 Shortly after 11pm, 2nd Destroyer Flotilla were passing up Channel, Portland to Firth of Forth, when *Blackwater* was in collision with SS *Hero* of Bristol. The scout *Forward* took *Blackwater* in tow, but she foundered 5 miles from Dungeness.

Footnote
The ''Mersey'' type trawler *William Inwood*, 324 gross registered tons, built in 1918 by Cochrane, was in 1920 renamed *Blackwater*. 1946 Sold and renamed *Spleis*.

HMS *Blackwater*

BLAZER

A P2000 Coastal Training Craft of 43 tonnes for the RNR. Built of GRP by Watercraft Ltd., Shoreham-by-Sea. Allocated to Sussex Division, RNR.

Description of Badge

Field:- Azure.
Badge:- A gold star irradiated in front of two smaller silver stars.

Motto

Battle Honours

Glückstadt   1814   Baltic   1855

Previous ships of the name

1. Gunvessel (Gunboat No. 12) 159 bm, 12 guns. Built by Dudman, Deptford. Launched 14.4.1797. 23.3.1801 Captured by the enemy at Copenhagen but, after the armistice, was returned to the British. 1.1803 Sold out of the service.

2. Gun-brig, 180 bm, 12 guns. Built by Pitcher, Northfleet. Launched 3.5.1804. 15.12.1814 Sold out of the service.

3. Wood paddlewheel sloop, 527 bm. Built in Chatham Dockyard. Launched 5.1834. 1.1843 Converted to Survey Ship. 18.. ..o established uniform but men of *Blazer* wore blue and white striped guernseys with jackets. 1853 Broken up at Portsmouth.

4. Mortar Vessel, 117 bm, 1 x 13" mortar. Built by Mare, Blackwall. Launched 5.5.1855. 19.10.1855 Renamed *MV 3*. 10.1867 Transferred to Thames Conservancy Board.

5. "Albacore" class wood steam gunboat, 232 bm, 1 x 68 pdr, 1 x 32 pdr and 2 x 20 pdr guns. Built by Wm Laird, Birkenhead. Launched 23.2.1856. 6.1868 Became *YC 29*, a dredger at Portsmouth. 1870 Towed to Gibraltar for similar service. 4.5.1877 Sold at Gibraltar.

6. "Ant" class iron steam gunboat, 254 tons, 1 x 10" gun. Built in Portsmouth Dockyard. Launched 7.12.1870. 1871-1904 At Portsmouth, as a sea-going tender for testing guns. 1904-14 At Sheerness. 8.1914 Reverted to gunboat. 19.8.1919 Sold to W. Loveridge for breaking up.

Footnote
a) There were 3 earlier ships named *Blaze*.
b) Tug, 283 tons, built in 1888. 4.12.1914 Hired. 1915 Renamed *Blazer*, to operate in the Examination Service. 9.11.1918 Wrecked in the Isles of Scilly.

BOXER

A Batch Two "stretched" "Broadsword" class Type 22 frigate, 4,100 tons (standard) 4,800 tons (full load). Built by Yarrow, Scotstoun, Glasgow. Launched 17.6.1981. Exocet SSM and Sea Wolf SAM systems; 2 x 40mm and 4 x 20mm guns; 6 TT; 1 helicopter (ability to carry 2); helicopter-carried A/S torpedoes.

Description of Badge

Field:- Red.
Badge:- A boxing glove apaumée white, laced and edged gold.

Motto

Praemonitus praemunitus — Forewarned is fore-armed.

Battle Honours

Crimea	1855	Salerno	1943
Sicily	1943	Anzio	1944

Previous ships of the name

1. Gunvessel (Gunboat No. 9) 161 bm, 12 guns. Built by Wells, Rotherhithe. Launched 11.4.1797. 1798 In raid on Ostend. 1800 Attacked French frigates in Dunkirk Roads. 7.1809 Sold out of the service.

2. Gun-brig, 182 bm, 12 guns. Built by Hobbs, Redbridge. Launched 25.7.1812. 5.9.1813 Captured by American *Enterprise* off Portland, Maine.

3. Paddlewheel packet, 159 bm. Formerly GPO Vessel *Ivanhoe*. 2.1837 Transferred to Admiralty for survey work. Sold c.1842.

4. "Dapper" class wood steam gunboat, 284 bm, 1 x 68 pdr and 2 x 24 pdr guns. Built by Pitcher, Northfleet. Launched 7.4.1855. Saw action against Russian shore installations during Crimean War. 1866 Broken up at Malta.

5. "Beacon" class composite steam gunvessel, 584 bm, 1 x 7" and 1 x 64 pdr guns. Built in Deptford Dockyard. Launched 15.1.1868. Spent most of her active life in the Pacific and on West Coast of Africa. 1877 Transitted lower reaches of river Niger. 1879 Employed to lodge protest against French occupation of Matacong. 1879-80 North America and West Indies Station. Off Haiti during a revolution there. 1881 In Reserve. 6.1887 Sold for breaking up.

6. Destroyer, 280 tons, 1 x 12 pdr and 5 x 6 pdr guns; 2 TT. Built by Thornycroft, Chiswick. Launched 28.11.1894. 1914 Paid off. Recommissioned on outbreak of war. Served with Portsmouth Local Defence Flotilla. 8.2.1918 Sunk in collision with SS *St Patrick* in the Channel.

7. Tank Landing Ship, 3,620 tons. Built by Harland and Wolff, Belfast. Launched 12.12.1942. Took part in amphibious operations at Sicily, Salerno and Anzio. 1944 Converted to Fighter Direction Ship. 1946 Converted at Portsmouth to Radar Training Ship. 10.1955 Reserve at Portsmouth. 5.12.1958 Arrived Barrow to be broken up by T. W. Ward.

Footnote
Wood paddlewheel gunvessel, 301 tons, was ordered from Chatham Dockyard; laid down in May, 1846 but cancelled in 6.1847.

BRAVE

A Batch Two "stretched" "Broadsword" class Type 22 frigate, 4,100 tons (standard), 4,850 tons (full load). Built by Yarrow, Scotstoun, Glasgow. Launched 19.11.1983. Exocet SSM and Sea Wolf SAM systems; 2 x 40mm guns; 6 TT; 1 helicopter (ability to carry 2); helicopter-carried A/S torpedoes.

Description of Badge
Field:- White.
Badge:- The head-dress of a Red Indian, proper.

Motto
Fortis fortuna adiuvat — fortune favours the brave.

Battle Honours

Armada	1588	South France	1944
Cadiz	1597		

Previous ships of the name

1. Ship, 160 bm. Hired in 1588—"set forth and paid upon the charge of the City of London" for the Armada campaign. 1596-7 Hired again for the Cadiz expedition.

2. Xebec (3 masted vessel) 154 bm. Captured 1747 by *Blandford* at Lisbon. 1748/9 Sold at Port Mahon.

3. Lugger, 12 guns. Hired 1798. 22.4.1799 Sunk in collision in the Channel; crew saved.

4. French third rate, 1,890 bm, 74 guns. Captured 6.2.1806 at San Domingo. 12.4.1806 Foundered off the Azores when on passage from Jamaica to UK.

5. French *Formidable*, third rate, 2,249 bm, 80 guns. Captured, 4.11.1805, in an action off the coast of Spain. 1.1808 Prison Ship in the River Tamar. 10.1814 Reduced to a powder hulk. 4.1816 Sold to be broken up.

6. "Albacore" class wood steam gunboat, 232 bm, 1 x 68 pdr, 1 x 32 pdr and 2 x 20 pdr guns. Built by Wm Laird, Birkenhead. Launched 11.2.1856. Never completed. 3.1869 Broken up at Portsmouth.

7. "Algerine" class minesweeper, 850 tons, 1 x 4" and 8 x 20mm guns. Built by Blyth S.B. and D.D. Co. Launched 4.2.1943. 1943-5 With 19th Minesweeping Flotilla in the Mediterranean. 5.1946 Returned to UK to enter Reserve at Chatham, then Harwich. 1951 to RNVR, Tyne, as the drillship *Satellite*. 25.11.1958 Arrived Dunston to be broken up by Clayton and Davie.

Footnote
a) Dutch *Braave*, fifth rate, 883 bm, 40 guns. Captured 17.8.1796 at Saldanha Bay. 1808 Reduced to Harbour Service. 20.7.1825 Sold out of the service.
b) An aircraft carrier was laid down as *Brave* by Harland and Wolff, Belfast, but was renamed *Warrior* in 1942 before launching 20.5.1944.

BRAZEN

A Batch One "Broadsword" class Type 22 frigate, 3,500 tons (standard), 4,200 tons (full load). Built by Yarrow, Scotstoun, Glasgow. Launched 4.3.1980. Exocet SSM and Sea Wolf SAM systems; 2 x 40mm AA and 4 x 20mm AA guns; 6 TT; helicopter-carried A/S torpedoes; 1 helicopter (ability to carry 2).

Description of Badge

Field:- Red.
Badge:- A trumpet gold.

Motto

Audax omnia perpeti — Daring to suffer all things.

Battle Honours

Norway   1940   English Ch   1940

Previous ships of the name

1. Cutter, 123 bm, 14 guns. Purchased 6.1781. 4.1799 Sold out of the service.

2. French sloop *Bonaparte,* a privateer, 363 bm, 18 guns. Captured 4.1799 by *Boadicea.* 26.1.1800 Wrecked near Brighton; only 1 survivor.

3. Sixth rate, 422 bm, 26 guns. Built in Portsmouth Dockyard. Launched 26.5.1808. Served on Jamaica Station, in English Channel, off Ireland and on West Coast of Africa. 1827 Converted to a Floating Chapel. Loaned to Episcopalian Church Society; moored in the Thames opposite Tower of London. 7.1848 Broken up.

4. "Albacore" class wood steam gunboat, 232 bm, 1 x 68 pdr, 1 x 32 pdr and 2 x 20 pdr guns. Built by Wm Laird, Birkenhead. Launched 8.3.1856. Never used in service. 8.1864 Broken up.

5. Destroyer, 390 tons, 1 x 12 pdr and 5 x 6 pdr guns; 2 TT. Built by J. and G. Thomson, Glasgow. Launched 3.7.1896. Completed at Clydebank Shipbuilding Company, Glasgow; then lay idle at Portsmouth. 1905 Reduced to Reserve. 1910 4th DF, Home Fleet; then 5th DF. 1911 6th DF at the Nore. 1914 Local Defence Flotilla at the Nore. 4.11.1919 Sold to J.H. Lee.

6. "Basilisk" class destroyer, 1,360 tons, 4 x 4.7" guns; 8 x 21" TT. Built by Palmer, Jarrow-on-Tyne. Launched 25.7.1930. 4.1940 Formed part of escort to first British troop convoy to Norway. 15.4.1940 With *Fearless,* assisted in sinking *U 49* with depth charges in Vaagsfiord. 20.7.1940 Off Dover, shot down 3 aircraft before she herself was hit and badly damaged. Impossible to take her in tow, so she was abandoned and sank some hours later.

Footnote
Sloop, 420 bm, 18 guns, was ordered from Portsmouth Dockyard in 1798 but cancelled in the following year.

BRECON

A "Hunt" class Mine Countermeasures Vessel, 615 tons (standard), 725 tons (full load); 1 x 40mm gun. Built of GRP by Vosper Thornycroft, Woolston, Southampton. Launched 21.6.1978.

Description of Badge

Field:- Barry wavy of four, blue and white.
Badge:- A cape red-lined and collared ermine and laced with a cord knotted or.

(From the Seal of Brecon, depicting the cloak of the Master of the Brecon Hunt).

Motto

By luck and good guidance.

Battle Honours

Sicily	1943	South France	1944
Salerno	1943	Aegean	1944
English Ch	1943	Atlantic	1945
Mediterranean	1944		

Previous ships of the name

1. "Hunt" class, Type 4, destroyer, 1,175 tons, 6 x 4" AA guns; 3 x 21" TT. Built by Thornycroft, Woolston, Southampton. Launched 27.6.1942. Served with Home Fleet until 6.1943 when she sailed for the Mediterranean. Took part in Operations 'Husky' and 'Avalanche', giving naval gunfire support to the landings in Sicily and Salerno. 1944 Saw extensive anti-submarine action in Mediterranean and took part in Operation 'Dragoon', the landings in South France. 1945 Refit in Malta; then cross-Channel escort work. 8.1945 Joined East Indies fleet. 12.1945 Placed in Reserve. 17.9.1962 Arrived Metal Industries, Faslane, to be broken up.

HMS *Brecon* (1943).

BRILLIANT

A Batch One "Broadsword" class Type 22 frigate, 3,500 tons (standard), 4,200 tons (full load). Built by Yarrow, Scotstoun, Glasgow. Launched 15.12.1978. Exocet SSM and Sea Wolf SAM systems; 2 x 40mm AA and 4 x 20mm AA guns; 6 TT; helicopter-carried A/S torpedoes; 1 helicopter (ability to carry 2).

Description of Badge

Field:- Black.
Badge:- A twelve-pointed star, gold.

Motto

Ea nostra vocamus — We call these ours.

Battle Honours

Belgian Coast	1914	Atlantic	1941-3
Zeebrugge	1918	North Africa	1942-3
Ostend	1918	Falkland Islands	1982
English Ch	1940-3		

Previous ships of the name

1. Sloop, 60 bm, 6 guns. Captured in 1696, but sold out of the service 2 years later.

2. Sloop, in service in 1729.

3. Fifth rate, 718 bm, 36 guns. Built in Plymouth Dockyard. Launched 28.10.1757. In the Channel over the Christmas period, 1757, forced the surrender of 2 French privateers, *Dragon*, 24, and *Intrepide*, 14. The latter scuttled herself. 1760 In company with *Pallas* and *Aeolus*, off the Isle of Man, forced 3 more French ships to surrender. 1.11.1776 Sold at Deptford.

4. Sixth rate, 600 bm, 28 guns. Built by H. Adams, Buckler's Hard. Launched 13.7.1779. 11.1811 Broken up at Portsmouth.

5. Fifth rate, 954 bm, 36 guns. Built by Lungley, Deptford. Launched 28.12.1814. 1843 Reduced to 22 guns. 1859 RNR Training Ship. 8.11.1889 Renamed *Briton*. 12.5.1908 Sold out of the service.

6. Cruiser, 3,600 tons, 2 x 6" and 6 x 4.7" guns. Built in Sheerness Dockyard. Launched 24.6.1891. 1.10.1901 Commissioned for Cruiser Squadron. 1904 Drill Ship for RN Reserve at Southampton. 1906 Detached for special duties in connection with the Newfoundland Fisheries. 1908 4th CS. 1912 Disposal List at Chatham. 25.8.1914 Recommissioned. 23.4.1918 Sunk as a blockship at Ostend.

7. "Basilisk" class destroyer, 1,360 tons, 4 x 4.7" guns; 8 x 21" TT. Built by Swan Hunter, Wallsend-on-Tyne. Launched 9.10.1930. 5.1940 Landed demolition team at Antwerp and evacuated 100 Britons before the port was overrun by the Germans. 1940 Hit by 2 bombs which passed through the quarterdeck without exploding. 1941 In South Atlantic assisted in the sinking of 2 German supply ships *Esso Hamburg* and *Egerland*. 1942 North Africa. Sank Vichy French sloop *La Surprise*. 1943-4 Gibraltar Force. 6.1945 Escorted *Jamaica* conveying HM King George VI to Jersey. 18.8.1947 Sold to Arnott Young and broken up at Troon.

Footnote
Fifth rate, 939 bm, 36 guns, was laid down by Brindley, Frindsbury, but renamed *Orontes* before being launched 29.6.1813.

BRISTOL

A Type 82 Guided Missile Destroyer, 6,300 tons (standard), 7,100 tons (full load). Built by Swan Hunter, Wallsend-on-Tyne. Launched 30.6.1969. Sea Dart SAM Ikara systems; 1 x 4.5"; 4 x 30mm and 2 x 20mm guns; 2 x 20mm Oerlikons.

Description of Badge

Field:- Gules.
Badge:- Sinister, a castle proper rising from a sea wavy barry, azure and argent, and issuing therefrom a ship in sail.
(Simplification of the Arms of the City of Bristol).

Motto

Battle Honours

Santa Cruz	1657	Texel	1673
Lowestoft	1665	Finisterre	1747
Four Days' Battle	1666	Falkland Islands	1914
Orfordness	1666	Falkland Islands	1982
Sole Bay	1672		

Previous ships of the name

1. Ship, 532 bm, 48 guns. Built in Portsmouth Dockyard in 1653. 1688 Channel Service. 1693 Rebuilt at Deptford as 670 bm. 12.4.1709 Captured by the French *La Goire*. 25.4.1709 Recaptured and sunk in the Channel.

2. Fourth rate, 703 bm, 50 guns. Built in Plymouth Dockyard. Launched 8.5.1711. 6.1741 Was one of the six ships left at Jamaica to protect the Island when Vice Admiral Vernon sailed from Port Royal for the unsuccessful attack on Cuba. 1742 Rebuilt at Woolwich as ship of 1,021 bm. Launched 9.7.1746. 1768 Broken up at Plymouth.

3. Fourth rate, 1,049 bm, 50 guns. Built in Sheerness Dockyard. Launched 25.10.1775. 1800 Became a Prison Ship at Chatham. 6.1810 Broken up.

4. East Indiaman *Earl Talbot* was purchased on the stocks to become third rate *Agincourt*, 1,440 bm, 64 guns. Built by Perry, Blackwall. Launched 23.7.1796. 6.1.1812 Became a Prison Ship and renamed *Bristol*. 15.12.1814 Sold out of the service.

5. Wood steam frigate, 4,020 tons. Built in Woolwich Dockyard. Launched 12.2.1861. Used as a sea-going Training Ship for Cadets. 1883 Sold out of the service.

6. Name ship of class of light cruisers, 4,800 tons, 2 x 6", 10 x 4" and 4 x 3 pdr guns, 2 x 18" TT. Built by J. Brown, Clydebank. Launched 23.2.1910. 1910-2 Home Fleet. 1913-4 Second Fleet. 1914 4th CS, North America and West Indies Station. 6.8.1914 In action with German light cruiser *Karlsruhe* off the Bahamas. 1914-5 South American waters. 8.12.1914 Falklands battle, capturing and sinking two transports. Continued afterwards to search for the German light cruiser *Dresden*. 1915-8 In Mediterranean and Adriatic. 15.5.1917 In action with Austrian light cruisers attacking the Otranto barrage. 1918 South Atlantic. 1919 In Reserve. 9.5.1921 Sold to T. W. Ward, Hayle, for breaking up.

BRITANNIA

The Royal Yacht, 3,990 tons (light), 4,961 tons (full load). Built by John Brown, Clydebank. Launched 16.4.1953. Designed as a medium sized naval hospital ship.

Description of Badge

Field:- White.
Badge:- In front of two anchors in saltire gold, a Tudor rose charged with the letters E II R, the whole within the Garter, surmounted by the Imperial Crown.

Motto

Honi soit qui mal y pense — Evil be to him who evil thinks.

Battle Honours

Barfleur	1692	St Vincent	1797
Ushant	1781	Trafalgar	1805
Genoa	1795	Crimea	1854

Previous ships of the name

1. First rate, 1,708 bm, 100 guns. Built in Chatham Dockyard. Launched 1682. 1692 Senior flagship in Anglo-Dutch operations against the French. 1696 In fleet operations along the French coast, Belle Ile to Ile de Ré. 1697 Laid up. 1715 Taken to pieces and frames used for the next ship.

2. First rate, 1,894 bm, 100 guns. Built in Woolwich Dockyard. Launched 3.10.1719. 1735 Flagship on Lisbon Station. 1745 Reduced to Harbour Service, and used as a Hospital Ship. 9.1749 Breaking up completed at Chatham.

3. First rate, 2,116 bm, 100 guns. Built in Portsmouth Dockyard. Launched (after 11 years on the stocks) 19.10.1762. 4.1781 At Relief of Gibraltar. Further distinguished career, included Trafalgar. 6.1.1812 Renamed *Princess Royal*. 18.1.1812 Renamed *St George*, for use as a Convalescent Ship. 2.6.1819 Renamed *Barfleur*. 2.1825 Broken up.

4. First rate, 4,700 tons, 120 guns. Built in Plymouth Dockyard. Launched (after 7 years on the stocks) 20.10.1820. For some years was Guardship at Plymouth. 1836 Flagship at Portsmouth. 1839 Flagship in the Mediterranean. 1854 Black Sea operations in the Russian War. 1.1.1859 Training Ship for Naval Cadets in Portsmouth. 1860 Moved to Dartmouth. 3.3.1869 Superseded by *Prince of Wales*. 20.11.1869 Breaking up completed at Devonport.

5. Steam first rate *Prince of Wales*, 6,201 tons, 121 guns. Built in Portsmouth Dockyard. Launched 25.1.1860. Renamed *Britannia* 3.3.1869. Lay in River Dart for 40 years as Cadet Training Ship. 13.11.1914 Sold to J.B. Garnham & Sons. Re-sold to Hughes Bolckow and arrived Blyth, 7.1916, to be broken up.

6. "King Edward VII" class battle ship, 15,630 tons, 4 x 12", 4 x 9.2" and 10 x 6" guns; 4 x 18" TT. Built in Portsmouth Dockyard. Launched 10.12.1904. In WW1 served in 3rd Battle Squadron and 9th Cruiser Squadron. 9.11.1918 Sunk by *UB 50* off Cape Trafalgar—the last British warship sunk in World War One.

Footnote

a) East India Company ship, 676 bm, built in 1761, was also named *Britannia*. 22.1.1794 Captured 2 large French privateers.
b) Storeship, 535 bm, 26 guns. Purchased 1780 for service in East Indies. 4.1782 Lost with all hands when wrecked on Kentish Knock.
c) Cutter, 69 bm, 6 x 3 pdr guns, was hired 1793-6 and again 1803 to 2.1811.

BROADSWORD

Name ship of the Class of Type 22 frigates, Batch One, 3,500 tons (standard), 4,200 tons (full load). Built by Yarrow, Scotstoun, Glasgow. Launched 12.5.1976. Exocet SSM and Sea Wolf SAM systems; 2 x 40mm; 4 x 20mm AA guns; 6 TT; helicopter-carried A/S torpedoes; 1 helicopter (ability to carry 2).

Description of Badge

Field:- Barry wavy of eight white and blue.
Badge:- In front of a roundel red, a broadsword in pale, point downwards, proper, pommel and hilt gold.

Motto

Battle Honours

Falkland Islands   1982

Previous ships of the name

1. Weapon class destroyer, 1,980 tons, 4 x 4″ guns; 10 x 21″ TT. Built by Yarrow, Scotstoun, Glasgow. Launched 5.2.1946. 1950 Attached to US Operational Development Force. 1953 Paid off into Reserve. 1957-8 Converted to Fleet Radar Picket at Rosyth. 30.9.1958 Commissioned for the 7th Destroyer Squadron on Home/Mediterranean Service. 1959 and 1961 Icelandic patrols. 1963 Reserve Fleet. 1964 Disposal List. 25.4.1968 Towed from Portsmouth to Rosyth to be used for Target Trials by the Naval Constructional Research Establishment. 8.10.1968 Arrived Inverkeithing for breaking up.

HMS *Broadsword* (May 1962).

BROCKLESBY

A "Hunt" class Mine Countermeasures Vessel; 615 tons (standard), 725 tons (full load); 1 x 40mm gun. Built of GRP by Vosper Thornycroft, Woolston, Southampton. Launched 12.1.1982.

Description of Badge

Field:- Red.
Badge:- A buckle gold.
(From the Arms of Pelham, Lord Yarborough).

Motto

Vincit amor patriae — Love of country conquers.

Battle Honours

Dieppe	1942	Sicily	1943
English Ch	1942-3	Salerno	1943
Atlantic	1943	Adriatic	1944

Previous ships of the name

1. "Hunt" class, Type 1, destroyer, 1,000 tons, 4 x 4" guns and 1 x 4 barrelled pom-pom. Built by Cammell Laird, Birkenhead. Launched 30.9.1940. 1942 In the attack on St Nazaire by *Campbeltown*, *Brocklesby* acted as escort to the expedition on its homeward passage. In 1943 conveyed Generals Eisenhower and Montgomery, and Admiral Sir Bertram Ramsay to Sicily after the Allied Landings there. 1945 At the end of the War, was sent to Wilhemshaven to "show the flag". 1946 Aircraft Target Training Ship at Rosyth and Portsmouth. 1947 Reserve at Portsmouth. 1951-2 Refit at Devonport. 1952 2nd Frigate Squadron at Devonport. 1955 Dis-armed for service at Portland as Asdic Training and Trials Ship. 22.6.1963 Arrived Portsmouth to pay off; the last "Hunt" class in commission. 28.10.1968 Arrived Faslane to be broken up.

HMS *Brocklesby* (December 1961).

BULLDOG

Name ship of the class of Coastal Survey Vessels, 800 tons (standard), 1,080 tons (full load). Built by Brooke Marine, Lowestoft. Launched 12.7.1967. Originally designed for service overseas. Built to commercial standards. Fitted for (but not with) 2 x 20mm guns.

Description of Badge

Field:- Black.
Badge:- A bulldog white.

Motto

Hold fast.

Battle Honours

St Lucia	1796	North Africa	1942
Baltic	1854-5	Arctic	1942-4
Dardanelles	1915-6	Atlantic	1942-5
English Ch	1940-5		

Previous ships of the name

1. Sloop, 317 bm, 16 guns. Built by Ladd, Dover. Launched 10.11.1782. 5.1798 Employed in the blockade of Naples. 28.11.1798 With 3 other ships, captured Spanish *San Leon,* 16 guns. 27.2.1801 to 16.9.1801 Was in French hands. Later reduced to a Powder Hulk. 12.1829 Breaking up completed at Portsmouth.

2. Gunvessel, 58 bm, 4 guns. A Dutch Hoy, purchased 3.1794. Sold later the same year.

3. Wood paddlewheel sloop, 1,124 bm. Built in Chatham Dockyard. Launched 2.10.1845. Distinguished career in the Baltic and West Indies. Captured 2 Russian Government schooners off Biörko. 23.10.1865 Stranded and destroyed while attacking rebel steamer in Haiti.

4. ''Ant'' class iron steam gunboat, 254 tons, 1 x 10" gun. Built by Cammell and Johnston, Woolwich. Launched 1.9.1872. 1872-82 Reserve at Portsmouth. 1882 At Devonport. 1884-1903 Tender to *Cambridge,* gunnery ship at Devonport. 16.7.1906 Sold out of the service.

5. Destroyer, 952 tons, 1 x 4" and 3 x 12 pdr guns; 2 TT. Built by J. Brown, Clydebank. Launched 13.11.1909. 1910-1 1st DF, Home Fleet. 1912 3rd DF. 1913 5th DF in the Mediterranean. 1915 Dardanelles. 1916 Evacuation at Gallipoli. 21.9.1920 Sold to T.W. Ward, Rainham, for breaking up.

6. ''Basilisk'' class destroyer, 1,360 tons, 4 x 4.7" guns; 8 x 21" TT. Built by Swan Hunter, Wallsend-on-Tyne. Launched 6.12.1930. 1939 In the Mediterranean, with aircraft carrier *Glorious.* 9.5.1940 Took the torpedoed *Kelly* in tow. 11.6.1940 Damaged by air attack off St Valery; immobilised; towed to Portsmouth. 9.5.1941 With other ships, destroyed *U 110*; tried to take the submarine in tow but she later sank. 2.5.1942 In action with 3 German destroyers. 26.6.1944 Sank *U 719* north west of Ireland. 9.5.1945 Instrument of surrender of German garrison in Channel Islands was signed on board. 15.1.1946 Sold to Metal Industries. 3.1946 Arrived Rosyth to be broken up.

Footnote
Trawler, 148 tons, built in 1892, was hired from 1917-9.

HMS *Bulldog* (July 1937).

CAMPBELTOWN

A Batch Three "Broadsword" class Type 22 frigate, 4,200 tons (standard), 4,900 tons (full load). Being built by Cammell Laird, Birkenhead. Harpoon SSM and Sea Wolf SAM systems; 1 x 4.5"; 1 Goalkeeper system; 2 x 30mm guns; 6 TT; helicopter-carried A/S torpedoes; ability to carry 2 helicopters.

Description of Badge

Field:- White.
Badge:- Within an annulet blue charged in base with a mullet white, a sprig of myrtle proper.

Motto

Battle Honours

Atlantic	1941-2	St Nazaire	1942

Previous ships of the name

1. Destroyer, ex-USS *Buchanan*, 1,090 tons, 3 x 4" and 1 x 3" guns; 6 TT. Built by Bath Iron Works, Maine, USA. Launched 2.1.1919. One of the 50 USN destroyers handed over to the RN in exchange for leases of naval and air bases in Newfoundland and West Indies. 29.9.1940 Arrived Devonport. Joined 7th Escort Group, Liverpool, and from Londonderry. 3.12.1940 In collision; repairs completed 3.1941. 1941 27th Escort Group, Greenock. 3 to 4.1941 Allocated to the Netherlands, then to Poland. 9.1941 Reverted to RN. Employed as Escort to Atlantic convoys. 10 to 19.3.1942 Fitted out at Devonport as an "expendable explosive destroyer" for the raid on St Nazaire. 27/28.3.1942 Expended at St Nazaire in demolishing the lock gates.

CARDIFF

A Batch One "Town" class Type 42 Guided Missile Destroyer, 3,500 tons (standard), 4,100 tons (full load). Built by Vickers, Barrow. Launched 22.2.1974. Sea Dart SAM system; 1 x 4.5"; 2 x 20mm Oerlikons; helicopter-launched Sea Skua missiles; 6 TT; 1 helicopter.

Description of Badge

Field:- Green.
Badge:- A castle gold, on three wavelets red and gold.

(The Arms of the City of Cardiff are red, three chevrons gold).

Motto

Acris in cardine rerum — Keen in emergency.

Battle Honours

Falkland Islands   1982

Previous ships of the name

1. Dutch pirate ship *Fortune,* 300 bm, 34 guns. Captured in the North Sea in 1652. Added to the Royal Navy as *Cardiff;* so named to commemorate the capture of Cardiff Castle during the Civil War. 1658 Sold at Jamaica.

2. "Ceres" class Light Cruiser, ex-*Caprice*, 4,190 tons, 5 x 6" and 2 x 3" AA guns; 8 x 21" TT. Built by Fairfield, Govan, Glasgow. Launched 12.4.1917. 17.11.1917 At Battle of Heligoland Bight. 21.11.1918 Led the German High Seas Fleet to their surrender rendezvous. Afterwards led 6th Cruiser Squadron to the Baltic to support Latvians and Estonians against the Bolsheviks. 1919-29 Flagship 3rd LCS, Mediterranean. 1929-31 Refit at Devonport. 1931-3 Africa Station. 1933-8 In Reserve; SORF, Nore. 1938-9 China Station. 1939 12th CS on Northern Patrol. 1940-5 Gunnery Training Ship in Clyde area. 3.9.1945 Reduced to Reserve in the Gareloch. 23.1.1946 Sold to Arnott Young to be broken up at Troon.

HMS Cardiff

CARRON

A "River" class Fleet Minesweeper, 890 tons (full load); 1 x 40mm gun. Built by Richards, Great Yarmouth. Launched 23.9.1983. Allocated to the Severn Division, RNR.

Description of Badge
Field:- Red.
Badge:- A fountain charged with a stag's head caboshed gold.
(The stag's head is from the Arms of Mackenzie).

Motto

Battle Honours
Baltic   1855

Previous ships of the name

1. Sixth rate, 460 bm, 20 guns. Built by H. Adams, Buckler's Hard. Launched 9.11.1813. 1814 Served in the American War. 6.7.1820 Wrecked near Puri Bay in India.

2. Wood paddlewheel vessel, 294 bm—converted on the stocks from a "Cherokee" class brig-sloop—built in Deptford Dockyard. Launched 9.1.1827. 1837 Converted to a Tug. 1846 Lent as a Coal Hulk. 1848 Used as a breakwater. 6.1877 Removed from the Navy List. 1.1885 Broken up at Devonport.

3. Mortar Vessel, 160 bm. Built by Wigram, Blackwall. Launched 28.4.1855. 19.10.1855 Renamed *MV 17*. 7.1866 Reduced to a hulk. 11.1884 Broken up at Devonport.

4. Destroyer from the "CA" group of the "C" class, 1,710 tons, 4 x 4.5", 4 x 40mm AA guns; 8 TT. Built by Scotts, Greenock. Launched 28.3.1944. Saw action with 6th Destroyer Flotilla in North Atlantic and off Norway. 1945-6 In Indian Ocean. 1946-54 In Reserve at Chatham. 8.1955 Completed conversion at Chatham. Joined Dartmouth Training Squadron. 7.1960 Transferred to Portsmouth as Navigational Training Ship attached to HMS *Dryad*. 29.3.1963 Paid off for disposal. 4.4.1967 Arrived Inverkeithing to be broken up by T.W. Ward.

Footnote
Motor Vessel commissioned into the RN for the period of World War I.

HMS *Carron,* at Dartmouth.

CATTISTOCK

A "Hunt" class Mine Countermeasures Vessel, 615 tons (standard), 725 tons (full load); 1 x 40mm gun. Built of GRP by Vosper Thornycroft, Woolston, Southampton. Launched 21.1.1981.

Description of Badge

Field:- Red.

Badge:- Upon a white roundel, a blue cornflower, stalked and leaved proper.

(Cornflower refers to the "True Blue", the old name of the Hunt).

Motto

Battle Honours

North Sea	1941-5	Normandy	1944
Atlantic	1942-4		

Previous ships of the name

1. Early "Hunt" class minesweeper, 750 tons, 2 x 12 pdr guns. Built by Clyde S.B. Co. Launched 21.2.1917. In World War 1, operated off Southern Ireland and in the North Sea. 1919 In the Baltic, operating against the Bolsheviks. 1920 Paid off. 22.2.1923 Sold to Alloa S. Bkg. Co. 8.1924 Arrived Charlestown, Fife, to be broken up.

2. "Hunt" class Type 1 "Atherstone" type destroyer, 907 tons; 4 x 4" guns and 1 x 4 barrelled pom-pom. Built by Yarrow, Scotstoun, Glasgow. Launched 22.2.1940. Served in the 21st Destroyer Flotilla on anti-E-boat patrols and was involved in cross-Channel escort duties during the build-up phase to the Normandy invasion. 29/30.8.1944 Was hit by 26 projectiles from German coastal batteries and her Commanding Officer, Lt. R.G.D. Keddie, D.S.C., was killed. After 7 weeks of repairs, she returned to escort and patrol duties. 8.1945 Portsmouth Command. 3.1946 Placed in Reserve at Devonport. Sold, and in 6.1957 arrived Newport to be broken up by J. Cashmore.

HMS *Cattistock*

CHALLENGER

A Seabed Operations Vessel, 6,500 tons (standard), 7,195, (full load). Built by Scotts, Greenock. Launched 19.5.1981. Accepted 13.7.1984.

Description of Badge

Field:- Blue.
Badge:- A stag statant on a mount, proper.
(From Landseer's picture ''The Challenger'', 1872).

Motto

Depugnare superbos — To fight the proud.

Battle Honours

San Sebastian   1813   Cameroons   1914

Previous ships of the name

1. Brig-sloop, 285 bm, 16 guns. Built of pitch pine by Wallis, Blackwall. Launched 30.7.1806. 12.3.1811 Captured by a French frigate off Mauritius.

2. ''Cruizer'' class brig-sloop, 384 bm, 18 guns. Built by Hobbs and Hillyer, Redbridge. Launched 15.5.1813. 1813 Helped capture San Sebastian. At Mouth of Bayonne River engaged a French ship which set fire to herself. 1820 Mooring Vessel. 3.1824 Sold at Trincomalee.

3. Sixth rate, 603 bm, 28 guns. Built in Portsmouth Dockyard. Launched 14.11.1826. 19.5.1835 Wrecked on west coast of Chile. Two lives lost.

4. Wood steam corvette, 2,306 tons, 8 guns. Built in Woolwich Dockyard. Launched 13.2.1858. 1860 Actions against Mexico and Fijians. 1872 Became a Survey Ship. Between 1872-6 crossed the Equator 8 times; ventured into Antarctic ice; and covered 68,000 miles in 1,000 days at sea. 1880 Coal Hulk. 6.1.1921 Sold to J.B. Garnham for breaking up.

5. Cruiser—name ship of class—5,880 tons, 11 x 6" guns; 2 x 18" TT. Built in Chatham Dockyard. Undocked 27.5.1902. 1904 Served with Imperial Squadron on the Australian Station. 1914-5 At Cameroons. 7.1915 Participated in destruction of *Königsberg*. 13.6.1916 With HMAS *Pioneer*, bombarded Dar-Es-Salaam. 1.4.1919 Paid off at Portsmouth. 31.5.1920 Sold to T.W. Ward, Preston, for breaking up.

6. Survey Ship, 1,140 tons. Built in Chatham Dockyard. Launched 1.6.1931. Originally designed as a Fishery Protection ship. 1933-9 Survey duties, mostly around UK coast. 1939-42 Portsmouth and Nore Command. 1942-5 With Eastern Fleet. 1947 Surveying Persian Gulf. 1950 Surveying West Indies and Far East. 1953 At Portsmouth. 12.1.1954 Arrived Dover Industries Ltd. to be broken up.

Footnote
a) Corvette, 18 guns, was ordered from Chatham Dockyard in 1845 but cancelled in 1848.
b) Trawler was hired into service 1917-9.

CHARGER

A Coastal Training Craft of 43 tonnes for the RNR. Being built of GRP by Watercraft Ltd., Shoreham-by-Sea. Allocated to London Division, RNR.

Description of Badge

Field:- Green.
Badge:- A horse courant white, caparisoned white, fimbriated gold.

Motto

Battle Honours

None.

Previous ships of the name

1. Gun-brig, 179 bm, 1 x 8" mortar, 10 x 18 pdr carronades, 2 x 18 pdr guns. Built by Dudman, Deptford. Launched 17.4.1801. 9.6.1808 While acting as convoy escort, was attacked by 25 Danish gunboats, but managed to beat them off and escape. 9.6.1814 Sold out of the service.

2. Wood paddlewheel packet, 733 bm, ex-*George IV*. 20.8.1830 Purchased and renamed *Courier*. 1831 Renamed *Hermes*. 1835 Renamed *Charger* and became a Coal Hulk at Woolwich. 1854 Broken up.

3. "Albacore" class wood steam gunboat, 232 bm, 1 x 68 pdr, 1 x 32 pdr and 2 x 20 pdr guns. Built by Pitcher, Northfleet. Launched 13.11.1855. In Reserve until 6.1866. Became a Buoy Boat at Halifax as *YC3*. 1869 Renamed *YC6*. 7.1887 Sold for mercantile service, and renamed *Rescue*. 1921 Broken up.

4. "A" class destroyer, 290 tons, 1 x 12 pdr gun; 2 TT. Built by Yarrow, Poplar. Launched 15.5.1894. On completion, lay at Portsmouth. 1899-1900 Refit at Earle's Shipbuilding Company, Hull. After a period at Devonport, was reduced to Reserve at Chatham. 1907 Commissioned for the Home Fleet at the Nore. 1911 Laid up at Sheerness. 14.5.1912 Sold at Chatham.

5. LST (3) 3026, 2,256 tons, 10 x 20mm AA guns. Built by Blyth S.B. and D.D. Co. Launched 30.10.1944. 1947 Renamed *Charger*. 1956 Renamed *Empire Nordic* with the Ministry of Transport. 1967 On Sales List.

Footnote

a) Escort Carrier, 8,200 tons, ex-mercantile *Rio de la Plata*; converted on the stocks by Sun S.B. and D.D. Co., Chester, Pennsylvania, USA. Launched 1.3.1941 for the RN, but retained by the USN as USS *Charger*, for pilot training at sea.
b) Escort Carrier, 11,420 tons. Laid down as *Charger* by Seattle, Tacoma, USA, but launched 16.7.1942 as *Ravager*.

CHARYBDIS

A Batch Three "Leander" class (broad-beamed) frigate, 2,500 tons. Built by Harland and Wolff, Belfast. Launched 28.2.1968. 1977-80 Exocet conversion at Devonport. New armament:- Exocet SSM and Sea Wolf SAM systems; A/S torpedo tubes; 2 x 20mm guns; 1 helicopter.

Description of Badge

Field:- White.

Badge:- Issuant from a whirlpool in base, a fig tree proper, suspended from the branches a bat inverted, gold.

(In Greek mythology, Charybdis was a beautiful goddess, the daughter of Gaia (the earth mother) and Poseidon (the sea god). The legend describes how Charybdis, having stolen the cattle of Heracles, was punished by being thrown into the Straits of Messina. There she was transformed into a whirlpool, a deadly hazard to unwary mariners).

Motto

Battle Honours

Malta Convoys	1942	Atlantic	1943
North Africa	1942	English Ch	1943
Salerno	1943	Biscay	1943

Previous ships of the name

1. "Cruizer" class brig-sloop, 385 bm, 18 guns. Built by Richards, Hythe. Launched 28.8.1809. 3.2.1819 Sold to Pittman.

2. "Cherokee" class brig-sloop, 232 bm, 10 guns. Built in Portsmouth Dockyard. Launched 27.2.1831. 7.11.1843 Sold to Beatson, Rotherhithe.

3. Wood steam corvette, 2,187 tons, 20 x 8" guns. Built in Chatham Dockyard. Launched 1.6.1859. 10.1880 to 8.1882 Lent to Canada as Training Ship. 1884 Sold at Halifax.

4. Cruiser, 4,360 tons, 2 x 6" and 8 x 4.7" guns. Built in Sheerness Dockyard. Launched 15.6.1893. 14.1.1896 Commissioned at Chatham for the Particular Service Squadron; then the Channel Squadron. 1898 Paid off at Devonport. 18.4.1900 Commissioned for the North America and West Indies Station. 3.5.1902 Recommissioned at Halifax. 1905 Paid off into Reserve at Chatham. 1907-12 Home Fleet at the Nore. 25.4.1913 Commissioned for the Third Fleet. 1915 Damaged in collision; laid up; then converted. 3.1918 Converted to Cargo Carrier on Bermuda-New York run. 12.1919 Returned to RN. 27.1.1922 Sold at Bermuda. 10.1923 Resold and broken up in Holland.

5. "Dido" class cruiser, 5,582 tons; 8 x 4.5" guns. Built by Cammell Laird, Birkenhead. Launched 17.9.1940. Played a vital part in several Malta Convoys. 1943 Landings at Salerno. 23.10.1943 With *Limbourne,* was engaged in an offensive sweep off French coast. In poor visibility, she was hit by a torpedo from German TBs. Five minutes later, hit by another. She turned over and sank. *Limbourne* was also sunk. Nearly 500 men died, some of the bodies coming ashore in the Channel Islands. In Guernsey, islanders turned out in large numbers for burials, despite German instructions to the contrary.

CHASER

An "Attacker" class Seamanship and Navigational Training Vessel of 34 tons for the RNR and University RN Units. Built by Fairey Allday Marine, Southampton. Completed 1983. Allocated to Aberdeen University.

Description of Badge

Field:- Per fess wavy white and green.
Badge:- A greyhound courant, proper.

Motto

Venando victor — Victorious by chasing.

Battle Honours

Atlantic	1943	Okinawa	1945
Arctic	1944		

Previous ships of the name

1. Sloop, 320 bm, 18 guns. Purchased 1.1.1781 in the East Indies. 25.2.1782 Captured by the French in the Bay of Bengal. 3.1783 Recaptured. 28.8.1784 Sold out of the service.

2. Escort Carrier, 11,420 tons, ex-mercantile *Mormacgulf,* converted on the stocks to USS *Breton.* Built by Ingalls S.B. Corp., Pascagoula, Miss., USA. Launched 19.6.1942. 9.4.1943 Transferred to RN on Lend-Lease. Carried RAF ground crews to Russia prior to FAA attack on *Tirpitz.* 3.1944 Escorting the westbound convoy RA 57 from Russia. Her aircraft were involved in the sinking of *U 472, U 366* and *U 973.* 1945 In British Pacific Fleet. 12.5.1946 Returned to the USN; sold as *Aagtekerk.*

3. LST (3) 3029, 2,256 tons, 10 x 20mm guns. Built by Alex Stephen, Linthouse, Glasgow. Launched 12.1.1945. 1947 Renamed *Chaser.* 1956-60 SO Submarines Ship at Portland. 1.2.1962 Sold. 28.3.1962 Arrived Spezia to be broken up.

HMS *Chaser*

CHATHAM

A Batch Three "Broadsword" class Type 22 frigate. 4,200 tons (standard), 4,900 tons (full load). Being built by Swan Hunter, Wallsend-on-Tyne. Harpoon SSM and Sea Wolf SAM systems; 1 x 4.5"; 1 Goalkeeper system; 2 x 30mm guns; 6 TT; helicopter-carried A/S torpedoes; 1 helicopter (ability to carry 2).

Description of Badge

Motto

Battle Honours
Quiberon Bay   1759   Dardanelles   1915-6

Previous ships of the name

1. Sloop, 50 bm, 4 guns. Built in Chatham Dockyard in 1673. 1677 Wrecked.

2. Fourth rate, 696 bm, 48 guns. Built in Chatham Dockyard. Launched 20.4.1691. 19.5.1692 In the defeat of the French off Barfleur. 7.1704 Off Lisbon. 1721 Rebuilt at Deptford as 756 bm. 1744 In Mediterranean. 5.1749 Sunk as a breakwater at Sheerness. 1762 Raised and rebuilt.

3. Sheer Hulk; actually built as a Hulk, 714 bm. Built in Chatham Dockyard. Launched 9.10.1694. 10.1813 Broken up at Chatham.

4. Yacht, 60 bm, 14 guns. Built in Chatham Dockyard. Launched 18.7.1716. Did duty as Commissioner's Yacht at Chatham. 28.3.1742 Sold out of the service.

5. Yacht, 74 bm, 6 guns. Built in Chatham Dockyard. Launched 1.10.1741. Assumed duties of previous vessel. 1793 Rebuilt at Chatham as 93 bm. 1842 Again rebuilt at Chatham, lengthened 10 feet, as 104 bm. 9.3.1867 Her breaking up at Chatham completed.

6. Fourth rate, 1,052 bm, 50 guns. Built in Portsmouth Dockyard. Launched 25.4.1758. 18.5.1759 Captured the French 36 guns *Aréthuse*. 2.9.1781 Took the French 32 guns frigate *Magicienne* in Boston Bay. 3.1793 Reduced to Harbour Service at Chatham. Used as Hospital Ship at Falmouth. 12.1805 Converted to Powder Hulk. 1810 Renamed *Tilbury*. 5.1814 Broken up at Chatham.

7. Survey Brig, 133 bm, 4 guns. Built by King, Dover, in 1788. Purchased into RN 12.2.1788. 1791-5 In Vancouver's voyage of discovery in the Pacific. 1830 Sold at Jamaica.

8. Sloop, 184 bm, 10 guns. Hired 1793-5.

9. Transport, 317 bm. Built by Brindley, Frindsbury. Launched 22.6.1811. 9.1825 Sunk as a breakwater.

10. Third rate, 1,860 bm, 74 guns. French *Royal Hollandais* captured on the stocks at Flushing 17.8.1809. Frames taken to Woolwich Dockyard. Launched 14.2.1812. 10.9.1817 Sold to J. Cristall.

11. Sheer Hulk, 1,691 bm. Built in Chatham Dockyard. Launched 2.4.1813. 5.8.1876 Her Breaking up completed at Chatham.

12. Name ship of class of light cruisers, 5,400 tons, 8 x 6" and 4 x 3 pdr guns; 2 x 21" TT. Built in Chatham Dockyard. Launched 9.11.1911. 1912-3 2nd BS, Home Fleet. 1913-4 In Mediterranean. 1914-5 Red Sea and East Indies. 19.10.1914 Captured the German SS *Präsident* in the Lindi River. 1915 Off the Rufiji River blockading the German *Königsberg*. 5.1915 Dardanelles operation. 1916-8 3rd LCS, Grand Fleet. 26.5.1916 Damaged by mine off the Norfolk coast. 1917 Scandinavian convoy escort. 1918-20 In Reserve. 1920-4 Loaned to the RNZN. 1924-5 Flagship, 4th LCS, East Indies. 1925-6 Again in Reserve. 13.7.1926 Sold to T.W. Ward, Pembroke.

Footnote
a) Sloop, 50 bm, 4 guns. Built in Chatham Dockyard in 1673 with a double hull. Known as *Chatham Double*.
b) Sloop, 65 bm, 8 guns. Captured from the French 3.1703, by *Chatham* (No. 2 above). Renamed *Chatham Prize*.

CHIDDINGFOLD

A "Hunt" class Mine Countermeasures Vessel, 615 tons (standard), 725 tons (full load). 1 x 40mm. Built of GRP by Vosper Thornycroft, Woolston, Southampton. Launched 6.10.1983.

Description of Badge

Field:- Blue.
Badge:- A stirrup and leather, white, and a spur, gold, interlaced and in saltire.
(From the Arms of Sadler, a Master of the Chiddingfold Hunt).

Motto

Battle Honours

Norway   1941   English Ch   1945

Previous ships of the name

1. "Hunt" class Type 2 "Blankney" type destroyer, 1,050 tons, 6 x 4" AA guns. Built by Scotts, Greenock. Launched 10.3.1941. Her two Battle Honours indicate her war service. 16.11.1945 Returned to Portsmouth from the East Indies; paid off into Reserve. 1950-2 Laid up at Harwich. 7.1952 Towed to Liverpool for refit. 27.10.1952 Loaned to the Indian Navy for 3 years; renamed *Ganga*; loan extended. 4.1959 Sold to the Indian Navy. 1975 Disposal List.

HMS *Chiddingfold*

CHURCHILL

Name ship of the class of nuclear powered Fleet Submarine, 4,300 tons (surfaced), 4,800 tons (submerged); 6 x 21" TT Built by Vickers, Barrow. Launched 20.12.1968.

Description of Badge

Field:- Barry wavy of six, white and blue.
Badge:- A lion rampant, guardant white, holding between the paws a staff gold, flying therefrom to the sinister, a flag red charged with a dexter hand couped white and charged on the body with a hurt thereon a mullet, also white.
(From the Arms of Churchill).

Motto

Veteris vestigia flammae — A spark of the old flame.

Battle Honours

Atlantic   1941-4

Previous ships of the name

1. Ex-USS *Herndon,* destroyer, 1,190 tons, 1 x 4" and 1 x 3" guns; 3 TT. One of the 50 American destroyers transferred to the RN in 1940. 9.9.1940 Commissioned into the RN. Mid-1941 Loaned to the RCN in Newfoundland Force. 1.1942 In UK with 26th Escort Group, Clyde. Took part in Atlantic Convoys, including one for the big build-up in North Africa after Operation 'Torch' in 1942. 3.1943 In Canadian C 4 Group at Londonderry. Early 1944 Reduced to Reserve. 16.7.1944 Transferred to the Russian Navy as *Deiatelnyi.* 16.1.1945 Sunk in Arctic Ocean by *U 956.*

HMS *Churchill* (1980).

CLEOPATRA

A Batch One ''Leander'' class frigate, 2,450 tons (standard). Built in Devonport Dockyard. Launched 25.3.1964. 1973-5 Exocet conversion at Devonport. New armament:- Exocet SSM and Sea Cat SAM systems; 2 x 40mm guns; 6 TT. Towed Array sonar system.

Description of Badge

Field:- Black.
Badge:- Cleopatra's head proper, crowned gold.

(Cleopatra was Queen of Egypt, distinguished for her beauty and her love affairs, who killed herself by self-inflicting the bite of an asp).

Motto

Invicta ut olin — Unconquered as ever.

Battle Honours

Dogger Bank	1781	Malta Convoys	1942
Martinique	1809	Sirte	1942
Burma	1853	Sicily	1943
Belgian Coast	1916		

Previous ships of the name

1. Fifth rate, 689 bm, 32 guns. Built by J.H. Hillhouse, Bristol. Launched 26.11.1779. 1796 Captured the French *Aurore* on American Station. 17.2.1805 Herself captured by *Ville de Milan* off Bermuda; but in French hands for only a week. 1809 Captured the French frigate *Topaz*. 21.9.1814 Breaking up at Deptford completed.

2. Sixth rate, 918 bm, 26 guns. Built at Pembroke Dock. Launched 28.4.1835. 1841 Captured Spanish slaver *Segundo Rosario*, with 284 slaves, in West Indies. 2.1862 Broken up by Messrs. Castle and Beech.

3. Paddlewheel sloop, built in 1839 by Pitcher, Northfleet. 14.4.1847 Foundered in the Indian Ocean.

4. Steam corvette, 2,380 tons, 2 x 7'' and 12 x 64 pdr guns. Built by Elder, Glasgow. Launched 1.8.1878. 1894 At intervention at Bluefields, Nicaragua. 1905 Reduced to Harbour Service. Used as overflow ship to *Defiance* in the Hamoaze, Devonport. 1.1922 Renamed *Defiance III*. 7.1931 Sold to Castle at Millbay, Plymouth, for breaking up.

5. ''Caroline'' class light cruiser, 3,750 tons, 2 x 6'', 8 x 4'' and 1 x 3'' AA guns; 4 x 21'' TT. Built in Devonport Dockyard. Launched 14.1.1915. Fitted with a flying-off platform and one seaplane. Platform removed in 1916. 25.3.1916 Rammed and sank the German destroyer *G 194*. 4.8.1916 Struck a British mine off the Dutch coast. 1918-9 7th LCS, Grand Fleet. 1919 To the Baltic. 1920-1 Atlantic Fleet. 1922-3 Reserve Fleet at the Nore. 1923-4 3rd LCS in the Mediterranean. 1926 Again in Reserve at the Nore. 1928-9 Trooping trips to the Mediterranean and China. 26.6.1931 Sold to Hughes Bolckow; broken up at Blyth.

6. ''Dido'' class cruiser, 5,582 tons, 10 x 5.25'' and 8 x 2 pdr AA guns; 6 x 21'' TT. Built by Hawthorn Leslie, Hebburn-on-Tyne. Launched 27.3.1940. 12.2.1942 Damaged by bomb off Grand Harbour, Malta. Repaired at Malta. 22.3.1942 Second Battle of Sirte. 7 to 9.1942 Operating in Eastern Mediterranean. 9.1942 Self refit at Massawa. No floating dock large enough; ship docked half at a time, during which she slipped off the blocks; suffered minor damage. 13.12.1942 With others, sank 3 enemy ships off North Africa. 7.7.1943 Invasion of Sicily. 16.7.1943 Damaged by torpedo from Italian submarine *Dandolo*. Repaired at Malta; then Gibraltar. 12.1943 to 18.10.1944 at Philadelphia, USA. 5.1.1945 to 1.3.1945 On the Clyde. 5.1945 In Mediterranean; then to East Indies. 1.9.1945 Arrived Penang for Japanese surrender. 7.2.1946 Arrived Portsmouth. 10.1953 Reserve Fleet, Chatham. 9.1954 to 11.1956 Accommodation Ship at Portsmouth. 15.12.1958 Arrived Newport to be broken up by J. Cashmore.

CONQUEROR

A "Churchill" class nuclear powered Fleet Submarine, 4,300 tons (surfaced), 4,500 tons (submerged). 6 x 21" TT. Built by Cammell Laird, Birkenhead. Launched 28.8.1969.

Description of Badge

Field:- Argent.

Badge:- A banner gules, fringed with or, and charged with a raven proper, the banner flying from a spear.

(The raven flag of the Norseman. The Bayeux tapestry shows William the Conqueror with a similar flag).

Motto

Battle Honours

Lagos	1759	English Ch	1943-5
The Saints	1782	Biscay	1944
Trafalgar	1805	Atlantic	1944-5
Jutland	1916	Falkland Islands	1982
North Sea	1942-3		

Previous ships of the name

1. French fireship *La Conquerante,* 308 bm, 8 guns. Captured 1745 by *Lowestoffe* in Mediterranean. 1746 Bought into RN as fireship *Conqueror;* never used as such. 7.3.1748 Sold.

2. Third rate, 1,432 bm, 70 guns. Built by Barnard, Harwich. Launched 24.5.1758. 26.10.1760 Wrecked in Plymouth Sound, when driven from her anchorage.

3. Third rate, 1,606 bm, 74 guns. Built in Plymouth Dockyard. Launched 18.10.1773. 11.1794 Broken up.

4. French third rate *La Conquerante,* 1,681 bm, 74 guns. Captured at Battle of the Nile, 1798. 1799 Reduced to Harbour Service. 3.1802 Broken up.

5. Third rate, 1,854 bm, 74 guns. Built by Graham, Harwich. Launched 23.11.1801. 7.1822 Broken up at Chatham.

6. First rate, steam, 3,225 bm, 101 guns. Built in Devonport Dockyard. Launched 2.5.1855. 29.12.1861 Wrecked on Rum Bay, near Nassau, in the Bahamas.

7. First rate, *Waterloo,* 2,694 bm, 120 guns. Built in Chatham Dockyard. Launched 10.6.1833. 12.11.1859 Undocked as steam ship. 1862 Renamed *Conqueror.* 11.8.1876 Renamed *Warspite,* Marine Society Training Ship. 20.1.1918 Burnt in the Thames.

8. Name ship of the class of Turret Ships, 6,200 tons, 2 x 12" and 4 x 6" guns. Built in Chatham Dockyard. Undocked 8.9.1881. On completion, lay at Chatham. 1887 To Devonport; acted as tender to *Cambridge,* Gunnery Ship. 1905 Laid up in Holy Loch. 9.4.1907 Sold to Castle for breaking up.

9. Battleship 22,500 tons, 10 x 13.5" and 16 x 4" guns. Built by Wm Beardmore, Dalmuir. Launched 1.5.1911. 23.11.1912 Commissioned at Devonport for 2nd BS. Wartime Service was spent in the 2nd BS, Grand Fleet. 18.8.1920 Reduced to Reserve complement at Portland. 29.6.1921 Recommissioned to become Flagship of Vice Admiral Commanding Reserve Fleet. 19.12.1922 Sold to Upnor Sbkg. Co.

Footnote

a) Yacht, 526 tons, was hired in 1915 as *Conqueror II,* patrol vessel. 26.9.1916 Sunk by gunfire from *U 52.*

b) Tug, 177 tons, was hired 1916-9.

c) Battleship, 40,000 tons, 9 x 16" and 16 x 5.25" guns, was ordered from J. Brown, Clydebank in 8.1939 but cancelled in 1940.

d) Yacht, 886 tons, ex-*Emerald,* was hired as A/S vessel, 1939-45.

e) Two French ships were seized at Falmouth 3.7.1940—Patrol Vessel *Le Conquerant* 374 tons, 2 x 3.9" guns; foundered in 1941; and a naval tug *La Conquerante,* 70 tons, which served in the RN on M/S duties. Returned 1945.

CORMORANT

Patrol Craft, former RAF Search and Rescue craft *Sunderland*. Built by James and Stone, Brightlingsea, in 1976. Commissioned into the RN in 1985. Based at Gibraltar.

Description of Badge

Field:- Blue.
Badge:- A cormorant on a rock gold, in his beak an eel, silver.

Motto

Laboris avidus — Greedy of work.

Battle Honours

Quebec	1759	China	1856-9
Minorca	1798		

Previous ships of the name

1. Fireship, 408 bm, 16 guns. Ex-French *Marchault*. Captured in 4.1757. 1759 At capture of Quebec. 23.12.1762 Sold out of the service.

2. Sloop, 304 bm, 14 guns. Built by Barnard, Ipswich. Launched 21.5.1776. 8.1778 In action with a French squadron off Pondicherry. 10.1778 At blockade and capture of Pondicherry. 24.8.1781 Captured by the French off Charleston Bar.

3. Brig-sloop, 198 bm, 12 guns. Ex-American *Rattlesnake*. Captured in 1781 by *Assurance*. 30.7.1782 Captured French 10 gun sloop *Temeraire*. 8.1783 Renamed *Rattlesnake*. 10.10.1786 Sold out of the service.

4. Sloop, 427 bm, 18 guns. Built by Randall, Rotherhithe. Launched 2.1.1794. 1796 Bombardment of Leogane, San Domingo. 1796 Captured French 14 gun sloop *Alerte* in West Indies. 24.12.1796 Accidentally blown up at Port-au-Prince, Haiti.

5. Sixth rate, 564 bm, 20 guns. Ex-French *Etna*. 13.11.1796 Captured by *Melampus* on coast of France. 1798 Engaged in the blockade of Cadiz. 2.1.1799 Captured the Spanish 12 gun *Valiente* off Malaga. 16.3.1799 With *Centaur* engaged and drove ashore the Spanish 34 gun frigate *Guadalupe*. 19.3.1799 Captured the Spanish 18 gun sloop *Vincenjo*. 20.5.1800 Wrecked on the coast of Egypt.

6. Sloop, 328 bm, 16 guns. Ex-*Blenheim*. Purchased in 6.1804. 4.12.1817 Sold out of the service.

7. Wood paddlewheel sloop, 1,057 bm. Built in Sheerness Dockyard. Launched 29.3.1842. 1849 Engaged in the suppression of slave-trade off south east coast of America. 1850 Her boats destroyed the famous slaver *Rival* in the Rio Frio. 1853-4 Broken up.

8. "Vigilant" class wood steam gunvessel, 675 bm, 1 x 110 pdr, 1 x 68 pdr and 2 x 20 pdr guns. Built by Fletcher, Limehouse. Launched 23.2.1856. 1858 Second China War, including bombardment and capture of Taku forts. 28.6.1859 Sunk in action with Peiho forts, China.

9. Name ship of class of wood steam sloops 695 bm, 2 x 68 pdr and 2 x 32 pdr guns. Built by Wigram, Blackwall. Launched 9.2.1860. 1862-70 China Station. 1870 Sold at Hong Kong.

10. "Osprey" class composite steam sloop, 1,130 tons, 2 x 7" and 4 x 64 pdr guns. Built in Chatham Dockyard. Launched 12.9.1877. 1878-82 Australia Station. 1879 Punitive expedition in New Hebrides. 1883-5 Reserve and refit. 1885 Channel Squadron. 1885-9 Pacific Station. 11.1889 Reduced to Harbour Service; machinery removed; became Receiving Ship at Gibraltar. 7.1946 Renamed *Rooke*. 1949 Broken up at Malaga, Spain.

Footnote
a) Trawler, 154 tons, built in 1891, was hired as *Cormorant II* 1915-9.
b) Drifter, 94 tons, built in 1907, was hired as *Cormorant III* 1915-9.
c) Trawler, 162 tons, built in 1897 was hired as *Cormorant IV* 1916-9.

CORNWALL

A Batch Three "Broadsword" class Type 22 frigate, 4,200 tons (standard), 4,900 tons (full load). Built by Yarrow, Scotstoun, Glasgow. Launched 14.10.1985. Harpoon SSM and Seawolf SAM systems; 1 x 4.5"; 1 Goalkeeper system; 2 x 30mm guns; 6 TT; helicopter-carried A/S torpedoes; 1 helicopter (ability to carry 2).

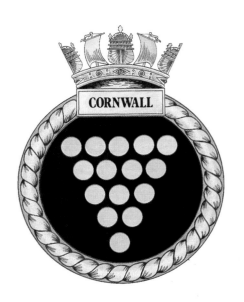

Description of Badge

Field:- Black.
Badge:- Fifteen bezants gold.
(The Arms and Motto of the Duchy of Cornwall).

Motto

One and all.

Battle Honours

Falkland Islands   1914   Dardanelles   1915

Previous ships of the name

1. Second rate, 1,186 bm, 80 guns. Built by Winter, Southampton. Launched 23.4.1692. 5.1692 In combined Anglo-Dutch fleet in action off Cape Barfleur. 1706 Rebuilt at Rotherhithe as 1,241 bm. 1707 Helped in Siege of Toulon. 1726 Rebuilt at Deptford as 1,350 bm. 1727 To Baltic. 1748 In Jamaica. 16.7.1761 Completed being broken up at Chatham.

2. Third rate, 1,634 bm, 74 guns. Built by Wells, Deptford. Launched 19.5.1761. 1778 In the War of American Colonies. 6.7.1779 In Battle of Grenada. 19.5.1780 Damaged in action with the French in the West Indies. 30.6.1780 Burnt at St Lucia, being considered unserviceable.

3. Third rate, 1,751 bm, 74 guns. Built by Barnard, Deptford. Launched 16.1.1812. 1831 Reduced to 50 guns. 1859 Training Ship for Boys at Purfleet, Essex. 1868 Renamed *Wellesley*, Industrial School on the Tyne. 18.1.1875 Breaking up at Sheerness completed.

4. Third rate, 1,746 bm, 74 guns. Built in Bombay Dockyard. Launched as *Wellesley* on 24.2.1815. 1854 Became Guardship. 18.6.1868 Renamed *Cornwall*, Training Ship on the Tyne. Ended her days as Juvenile Reformatory Ship at Gravesend. 24.9.1940 Sunk in the Thames by air attack.

5. Armoured Cruiser, 9,800 tons, 14 x 6" guns; 2 x 18" TT. Built at Pembroke Dock. Launched 29.10.1902. 1904-6 Atlantic Fleet. 1908 Cadets' Training Ship. 6.8.1911 Ran aground on Pinnacle Rock off Cape Sable, while going to the assistance of HM Canadian Ship *Niobe* which had also run aground. Both ships were refloated. 6.8.1914 Captured the German SS *Syra*. 8.12.1914 Battle of Falklands. With *Glasgow*, sank the German cruiser *Leipzig*. 1915 In the blockade of the German *Königsberg* in Rufiji River. 1915 Dardanelles. 1916 China. 1917 Atlantic convoy duty. 1917-8 North America and West Indies Station. 1919 Cadets' Training Ship. 7.7.1920 Sold to T.W. Ward, Briton Ferry, for breaking up.

6. "Kent" class cruiser, 10,000 tons, 8 x 8" and 4 x 4" AA guns; 8 x 21" TT. Built in Devonport Dockyard. Launched 11.3.1926. 1928-36 Spent 3 commissions on China Station. 1937-9 Boys' Seagoing Training Ship. 19.9.1940 With *Delhi*, intercepted French cruiser *Primaguet* and tanker *Tarn*, and escorted them into Casablanca. 7.5.1941 Attacked German raider *Pinguin*; *Cornwall*'s steering was damaged by a shell from *Pinguin*, but *Pinguin* blew up and sank. 6.1941 to 3.1942 Convoy and Patrol duties in Indian Ocean. 5.4.1942 In company with *Dorsetshire*, was sunk off Colombo in an attack from 53 dive bombers from Japanese aircraft carriers.

COTTESMORE

A "Hunt" class Mine Countermeasures Vessel, 615 tons (standard), 725 tons (full load); 1 x 40mm gun. Built of GRP by Yarrow, Scotstoun, Glasgow. Launched 9.2.1982.

Description of Badge

Field:- Red.
Badge:- A lozenge gold, charged with a fret red, surmounted by an annulet black.

(Annulets from the Arms of Lowther; Or fretty gules from the Arms of Noel, Master of the Pack).

Motto

Battle Honours

North Sea	1941-5	Normandy	1944
English Ch	1942-4		

Previous ships of the name

1. Early "Hunt" class minesweeper, 750 tons, 2 x 12 pdr guns. Built by Bow Mclachlan. Launched 9.2.1917. 1920 Paid off and laid up at Harwich. 18.1.1923 Sold to Alloa Sbkg. Co., Charlestown, Fife.

2. "Hunt" class, Type I, "Atherstone" type, destroyer; 907 tons, 4 x 4" guns and 1 x 4 barrelled pom-pom. Built by Yarrow, Scotstoun, Glasgow. Launched 5.9.1940. 10.1942 One of a force of 5 destroyers and 8 MTBs which foiled an enemy attempt to take the auxiliary cruiser *Schiff 45 Komet* through the Channel from Le Havre. 6.1944 Part of Force K at D-Day landings. 17.9.1950 Sold to Egyptian Navy. Refitted at Cowes. Renamed *Ibraham el Awal*. Renamed, about 1951, *Mohamed Ali el Kebir*. 1969 Renamed *Port Said*. 1985 Still in service.

HMS *Cottesmore*

COURAGEOUS

A ''Churchill'' class nuclear powered Fleet Submarine, 4,300 tons (surfaced), 4,800 tons (submerged); 6 x 21" TT. Built by Vickers, Barrow. Launched 7.3.1970.

Description of Badge

Field:- Black.
Badge:- A right arm proper, the hand grasping a serpent green.

Motto

Fortiter in augustis — Bravely in difficulties.

Battle Honours

Ushant	1781	Bay of Biscay	1805
Genoa	1795	Falkland Islands	1982

(The first three won by *Courageux*).

Previous ships of the name

1. French third rate, *Courageux*, 1,721 bm, 74 guns. Captured by *Bellona* 15.8.1761—taken in to Lisbon. Commissioned in to RN. 1794 In action off Corsica. 1795 With Vice Admiral Hotham's action with the French fleet off Genoa. 18.12.1796 Lost in a gale off Gibraltar.

2. French fifth rate *Courageuse*, 932 bm, 32 guns. Captured 18.6.1799 by a squadron in the Mediterranean. Still in service in 1803.

3. Third rate *Courageux*, 772 bm, 74 guns. Built in Deptford Dockyard. Launched 26.3.1800. 11.1805 Took part in Sir Richard Strachan's victory over Dumanoir's squadron. 2.1814 Reduced to Harbour Service. 10.1832 Broken up at Chatham.

4. Battle-cruiser *Courageous,* 18,600 tons, 4 x 15", 18 x 4" and 2 x 3" AA guns; 2 x 21" TT. (12 more added in 1917). Built by Armstrong, Elswick. Launched 5.2.1916. 1917-8 3rd LCS and 1st CS in Grand Fleet. 27.11.1917 In action with enemy light forces; damaged and suffered casualties. 1918-24 Flagship of Reserve Fleet, Portsmouth. 25.3.1928 Boiler Room explosion at Devonport; 1 killed. 5.1928 After 4 year refit at Devonport, emerged as an aircraft carrier, 22,500 tons, 16 x 4.7" guns and 48 aircraft. 1928-9 In Mediterranean. 1929-35 Atlantic and Home Fleets. 1938-9 Flagship, Aircraft Carriers, Home Fleet. 1939 Had just been paid off into Reserve but brought forward for war service. 16.9.1939 Left Devonport under Escort for Offensive Patrol. Next day when turning into wind to recover her aircraft, she was hit by 2 torpedoes from *U 29* in the Atlantic and sank within 15 minutes.

HMS *Courageous*

COVENTRY

A Batch Two "Broadsword" class Type 22 frigate, 4,100 tons (standard), 4,800 tons (full load). Built by Swan Hunter, Wallsend-on-Tyne. Exocet SSM and Sea Wolf SAM systems; 2 x 40mm and 4 x 20mm guns; 6 TT; 1 helicopter (ability to carry 2); helicopter carried A/S torpedoes. Launched 8.4.1986.

Description of Badge

Field:- Per pale red and green.
Badge:- An elephant bearing a castle gold.

Motto

Fortis fert securitatem — The strong carries safety.

Battle Honours

Quiberon Bay	1759	Greece	1941
Trincomalee	1782	Crete	1941
Norway	1940	Libya	1941
Spartivento	1940	Mediterranean	1941
Atlantic	1941	Falkland Islands	1982

Previous ships of the name

1. Spanish ship *San Miguel,* 191 bm, 20 guns. Captured in 1658. 1666 Captured by the French.

2. Fourth rate, 670 bm, 48 guns. Built at Deptford in 1695. 24.7.1704 Captured by the French *Le Jason* off the Isles of Scilly. 3.5.1709 Recaptured and broken up.

3. Sixth rate, 599 bm, 28 guns. Built by H. Adams, Buckler's Hard. Launched 20.5.1757. 10.1.1783 Captured by De Suffren's fleet at Grandjam, Orissa coast, after mistaking them for British and anchoring amongst them.

4. "Ceres" class cruiser, 4,190 tons (standard), 5 x 6" and 2 x 3" AA guns; 8 x 21" TT. Ex-*Corsair*, renamed 1916. Built by Swan Hunter, Wallsend-on-Tyne. Launched 6.7.1917. 1918-9 Harwich Force. 1920-4 Atlantic. 8.3.1923 Torpedo exploded on board at Malta; 2 killed. 1924-8 and 1930-4 In Mediterranean. 1935-6 Converted to AA role. 1937-9 In Reserve. 1940 Narvik. Then convoy escort in Mediterranean. In attack on Benghazi. 13.12.1940 Torpedoed by Italian submarine *Neghelli*. 3.1941 Escort to troop convoy to Greece. Supported Commando raid on Bardia. Later covered evacuation from Greece and Crete, where she rescued survivors from *Calcutta*. 14.9.1942 While supporting an abortive raid on Tobruk, she was hit by 4 large bombs. *Zulu* fired 2 torpedoes into her port side and *Coventry* sank.

5. Type 42 destroyer, 4,100 tons, 1 x Twin Sea Dart; 1 x 4.5" gun; 2 x 20mm Oerlikons; 6 TT. Built by Cammell Laird, Birkenhead. Launched 21.6.1974. First commissioned on 10.11.1978. 1980 One of the 9 RN ships on Far East tour. 10.1980 In Gulf of Oman. 4.1982 Amongst first ships to head south in the Falklands campaign. 1.5.1982 First ship to enter Total Exclusion Zone. In 4 weeks of war, she shot down 5 fighter bombers and a helicopter; sunk a patrol boat and co-ordinated the air defence of the amphibious fleet and landing force. 25.5.1982 Hit by 3 bombs and capsized and sank within 30 minutes. Nineteen men lost their lives.

Footnote
Type 61 frigate was laid down as *Coventry* by Vickers Armstrong, Newcastle-on-Tyne, but during building, plans were changed to a "Leander" class and she was renamed *Penelope* before launching 17.8.1962.

CUMBERLAND

A Batch Three "Broadsword" class Type 22 frigate, 4,200 tons (standard), 4,900 tons (full load). Built by Yarrow, Scotstoun, Glasgow. Laid down 12.10.1984. Harpoon SSM and Sea Wolf SAM systems; 1 x 4.5"; 1 Goalkeeper system; 2 x 30mm; 6 TT; helicopter-carried A/S torpedoes; 1 helicopter (ability to carry 2).

Description of Badge

Field:- Red.

Badge:- A rose gold, with red and gold centre.
(Part of the Arms and Motto of the County of Cumberland).

Motto

Justitiae tenax — Tenacious of Justice.

Battle Honours

Sadras	1758	Cameroons	1914
Negapatam	1758	North Africa	1942
Porto Novo	1759	Arctic	1942-3
St Vincent	1780	Sabang	1944
Baltic	1854	Burma	1945

Previous ships of the name

1. Third rate, 1,219 bm, 80 guns. Built by Wyatt, Bursledon. Launched 12.11.1695. 10.10.1707 Captured by the French. Sold to the Spanish Navy as *Principe de Asturias*. 1718 Recaptured by 2 English 70 gun ships *Breda* and *Captain*. Fate unknown.

2. Third rate, 1,308 bm, 80 guns. Built in Deptford Dockyard in 1710. Spent most of her time in the Baltic, but saw no action. 1731 Taken to pieces. 1739 Rebuilt in Woolwich Dockyard as 1,401 bm, 66 guns. 1754-6 Played prominent part in struggle with the French for the possession of India. 2.11.1760 Foundered while at anchor at Goa; deemed due to decay.

3. Bomb Vessel, 181 bm, 8 guns; ex-*Alex Robert*. Purchased 29.6.1739. 31.3.1742 Breaking up completed at Sheerness.

4. Third rate, 1,674 bm, 74 guns. Built in Deptford Dockyard. Launched 29.3.1774. 7.1778 In the indecisive action with the French off Ushant. 1781 Captured French privateer, 16 guns, *Duc de Chatres*. 1804 Broken up after 30 years distinguished service.

5. Schooner, 30 bm. Purchased by Commander Flinders at Port Jackson in 1803. Conveyed him from Australia to Mauritius. 1804-9 In French hands. 1810 Sold out of the service.

6. Third rate, 1,718 bm, 74 guns. Built by Pitcher, Northfleet. Launched 19.8.1807. Served under Collingwood in the Mediterranean. Later became a Convict Ship at Sheerness. 15.11.1833 Renamed *Fortitude*. 1870 Sold out of the service.

7. Third rate, 2,214 bm, 70 guns. Built in Chatham Dockyard. Launched 21.10.1842. 1870 Taken over by Clyde Training Ship Association. 17.2.1889 Burnt on the Clyde. Wreck broken up in Rosneath Bay.

8. "Monmouth" class armoured cruiser, 9,800 tons; 14 x 6" guns; 2 x 18" TT. Built by London and Glasgow Co., Govan. Launched 16.12.1902. 1904-6 2nd Cruiser Squadron, Atlantic Fleet. 1907-14 Cadet Training Ship. 1.1913 Cruise to West Indies; amongst the cadets on board was HRH Prince Albert, second son of King George V. 27.9.1914 Captured 10 German merchantmen at Duala. 1915-8 Atlantic convoy duties. 1918-20 At Spike Island, Queenstown; base ship for 4th Batt. RMs. 9.5.1921 Sold to T.W. Ward. 28.3.1923 Arrived Briton Ferry to be broken up.

9. "Kent" class cruiser, 10,000 tons, 8 x 8" and 4 x 4" AA guns; 8 x 21" TT. Built by Vickers Armstrong, Barrow. Launched 16.3.1926. 1928-34 and 1936-8 5th CS, China Station. 17.12.1939 Witnessed the sinking of the *Admiral Graf Spee*. 1941 Covered convoys to Russia. 1942-3 Service off Iceland. 1944 Eastern Fleet. 1945-6 Trooping. 6.1946 Laid up. 1949-51 Converted at Devonport to Trials Cruiser. 1951-8 Prolonged series of Gunnery Trials. 14.1.1959 Paid off and laid up. 3.11.1959 Arrived Newport to be broken up by J. Cashmore.

Footnote

a) There were 3 armed cutters named *Duchess of Cumberland*—i) purchased 1781; ii) hired 1783; iii) entered into the Navy in 1793.

b) An E.I. Co. ship, 36 guns, was in action with the French in 1804.

CYGNET

A ''Bird'' class Patrol Boat, 194 tons (full load); 1 x 40mm gun. Built by R. Dunston, Hessle, Humberside. Launched 6.10.1975. Based on ''Seal'' class RAF launches.

Description of Badge

Field:- Black.
Badge:- A cygnet silver on wavelets gold and blue.

Motto

Inter pares insignis — Notable among her fellows.

Battle Honours

Armada	1588	Alexandria	1882
Portland	1653	Sicily	1943
Havana	1762	Atlantic	1943-4
Guadeloupe	1810	Arctic	1944-5

Previous ships of the name

1. Pink, 30 bm, 3 guns. Built in 1585. Took part in Drake's expedition to Cadiz. 1588 Armada. 1603 Condemned.

2. Dunkirk privateer, 233 bm, 10 guns. Believed purchased in 1643. Served on Guard duties. 1654 Sold out of the service.

3. Sloop, 58 bm, 8 guns. Built in Chatham Dockyard in 1657. 1664 Sold out of the service.

4. Survey vessel, purchased in 9.1684. 1687 Foundered off Madagascar.

5. Fireship, 100 bm, 8 guns. Purchased in 1688. 20.9.1693 Captured by 2 French privateers off Cape Clear.

6. French sloop *Guirlande,* 386 bm, 18 guns. Captured 1.1759. 1768 Sold in South Carolina.

7. Sloop, 301 bm, 14 guns. Built in Portsmouth Dockyard. Launched 24.1.1776. 1776-83 In War of American Independence. 8.1802 Sold out of the service.

8. Sloop, 365 bm, 16 guns. Built by Palmer, Yarmouth. Launched 6.9.1804. 1806 Captured a French ship off Dominica. 1809 Received medal for destroying 2 French frigates. 7.3.1815 Wrecked in the Courantine River, French Guiana.

9. ''Cherokee'' class brig-sloop, 237 bm, 10 guns. Built in Portsmouth Dockyard. Launched 11.5.1819. 6.8.1835 Sold out of the service.

10. Brig, 359 bm, 8 guns. Built in Woolwich Dockyard. Launched 6.4.1840. 5.1863 Renamed *WV 30;* a Coastguard Vessel stationed in Chichester Harbour. 3.1.1877 Her breaking up completed at Portsmouth.

11. ''Philomel'' class wood steam gunvessel, 428 bm, 1 x 68 pdr and 4 x 24 pdr guns. Built by Wigram, Northam. Launched 6.6.1860. 1861-7 North America and West Indies Station. 8.1868 Broken up at Portsmouth.

12. Name ship of class of composite steam gunboat, 455 tons; 2 x 64 pdr and 2 x 20 pdr guns. Built by Wm Doxford, Sunderland. Launched 30.5.1874. 1876 Niger expedition. 1877-87 In Mediterranean. 11.7.1882 Present at the Bombardment of Alexandria. 1884-5 Sudan War. 1889 Broken up.

13. Destroyer, 355 tons, 1 x 12 pdr and 5 x 6 pdr guns; 2 TT. Built by Thornycroft, Chiswick. Launched 8.1.1898. In WW1, was in the Local Defence Flotilla, Nore. 29.4.1920 Sold to T.W. Ward, Rainham, for breaking up.

14. ''Crescent'' class destroyer, 1,375 tons; 4 x 4.7" and 1 x 3" AA guns; 8 x 21" TT. Built by Vickers Armstrong, Barrow. Launched 29.9.1931. 17.2.1937 Renamed *St Laurent* in RCN. 1947 Sold out of the service.

15. Modified ''Black Swan'' class sloop, 1,350 tons; 6 x 4" and 12 x 20mm guns. Built by Cammell Laird, Birkenhead. Launched 28.7.1942. Joined 2nd Support Group on convoy escort duties. 7.1943 Invasion of Sicily. 8.4.1944 With *Crane,* sank *U 962.* 1944-5 Escort to Russian Convoys. 16.3.1956 Arrived Rosyth to be broken up.

Footnote
a) Cutter, 120 bm, 10 guns. Hired 1796-9.
b) Trawler, 300 tons, built in 1907, was hired as the minesweeper *Cygnet II,* 1914-9.
c) Trawler, 138 tons, built in 1893, was hired as *Cygnet III,* 1917-9.

DANAE

A Batch Two "Leander" class frigate, 2,450 tons (standard). Built in Devonport Dockyard. Launched 21.10.1965. 1977-80 Exocet conversion at Devonport. New armament:- Exocet SSM and Sea Cat SAM systems; 2 x 40mm guns; 6 TT; 1 helicopter.

Description of Badge

Field:- Black.
Badge:- A castle gold.

(Danae was confined by her father in a tower of brass. Jupiter visited her in a shower of gold).

Motto

Timeant danaides — Let them fear those belonging to Danae.

Battle Honours

Normandy   1944

Previous ships of the name

1. French fifth rate, 941 bm, 38 guns. Captured 28.3.1759 by *Southampton* and *Melampe*. 14.6.1771 Her breaking up completed at Chatham.

2. French fifth rate, 689 bm, 32 guns. Captured 13.5.1779 when stranded and abandoned near St Malo. 10.1797 Sold out of the service.

3. French sixth rate, *Vaillante*. 508 bm, 20 guns. Captured 7.8.1798 by *Indefatigable* in the Bay of Biscay. 14.3.1800 Taken into Brest by her mutinous crew who handed her back to the French three days later.

4. "Eclipse" class corvette (sail and steam), 1,760 tons, 2 x 7" guns. Built in Portsmouth Dockyard. Launched 21.5.1867. 1886 Lent to the War Department as a Storeship. 15.5.1906 Sold out of the service.

5. "D" class Light Cruiser, First Group, 4,850 tons, 6 x 6" and 2 x 3" AA guns; 12 x 21" TT. Built by Armstrong Whitworth on the Tyne. Launched 26.1.1918. Closing stages of WW1 were spent in the Harwich Force's 5th Light Cruiser Squadron. 1919-23 Atlantic Fleet. 27.11.1923 Left Devonport with *Hood* and *Repulse* for world cruise. 1925-9 1st CS, Mediterranean. 1929-30 Refit. 1930-5 8th CS, North America and West Indies Station. 11.1935 Reserve at Devonport. 1936-7 5th CS, China Station. 1938-9 Reserve at Portsmouth. 1939-41 China Station. 1942 East Indies Fleet. 7.8.1942 to 2.7.1943 Refit on the Tyne. 10.1943 Returned to East Indies. 6.1944 Bombarding role at Normandy. 4.10.1944 to 28.9.1946 Loaned to Polish Navy as *Conrad*. 1946-7 In Reserve. 22.1.1948 Sold. 27.3.1948 Arrived Barrow to be broken up by T.W. Ward.

Footnote
The destroyer *Vimiera*, 2,610 tons, was renamed *Danae* in 3.1945. Was to be built at Cammell Laird, Birkenhead, but the order was cancelled in 1.1946.

DASHER

A P2000 Coastal Training Craft of 43 tonnes for the RNR, being built of GRP by Watercraft Ltd., Shoreham-by-Sea. Allocated to Severn Division, RNR.

Description of Badge

Field:- White.
Badge:- A ship's figurehead composed of the head and flowing mane of a horse depicted sable affixed to a ship's prow, tinctured gold.

Motto

Battle Honours

Java	1811	Atlantic	1942
North Africa	1942	Arctic	1943

Previous ships of the name

1. Sloop, 402 bm, 18 guns. Built by Goodrich, Bermuda in 1797. For some years was transferred for use by the Army in the West Indies. 1832 Used as a Convict Hulk. 3.1838 Broken up.

2. Wood paddlewheel packet, 260 bm, 2 guns. Built in Chatham Dockyard. Launched 12.1837. Employed on Packet Service from Weymouth and as Channel Islands Guardship. 1885 Sold out of the service.

3. Destroyer, 290 tons, 1 x 12 pdr gun; 2 TT. Built by Yarrow, Poplar. Launched 28.11.1894. On completion, lay at Portsmouth until 1899; then to Chatham. 1902 In commission at Devonport. 1904 In Reserve at Chatham. 1906 Commissioned at Chatham for Home Fleet at the Nore. 1910 6th DF. 1911 Paid off; Laid up at Sheerness. 14.5.1912 Sold at Chatham to King and Sons, for breaking up.

4. Escort Carrier, 8,200 tons, Ex-mercantile hull, *Rio de Janeiro.* Built by Sun S.B. and D.D. Company, Chester, Pennsylvania, USA. Launched 12.4.1941. Converted by Tietjens and Lang Dry Dock Co., Brooklyn, New York. 2.7.1942 Transferred to RN on Lend-Lease. 8.11.1942 Operation 'Torch'. At first light, aircraft from *Dasher* and *Biter* dropped propaganda leaflets over Oran. 2.1943 Damaged in heavy weather when on convoy duty; had to return to base. 27.3.1943 Lost by internal petrol explosion while exercising south of the Cumbraes. Sank with the loss of 378 of her ship's company.

DIOMEDE

A Batch Three "Leander" class (broad-beamed) frigate, 2,500 tons. Built by Yarrow, Scotstoun, Glasgow. Launched 15.4.1969. Sea Cat SAM system; A/S mortars; 2 x 4.5"; 2 x 20mm guns; 1 helicopter.

Description of Badge

Field:- Green.
Badge:- A white horse rampant with hooves gold.
(The wild mares of the Thracian Diomede were tamed by Hercules).

Motto

Fortibus feroces fragentur — The fierce are broken by the brave.

Battle Honours

Cape of Good Hope   1806

Previous ships of the name

1. Fifth rate, 891 bm, 44 guns. Built by J.H. Hillhouse, Bristol. Launched 18.10.1781. 2.8.1795 Wrecked near Trincomalee.

2. Fourth rate, 1,123 bm, 50 guns. Was ordered as the *Firm* but renamed *Diomede* in 1794. Built in Deptford Dockyard. Launched 17.1.1798. This ship gained the only Battle Honour when in Sir Hope Popham's squadron at capture of Cape of Good Hope in January, 1806. 8.1815 Sold out of the service.

3. "D" class, light cruiser, second group, 4,850 tons, 6 x 6" and 2 x 4" AA guns; 12 x 21" TT. Built by Vickers, Barrow. Launched 29.4.1919. 1922-5 5th LCS, China Station. 1925-9 With RNZN. 1929-30 Refit at Chatham. 1930-6 Again with the RNZN. 9.1935 In the Mediterranean for Abyssinian crisis. 3.1936 Returned to Chatham. 1936-7 In Reserve. 1937 Trooping to China. 1937-8 In Reserve. 1939 7th CS.20.2.1942 In US Task Force, South Atlantic, to protect Falkland Islands. 1942-4 Home Fleet. 8.1944 Refit at Rosyth. 10.1945 Reduced to Reserve at Plymouth; then to Falmouth. 5.4.1946 Sold to Arnott Young. 13.5.1946 Arrived Dalmuir to be broken up.

HMS *Diomede*

DOVEY

A "River" class Fleet Minesweeper, 890 tons (full load); 1 x 40mm gun. Built by Richards, Great Yarmouth. Launched 7.12.1983. Allocated to Clyde Division, RNR.

Description of Badge

Field:- Argent.
Badge:- In front of a shake-fork sable, a dove volant proper.

Motto

Battle Honours

Atlantic   1944

Previous ships of the name

1. "River" class frigate, 1,375 tons, 2 x 4" and 10 x 20mm guns. Ex-*Lambourne* renamed in 10.1942. Built by Fleming and Ferguson, Paisley. Launched 14.10.1943. Not commissioned after the war. 1949-52 Reserve at Harwich. 1953-5 Reserve at Barrow-in-Furness. 2.11.1955 Arrived Preston to be broken up by T.W. Ward.

HMS *Dovey*

DULVERTON

A ''Hunt'' class Mine Countermeasures Vessel, 615 tons (standard), 725 tons (full load); 1 x 40mm gun. Built of GRP by Vosper Thornycroft, Woolston, Southampton. Launched 3.11.1982.

Description of Badge

Field:- Barry wavy of six white and blue.
Badge:- Within an annulet per fess red and green, a griffin's claw erased red, grasping a riding whip and an axe in saltire gold.

(An allusion to the Crest of Lord Dulverton, Master of the Hunt, 1908-10).

Motto

Battle Honours

Libya	1942	Sicily	1943
Sirte	1942	Salerno	1943
Mediterranean	1942	Aegean	1943
Malta Convoys	1942		

Previous ships of the name

1. ''Hunt'' class, Type 2 ''Blankney'' type, destroyer, 1,050 tons, 6 x 4" AA guns. Built by Alex Stephen, Linthouse, Glasgow. Launched 1.4.1941. Had a short but distinguished career which gained her a surprising number of battle honours. 13.11.1943 When off Kos in the Dodecanese was hit by a glider bomb from German aircraft and sank. Three officers and 75 men were lost.

HMS *Dulverton*

DUMBARTON CASTLE

A "Castle" class Offshore Patrol Vessel, 1,427 tons. 1 x 40/60mm close-range gun. Built by Hall Russell, Aberdeen. Launched 3.6.1981. Design includes an ability to lay mines in wartime.

Description of Badge

Field:- Blue.

Badge:- A cloven rock proper, the cleft filled by a portcullis, gold over all. To the dexter a sword, point upwards proper, pommel and hilt gold, and to the sinister, a sceptre erect and gold.

(Dumbarton Castle is built on a rock cleft in two. Sword and sceptre are taken from the Royal Crest of Scotland and are significant of the Royal associations with the castle).

Motto

Battle Honours

Atlantic   1944-5   Falkland Islands   1982

Previous ships of the name

1. Sixth rate frigate, 24 guns. Originally of the Scots Navy, she was added to the List of the Royal Navy on 29.11.1707. 26.4.1708 Captured by the 44 gun French privateer *Le Jersey* off Waterford, whilst engaged on convoy duty.

2. "Castle" class corvette, 1,060 tons, 1 x 4" and 6 x 40mm guns. Built by Caledon S.B. Co., Dundee. Launched 28.9.1943. Spent most of the war in the North Atlantic on anti-submarine operations. After the war, was engaged in Air-Sea Rescue duties. 1946 Into Reserve. 16.11.1960 Sold. 3.1961 Broken up at Gateshead.

HMS *Dumbarton Castle*

EDINBURGH

A Batch Three "Town" class Type 42 Guided Missile destroyer (stretched version); 4,775 tons (full load). Built by Cammell Laird, Birkenhead. Launched 14.4.1983. Sea Dart SAM system; 1 x 4.5"; 2 x 20mm Oerlikons; helicopter-launched Sea Skua missiles; 6 TT; 1 helicopter.

Description of Badge

Field:- White.
Badge:- Upon a mount of rock in base proper, a castle triple towered black, masoned white, the flags, windows and portcullis red.
(From the Arms of the City of Edinburgh).

Motto

Battle Honours

Ushant	1747	*Bismarck*	1941
Cape Francois	1757	Atlantic	1941
Syria	1840	Malta Convoys	1941
Baltic	1854-5	Arctic	1941-2
Norway	1940-1		

Previous ships of the name

1. Fifth rate, 364 bm, 32 guns. Formerly the Scottish *Royal William*; transferred 5.8.1707. 10.8.1709 Sunk as a breakwater at Harwich.

2. Third rate, 898 bm, 70 guns. Built by Johnson and Castle, Blackwall. 8.6.1666 Launched as *Warspite*. 1702 Rebuilt at Rotherhithe as 952 bm. 2.1.1716 Renamed *Edinburgh*. 1721 Rebuilt at Chatham as 1,119 bm. 1726-7 In Baltic. 1744 Again rebuilt at Chatham as 1,286 bm, 64 guns. 1747 With other ships captured French frigate *Bellone*, 36 guns. 1748 Assisted in the capture of a Spanish convoy. 12.1771 Finally broken up at Plymouth.

3. Third rate, 1,772 bm, 74 guns. Built by Brent, Rotherhithe. Launched 26.1.1811. 31.12.1846 undocked after having been converted to steam. 1866 Sold to Messrs Castle and Beech for breaking up.

4. "Colossus" class Turret Ship, 9,420 tons, 4 x 12" and 5 x 6" guns. Laid down at Pembroke Dock as the *Majestic*, but two days before launching was renamed *Edinburgh*. Launched 18.3.1882. This class were the first British battleships to be built of steel. Also introduced large calibre breech-loading guns. 11.10.1910 Sold to T.W. Ward for breaking up.

5. Improved "Southampton" class cruiser—sister ship to *Belfast*, the Museum Ship in the Thames; 10,260 tons, 12 x 6" and 12 x 4" AA guns; 6 x 21" TT. Built by Swan Hunter, Wallsend-on-Tyne. Launched 31.3.1938. 16.10.1939 Suffered splinter damage from near misses by three 500lb bombs during air attack at Rosyth. 3.1941 Escort to forces on Lofoten Islands raid. 5.1941 *Bismarck* operation. 30.4.1942 Hit by 2 torpedoes which ripped off her stern. Did not sink, so attempts were made to tow her back to Russia. 2.5.1942 Third torpedo struck her, almost cut her in two. Still stayed afloat, but finally *Foresight* fired 3 torpedoes into her to send her to the bottom. Minesweepers *Harrier* and *Gossamer* took off survivors. At the time *Edinburgh* was transporting 5 tonnes of gold ingots—a payment from Russia for Western military supplies. Worth about £44 million, all but £4 million was recovered in 1981.

ENDURANCE

Ice Patrol Ship, 3,600 tons. Originally the Danish vessel *Anita Dan* built in 1956 by Krögerwerft, Rendsburg. Purchased from J. Lauritzen Lines, Copenhagen, in 1967. Converted by Harland and Wolff, Belfast, including installation of scientific and surveying equipment, and a flight deck and hangar for two helicopters.

Description of Badge

Field:- Azure.

Badge:- A wandering albatross proper, in flight above four bars wavy barry blue and argent, on which floats an ice floe proper.

(The albatross represents endurance and the ice floe, the Antarctic).

Motto

By endurance we conquer.

(The Shackleton family).

Battle Honours

Falkland Islands   1982

Previous ships of the name

None.

HMS *Endurance*

EURYALUS

A Batch One "Leander" class frigate, 2,450 tons (standard). Built by Scotts, Greenock. Launched 6.6.1963. 1973-6 Ikara conversion at Devonport. New armament:- Ikara A/S missiles (forward); Sea Cat SAM system; 2 x 40mm guns; Limbo A/S mortars (aft); 1 helicopter.

Description of Badge

Field:- Blue.
Badge:- The head and shoulders of a Greek warrior, gold.

(Derived from Greek mythology. Euryalus was a great friend of Nisus and one of the followers of Aeneas).

Motto

Omnia audax — Bold in all things.

Battle Honours

Trafalgar	1805	Mediterranean	1941-3
Baltic	1854-5	Sirte	1942
Heligoland	1914	Salerno	1943
Dardanelles	1915	Sicily	1943
Malta Convoys	1941-2	Okinawa	1945

Previous ships of the name

1. Fifth rate, 946 bm, 36 guns. Built by H. Adams, Buckler's Hard. Launched 6.6.1803. 1805 At Trafalgar, shadowed French and Spanish fleets as they left Cadiz. During the battle, rescued seamen from the water. Afterwards took the badly damaged *Royal Sovereign* in tow. 1826-44 Prison Ship at Chatham. 1845-59 Similar role at Gibraltar. 1859 Renamed *Africa*. 16.8.1860 Sold to Mr Recano at Gibraltar.

2. Wood steam frigate, 2,371 bm, 51 guns. Built in Chatham Dockyard. Launched 5.10.1853. During 1860s was in action in China and Japan during which one of her Midshipmen, Duncan Boyes, won the Victoria Cross when a landing party from the ship assaulted Japanese guns at Toyura. 3.1867 Sold to Messrs Castle and Beech.

3. "Bacchante" class iron steam corvette, 4,140 tons, 14 x 7" and 2 x 6" guns. Built in Chatham Dockyard. Launched 31.1.1877. 8.1882 Landed men to defend the Suez Canal. 1882-5 Spent four years as Flagship for East Indies. 10.5.1897 Sold to Cohen, Blackwall.

4. "Cressy" class armoured cruiser, 12,000 tons, 2 x 9.2" and 12 x 6" guns; 2 x 18" TT. Built by Vickers, Barrow. Launched 20.5.1901. Her completion was delayed due to damage caused by a fire in 6.1901. In dry dock, she slipped off the blocks, receiving severe underwater damage. 27.6.1903 Rammed by Special Service vessel *Traveller*. 1904-6 Flagship on the Australian Station. 1906 In Reserve. 1906-9 North America and West Indies Station. 1909-14 In Reserve. 1914 Grand Fleet. 1915 In the Dardanelles; at landing on 'W' beach. 1916-8 Flagship in the East Indies. 1918 Proposed conversion to a minelayer not completed. 1919 In Reserve. 1.7.1920 Sold to Castle and Sons; broken up in Germany.

5. "Dido" class cruiser, 5,450 tons, 10 x 5.25" and 8 x 2 pdr AA guns; 6 x 21" TT. Built in Chatham Dockyard. Launched 6.6.1939. The last cruiser built at Chatham. 9.1941 to Mediterranean. 3.1942 Battle of Sirte. Straddled by 15" shells from Italian battleship *Littorio,* but without serious damage. 15.9.1942 Flagship of 15th CS. 13.12.1942 With others, sank 3 enemy supply ships off North Africa. 7.1943 Invasion of Sicily. 9.1943 Salerno landings. 16.9.1943 When *Warspite* was hit off Salerno, *Euryalus* tried to take her in tow, but wire parted. Tugs took over. 10.1943 to 7.1944 Refit at John Brown's. 4.9.1944 Collided with *Black Ranger*. 16.12.1944 Left Liverpool to join British Pacific Fleet at Colombo. 29.1.1945 During air attack two shells from *Euryalus* landed on flight deck of *Illustrious;* killed 12. 4.2.1946 At Shanghai. 17.2.1947 Arrived Sheerness. Reduced to Reserve at Chatham, then Rosyth. 8.1947 to 1.1948 Refit at Rosyth, then to Mediterranean. 3.1953 Transferred to South Atlantic Station. 19.8.1954 Arrived Devonport to pay off into Extended Reserve. 18.7.1959 Arrived Blyth to be broken up by Hughes Bolckow.

EXETER

A Batch Two, Town class, Type 42 Guided Missile destroyer, 3,800 tons (standard), 4,250 tons (full load). Built by Swan Hunter, Newcastle-upon-Tyne. Launched 25.4.1978. Sea Dart SAM system; 1 x 4.5"; 2 x 20mm Oerlikons; helicopter-launched Sea Skua missiles; 1 helicopter.

Description of Badge

Field:— White.

Badge:— A demi-lion red, crowned gold, holding an orb gold, over wavelets gold and blue.

(Derived from the Crest and Motto of the Arms of the City of Exeter).

Motto

Semper fidelis — Always faithful.

Battle Honours

Sadras	1782	River Plate	1939
Providien	1782	Sunda Strait	1942
Negapatam	1782	Falkland Islands	1982
Trincomalee	1782		

Previous ships of the name

1. Third rate, 1,070 bm, 70 guns. Built in Sir Henry Johnson's Yard, Blackwall. Launched 1680. 30.6.1690 Fought in Anglo-Dutch fleet against the French off Beachy Head. 12.9.1691 Damaged by an explosion at Plymouth. 1697 Classed as a Hulk. 24.5.1717 Ordered to be broken up at Portsmouth.

2. Fourth rate, 949 bm, 60 guns. Built in Portsmouth Dockyard. Launched 26.5.1697. 1702 In action against the French off Newfoundland. 1711 In Mediterranean. 1740-4 Rebuilt in Plymouth Dockyard as 58 guns ship of 1,068 bm. 1.10.1746 Drove ashore the French 64 guns ship *Ardent*. 1748 At Siege of Pondicherry in S.E. India. 11.1763 Broken up at Portsmouth.

3. Third rate, 1,340 bm, 64 guns. Built by Henniker, Chatham. Launched 26.7.1763. 27.7.1778 Fought against the French in Battle of Ushant. 1779-83 In action against the French around India. Operational damage sustained rendered her unseaworthy. 12.2.1784 Condemned and destroyed by burning off Cape of Good Hope.

4. "York" class cruiser, 8,390 tons, 6 x 8" and 4 x 4" AA guns; 6 x 21" TT. Built in Devonport Dockyard. Launched 18.7.1929. 1933-9 Commodore's Ship on America and West Indies Station. 13.12.1939 In Battle of River Plate; badly damaged. Temporary repairs carried out at Port Stanley, Falkland Islands. 15.2.1940 Arrived Devonport for refit. 24.3.1941 Left Devonport incomplete to avoid air attacks. 5.1941 *Bismarck* operations. 7.1941 To Far East on convoy escort duties. 1.3.1942 Scuttled by her own ship's company after heroic action against overwhelming Japanese forces in the in the Java Sea while heading for Sunda Strait.

Footnote

a) Trawler, 165 tons, built in 1897, was hired for service 1917-9.

b) Frigate, 2,170 tons, was ordered from Fairfield, Govan, Glasgow, in 1956 but was cancelled.

FAWN

A "Bulldog" class Coastal Survey Vessel, 800 tons (standard), 1,088 tons (full load). Built by Brooke Marine, Lowestoft. Launched 29.2.1968. Originally designed for service overseas. Built to commercial standards. Fitted for (but not with) 2 x 20mm guns.

Description of Badge

Field:— Blue.
Badge:— Infront of a sextant, gold, a fawn statant proper.

Motto

Battle Honours

Martinique	1809	Belgian Coast	1914-8
Guadeloupe	1810		

Previous ships of the name

1. French brig-sloop *Faune,* 16 guns. Captured by *Goliath* and *Camilla,* west of Rochefort, on 15.8.1805. In service in 1806.

2. Sloop, 424 bm, 18 guns. Built by Owen, Topsham. Launched 22.4.1807. 28.5.1808 Her boats, off Puerto Rico, captured a Spanish privateer schooner and 3 merchant vessels. 11.10.1810 Captured, in the West Indies, the French 10 gun privateer schooner *Temeraire.* 20.8.1818 Sold out of the service.

3. Brigantine, ex-slaver *Caroline,* 169 bm, 6 guns. Purchased at Rio de Janeiro on 27.5.1840. 1842 Acted as a Tank Vessel at Cape of Good Hope. 5.1847 Sold to the Natal Colonial Government.

4. Wood steam sloop, 1,045 tons, 17 x 32 pdr guns. Built in Deptford Dockyard. Launched 30.9.1856. 6.1876 Became a Survey Ship. Performed many useful surveys, particularly in the Sea of Marmora. 12.1884 Sold out of the service.

5. Destroyer, 300 tons, 1 x 12 pdr and 5 x 6 pdr guns; 2 TT. Built by Palmer, Jarrow-on-Tyne. Launched 13.4.1897. 23.8.1914 Captured Austrian SS *Stephnia.* 1914-7 Dover Patrol. 3.1915 Sank submarine *U 8* in the Dover Straits. 1918 Humber Force. 5.1919 Sales List. 23.7.1919 Sold to T.W. Ward, New Holland, for breaking up.

Footnote
a) Trawler was hired 1918-9.
b) Trawler, 143 tons, built in 1897, was hired as a de-gaussing vessel from 12.1941 to 1945.
c) Drifter, ex-*Primrose*, 89 tons, built in 1915, was hired for A/S duties from 25.12.1939 to 1945.

HMS Fawn

FEARLESS

An Assault Ship (LPD); 11,060 tons (standard), 12,120 tons (full load). Built by Harland and Wolff, Belfast. Launched 19.12.1963. 4 Seacat SAM systems; 2 x 40mm Bofors AA guns; one flight of Assault helicopters.

Description of Badge

Field:— Blue.
Badge:— A lion's head, gold.

Motto

Explicit nomen — The name explains itself.

Battle Honours

Heligoland	1914	Malta Convoys	1941
Jutland	1916	Atlantic	1941
Norway	1940	Falkland Islands	1982
Mediterranean	1941		

Previous ships of the name

1. Gunvessel, 149 bm, 12 guns. Built by Cleverley, Gravesend. Launched 6.1794. 19.1.1804 Wrecked in Cawsand Bay, Plymouth Sound.

2. Gun-brig, 180 bm, 12 guns. Built by Graham, Harwich. Launched 18.12.1804. 1807 At Copenhagen. 8.12.1812 Wrecked on rocks of St Sebastian, near Cadiz.

3. Wood paddlewheel survey vessel, ex-GPO vessel *Flamer,* 165 bm Built by Fletcher and Fearnall, Limehouse. Renamed *Fearless* when the Admiralty took over the Packet Service in 1837. Broken up by Admiralty Order dated 9.6.1875.

4. Torpedo Cruiser, 1,580 tons, 4 x 5″ guns; 3 TT. Built by Barrow S.B. (Vickers). Launched 20.3.1886. 1.3.1888 Commissioned at Portsmouth for the Mediterranean. Recommissioned at Malta on 24.6.1891; 30.10.1894 and 30.11.1897. 1899 Temporarily detached to the Cape of Good Hope. 1900 Paid off at Portsmouth. 20.11.1901 Commissioned at Sheerness for China. 1905 Laid up at Portsmouth.
11.7.1905 Sold at Portsmouth.

5. ''Active'' class scout cruiser, 3,440 tons, 10 x 4″ and 4 x 3 pdr guns; 2 x 21″ TT. Built at Pembroke Dock. Launched 12.6.1912. 1913-4 1st DF, Home Fleet. 1914-5 At Harwich. 18.8.1914 In action with German light cruiser *Rostock* off the Dutch coast. 28.8.1914 In action off Heligoland; at sinking of German destroyer *V 187.* 31.5.1916 Battle of Jutland. 1916-8 Attached to the 12th Submarine Flotilla. 31.1.1918 'Battle' of May Island in the Firth of Forth. 8.11.1921 Sold to Slough T.C.; broken up in Germany.

6. ''F'' class destroyer, 1,375 tons, 4 x 4.7″ guns; 8 x 21″ TT. Built by Cammell Laird, Birkenhead. Launched 12.5.1934. 1937 Spanish Civil War. 4.1940 With *Brazen* sank *U 49* off Harstad. 6.1941 With other ships, sank *U 138* west of Cape Trafalgar. 23.7.1941 Whilst screening *Ark Royal,* was hit by a torpedo from Italian aircraft. Badly on fire, the ship lost power. Towing was not considered justified, so she was sunk north of Bone, by *Forester.*

Footnote
Drifter, 81 tons, built in 1907, was hired as *Fearless II* from 11.1914 to 1919.

FENCER

An ''Attacker'' class Seamanship and Navigational Training Vessel of 34 tons for the RNR and RN University Units. Built by Fairey Allday Marine, Southampton. Delivered 21.3.1983. Allocated to Southampton University Unit.

Description of Badge

Field:— Blue.
Badge:— In front of two fencing foils in saltire gold, a fencing mask also gold.

Motto

En garde — On guard.

Battle Honours

Atlantic	1943-4	North Sea	1944
Arctic	1944	Norway	1944

Previous ships of the name

1. An Escort Carrier, 11,420 tons, 18 aircraft; ex-USS *Croaton*. Built by Western Pipe and Steel Co., San Francisco, California, USA. Launched 4.4.1942. 27.2.1943 Transferred to RN on Lend-Lease. Employed on convoy protection. Her Swordfish aircraft, armed with rockets, were responsible for the destruction of four U-boats—10.2.1944 *U 666* in North Atlantic; 1.5.1944 *U 277* in Arctic Ocean; and 2.5.1944 *U 674* and *U 959* in Arctic Ocean. 10.1944 With *Striker*, left Glasgow for the Pacific theatre of war. 11.12.1946 Returned to the US Navy. 1951 Sold to mercantile sources as *Sydney*.

HMS *Fencer* (May 1983).

FIFE

A County Class Guided Missile destroyer, 5,440 tons (standard), 6,200 tons (full load). Built by Fairfield, Govan, Glasgow. Launched 9.7.1964. Exocet SSM, Sea Slug SAM and Sea Cat missile systems; 2 x 4.5″ guns; 6 TT; 1 helicopter.

Description of Badge

Field:— Blue.
Badge:— A base barry wavy of four white and blue overall, a knight in armour on a horse courant, in his dexter hand, a sword erect, all proper, his surcoat argent. On his sinister arm a shield, gold, charged with a lion rampant red, on the helm a wreath gold and red, rising therefrom a demi-lion red, the caparisons of the horse red, fimbriated gold, thereon six shields gold, each charged with a lion rampant red.

Motto

Tam ratione quam vi — As much by reason as by strength.

Battle Honours

None.

Previous ships of the name

None.

HMS *Fife*

FOX

A "Bulldog" class Coastal Survey Vessel, 800 tons (standard), 1,088 tons (full load). Built by Brooke Marine, Lowestoft. Launched 6.11.1967. Originally designed for service overseas. Built to commercial standards. Fitted for (but not with) 2 x 20mm guns.

Description of Badge

Field:— Blue.
Badge:— In front of a sextant gold, a fox passant guardant proper.

Motto

Battle Honours

Gabbard	1653	St Vincent	1797
Orfordness	1666	Egypt	1801
Barfleur	1692	Burma	1852-3
Genoa	1795		

Previous ships of the name

1. French 22 gun ship captured in 1650. 1656 Expended as a fireship at Malaga.

2. Ostender *St Anthony,* 203 bm, 14 guns. Captured in 1658. 1666 Expended as a fireship.

3. Fireship, 263 bm, 8 guns. Built by Barrett, Shoreham, in 1690. 19.5.1692 Expended at La Hogue.

4. Sloop, 68 bm, 6 guns. Built in Sheerness Dockyard in 1699. 2.12.1699 Wrecked on the coast of Ireland.

5. Sixth rate, 273 bm, 24 guns. A French prize captured 5.1705 by *Tryton.* 28.8.1706 Wrecked in Holyhead Bay.

6. Sixth rate, 251 bm, 24 guns. Built in Chatham Dockyard. Launched 16.12.1702 as *Nightingale.* 26.8.1707 Captured by the French. 12.1707 Recaptured as *Rossignol;* renamed *Fox.* 1727 Rebuilt at Deptford as 375 bm. 1.1737 Broken up at Deptford.

7. Sixth rate, 440 bm, 24 guns. Built by Buxton, Rotherhithe. Launched 1.5.1740. 14.11.1745 Foundered off Dunbar and lost with all hands.

8. Sixth rate, 503 bm, 24 guns. Built by Horn and Ewer, Bursledon. Launched 26.4.1746. 11.9.1751 Foundered in a hurricane off Jamaica.

9. Sixth rate, 585 bm, 28 guns. Built by Calhoun, Northam. Launched 2.9.1773. 7.6.1777 Captured by the American *Hancock.* 20.8.1777 Recaptured by *Flora.* 10.9.1778 Captured by French *Junon.*

10. Fifth rate, 697 bm, 32 guns. Built by Parsons, Bursledon. Launched 2.6.1780. 4.1816 Broken up.

11. Cutter, 104 bm, 10 guns. Purchased 1794. 24.7.1797 Sunk in action with the Spanish at Santa Cruz.

12. Schooner, 150 bm, 14 guns. An ex-French prize, purchased 1799. 28.9.1799 Wrecked in the Gulf of Mexico.

13. Fifth rate, 1,080 bm, 46 guns. Built in Portsmouth Dockyard. Launched 17.8.1829. 18.3.1856 Undocked as a steam frigate. 3.1862 Converted to Storeship. 3.1882 Broken up at Devonport.

14. "Astraea" class cruiser, 4,360 tons, 2 x 6", 8 x 4.7" and 8 x 6 pdr guns. Built in Portsmouth dockyard. Launched 15.6.1893. 1898 Bumpeh River expedition. 1901-4 and 1908-10 In East Indies. 1915 Off East Africa, in action against supply ships serving German cruiser *Königsberg.* 1916-8 Patrols in Red Sea. 14.7.1920 Sold to Cardiff Marine Stores.

Footnote

a) Between 1780-1800 seven cutters were hired for service over varying periods.
b) Ketch, 8 guns, built in Bombay Dockyard in 1766, and still listed in 1772, belonged to the Bombay Marine.

GALATEA

A Batch One "Leander" class frigate, 2,450 tons (standard). Built by Swan Hunter, Wallsend-on-Tyne. Launched 23.5.1963. 1974 Ikara installation completed at Devonport. New armament:- Ikara A/S missiles (forward); Sea Cat SAM system; 2 x 40mm guns; Limbo A/S mortars (aft); 1 helicopter.

Description of Badge

Field:— Blue.

Badge:— A female head proper, crowned with scallop shells gold.

(Galatea was the daughter of the sea-god Nereus).

Motto

Nobis mare patria — The sea is our Fatherland.

Battle Honours

Groix Island	1795	Norway	1940
Lynx	1807	*Bismarck*	1941
Tamatave	1811	Mediterranean	1941
Jutland	1916		

Previous ships of the name

1. French frigate, 22 guns, *Galathee*. Captured in 1758, whilst escorting a convoy of 12 transports, by *Essex* and *Pluto*. Renamed under the British flag.

2. Sixth rate, 429 bm, 20 guns. Built in Deptford Dockyard in 1776. 1780 With another vessel, captured 9 privateers off the American coast during the War of Independence. 4.1783 Broken up.

3. Fifth rate, 808 bm, 32 guns. Built by Parsons, Bursledon. Launched 17.5.1794. 21.10.1794 In the force which captured the French *Revolutionnaire*, 44 guns. 20.3.1796 Forced French storeship *Etoile*, 28 guns, to strike off the Saints. 21.1.1807 Her boats captured French brig *Lynx*, 14 guns, off Caraccas. 5.1809 Broken up.

4. Fifth rate, 947 bm, 36 guns. Built in Deptford Dockyard. Launched 31.8.1810. 1811 Severely damaged in action with 3 French frigates. 1814-24 Laid up at Plymouth. 1838 Reduced to Coal Depot Ship at Jamaica. 1849 Broken up there.

5. Wood steam frigate, 3,227 tons, 24 x 10" guns. Built in Woolwich Dockyard. Launched 14.9.1859. Saw action in the West Indies. 1870 Brought home from Calcutta, an elephant bound for London Zoo. Broken up c.1882.

6. "Orlando" class armoured cruiser, 5,600 tons, 2 x 9.2" and 10 x 6" guns. Built by Napier, Dalmuir. Launched 10.3.1887. 1893-5 Coastguard ship at Queensferry. 1895-1903 Coastguard service at Hull. 4.4.1905 Sold after a 9.2" gun had exploded and caused considerable damage.

7. "Arethusa" class light cruiser, 3,500 tons, 2 x 6", 6 x 4"and 1 x 4" AA guns; 4 x 21" TT. Built by Wm. Beardmore, Dalmuir. Launched 14.5.1914. 1914-5 Leader of 2nd DF. 1915-8 1st LCS. 4.5.1916 With *Phaeton* shot down Zeppelin L7. 31.5.1916 Battle of Jutland; exchanged opening shots of the battle with *Elbing*. 10.2.1918 Collided with, and sank, SS *Moto* near Coquet Island off the Northumberland coast. 1919 1st LCS, Baltic operations. 1919-20 2nd LCS. 1920 In Reserve. 25.10.1921 Sold, to be broken up by Multilocular Sbkg. Co.

8. "Arethusa" class cruiser, 5,220 tons, 6 x 6" and 8 x 4" AA guns; 6 x 21" TT. Built by Scotts, Greenock. Launched 9.8.1934. 1935-8 Rear Admiral, Destroyers, Mediterranean. 1940 Norwegian campaign. 1941 Involved in pursuit of *Bismarck*. 13.12.1941 Left Alexandria for attack on supply convoys to North Africa. Operations abandoned. 14/15.12.1941 Just before midnight, as she approached Alexandria, she was hit by 2 torpedoes from *U 557* and sank.

Footnote

a) The Dutch sloop *Galathee*, 16 guns, was captured on 30.8.1799 and was on Navy List until 1806.

b) Lugger was hired 1795-1805.

c) Ship, 596 tons, built in 1906, was hired in 8.1940 for Examination Service. 1941 Renamed *Pygmalion*. 1946 Returned to owners.

GLAMORGAN

A ''County'' class Guided Missile destroyer, 5,440 tons (standard), 6,200 tons (full load). Built by Vickers Armstrong, Newcastle-on-Tyne. Launched 9.7.1964. Exocet SSM and Sea Slug SAM systems; 2 x 4.5" and 2 x 40mm guns; 6 TT; 1 helicopter.

Description of Badge

Field:- Barry wavy white and blue.
Badge:- A demi-dragon red, between two clarions gold.

Motto

Battle Honours

Falkland Islands   1982

Previous ships of the name

None.

HMS *Glamorgan*, at Malta.

GLASGOW

A Batch One "Town" class Type 42 Guided Missile destroyer, 3,500 tons (standard), 4,100 tons (full load). Built by Swan Hunter, Wallsend-on-Tyne. Launched 14.4.1976. Sea Dart SAM system; 1 x 4.5"; 2 x 20mm Oerlikons; helicopter-launched Sea Skua missiles; 6 TT; 1 helicopter.

Description of Badge

Field:- Blue.
Badge:- The figure of St Kentigern, gold
(Derived from the Arms of the City of Glasgow).

Motto

Memor es tuorum — Be mindful of your ancestors.

Battle Honours

Lagos	1759	Norway	1940
Havana	1762	Arctic	1943
Algiers	1816	Biscay	1943
Navarino	1827	Normandy	1944
Falkland Islands	1914	Falkland Islands	1982

Previous ships of the name

1. Sixth rate, 284 bm, 24 guns. Originally the *Royal Mary* of the Scots Navy, built in London and first commissioned in 6.1696. After the Union in 1707, she was absorbed into the Royal Navy and renamed *Glasgow*. 20.8.1719 Sold out of the service.

2. Sixth rate, 504 bm, 24 guns. Built by Reed, Hull. Launched 22.5.1745. 8.4.1756 Sold out of the service.

3. Sixth rate, 452 bm, 20 guns. Built by Blaydes, Hull. Launched 31.8.1757. 19.6.1779 Accidentally set on fire and destroyed in Montego Bay, Jamaica.

4. Fourth rate, 1,260 bm, 50 guns. Built by Wigram and Green, Blackwall. Launched 21.2.1814. Broken up at Chatham, the work being completed 29.1.1829.

5. Wood steam frigate, 3,984 tons 30 x 8" guns. Built in Portsmouth Dockyard. Launched 28.3.1861. 1871-5 Was her only commission—in East Indies. 12.1884 Sold out of the service.

6. "Bristol" class cruiser, 4,800 tons, 2 x 6", 10 x 4" and 4 x 3 pdr guns; 2 x 18" TT. Built by Fairfield, Govan, Glasgow. Launched 30.9.1909. 1910-4 Served on S.E. Coast of South America. 16.8.1914 Captured the German steamer *Santa Catherina*. 1.11.1914 Battle of Coronel; suffered slight damage. 8.12.1914 Battle of the Falklands; assisted in the sinking of the light cruiser *Leipzig*, but was herself damaged. *Glasgow* was the only British ship in both the above actions. 14.3.1915 With *Kent*, sank the light cruiser *Dresden* at Mas a Tierra. 1918 8th LCS in the Adriatic. 1921-6 Training Ship for Stokers at Portsmouth. 29.4.1927 Sold to T.W. Ward, Morecambe, for breaking up.

7. "Southampton" class cruiser, 9,100 tons, 12 x 6" and 8 x 4" AA guns; 6 x 21" TT. Built by Scotts, Greenock. Launched 20.6.1936. 16.7.1940 In collision with destroyer *Imogen* in Pentland Firth in fog. *Imogen* caught fire and blew up. 3.12.1940 Hit by 2 torpedoes while at anchor in Suda Bay. 30.3.1943 Intercepted German blockade runner *Regensburg* in Denmark Strait which scuttled herself. 28.12.1943 In Bay of Biscay, with *Enterprise*, intercepted 10 German destroyers and sank three. 26.6.1944 Off Normandy, hit by 2 shells from shore batteries. Under repair until 7.1945. 1949-51 West Indies cruises. 1.1951 At Chatham reducing to Reserve. 17.12.1951 Arrived Malta to join the 1st Cruiser Squadron. 15.6.1953 Coronation Review at Spithead. 5.1954 Acted as escort to Royal Yacht *Britannia*. 11.1956 Reduced to Reserve at Portsmouth. 8.7.1958 Arrived Blyth to be broken up by Hughes Bolckow.

GLEANER

An Inshore Survey Motor Launch, 22 tons. Built by Emsworth Shipbuilders. Delivered 1.12.1983. Commissioned into Naval Service on 5.12.1983.

Description of Badge

Field:- Red.
Badge:- Eight ears of wheat, fretted gold.

Motto

Fruges consumere nati — Born to reap its reward.

Battle Honours

Baltic	1855	Arctic	1942-4
Atlantic	1940-1	Normandy	1944
North Sea	1941-2		

Previous ships of the name

1. Survey ketch, 154 bm. 12.7.1808 Hired, but purchased the following year. 8.1811 Converted to Dockyard lighter. 2.4.1814 Lost.

2. Wood paddlewheel gunvessel, 351 bm, 3 x 18 pdr guns. Built in Chatham Dockyard. Launched 30.9.1833 as *Gulnare*. 1838 Rebuilt and renamed *Gleaner*. 1849 Broken up at Deptford.

3. Name ship of class of wood steam gunboats, 216 bm, 1 x 68 pdr and 1 x 32 pdr guns; 2 x 24 pdr howitzers. Built in Deptford Dockyard. Launched 7.10.1854. 1855 In Baltic. 9/10.8.1855 took part in attack on Sveaborg. 1856 At Spithead Review on St George's Day. Some years in Reserve, then sent to South America. 4.1868 Sold at Montevideo.

4. Torpedo Gunboat, 735 tons, 2 x 4.7″ and 4 x 3 pdr guns; 5 TT. Built in dock in Sheerness Dockyard. Floated out 9.1.1890. 4.4.1905 Sold to G. Cohen.

5. Tender, 160 tons. War Department vessel *General Stothard*. 1906 Transferred to RN 26.11.1906 Renamed *Gleaner*. 2.11.1921 Sold to M.S. Hilton.

6. Survey Vessel, 835 tons. Built by Wm Gray and Co., West Hartlepool. Launched 10.6.1937. 14.3.1939 Commissioned for survey service in Home waters. 9.9.1939 Conversion to A/S vessel completed at Devonport. 12.2.1940 In Firth of Clyde, depth charged *U 33*; brought her to the surface; fired 5 rounds of 4″ and turned to ram; *U 33* surrendered and then sank. 31.8.1940 Whilst escorting convoy 'OA 204', was torpedoed, and forced to return to the Clyde. Repaired at Rosyth. 10.2.1942 to 20.5.1942 Converted to Minesweeper by Robb Leith. 25.8.1944 Damaged by a near miss mine explosion off Normandy; engines out of action; taken in tow. Repaired on the Thames. 14.3.1945 Collided with Pilot Vessel in North Sea; hole 6 feet long at deck level. Repaired at Chatham. 6.1946 Reduced to Reserve at Devonport. 2.9.1946 To Falmouth Reserve. 20.4.1950 Sold to T.W. Ward. 14.5.1950 Arrived Preston to be broken up.

HMS *Gleaner* (November 1945).

GLOUCESTER

A Batch Three ''Town'' class Type 42 Guided Missile destroyer (stretched version) 4,775 tons (full load). Built by Vosper Thornycroft, Woolston, Southampton. Launched 2.11.1982. Sea Dart SAM system; 1 x 4.5"; 2 x 20mm Oerlikons; helicopter-launched Sea Skua missiles; 6 TT; 1 helicopter.

Description of Badge

Field:- Blue.
Badge:- A trident white, enfiled by a horseshoe, gold.
(Derived from the Arms of the City of Gloucester.)

Motto

Prorsum — Onwards.

Battle Honours

Lowestoft	1665	Jutland	1916
4 Days' Battle	1666	Calabria	1940
Orfordness	1666	Matapan	1941
Sole Bay	1672	Crete	1941
Schooneveld	1673	Mediterranean	1941
Texel	1673	Malta Convoys	1941
Ushant	1747		

Previous ships of the name

1. Third rate, 755 bm, 54 guns. Built by Graves, Limehouse, in 1654. Saw much action, winning the first 6 battle honours. 6.5.1682 Wrecked off Yarmouth.

HMS *Gloucester* (March 1939).

2. Fourth rate, 896 bm, 60 guns. Built by Clements, Bristol. Launched 5.2.1695. Useful, but quite undistinguished service, including some in the West Indies. 1706 Reduced to Harbour Service at Deptford. 10.1731 Broken up.

3. Fourth rate, 923 bm, 60 guns. Built by Burchett, Rotherhithe. Launched 25.7.1709. 26.10.1709 When in charge of a convoy off Cape Clear, Southern Ireland, surrendered to a superior French force, commanded by Admiral Du Guay Trouin in the *Lys*. In French service until 1711. Then became Spanish *Conquistador*.

4. Fourth rate, 714 bm, 50 guns. Built at Deptford. Launched 4.10.1711. Spent several years in the Baltic. Broken up at Sheerness; the work being completed by 20.1.1724.

5. Fourth rate, 866 bm, 50 guns. Built in Sheerness Dockyard. Launched 22.3.1737. 7.1742 Damaged in a storm. 15/16.8.1742 Burned, near the Ladrones, to avoid capture by the Spanish.

6. Fourth rate, 986 bm, 50 guns. Built by Whitston and Greville, Rotherhithe. Launched 23.3.1745. 1746 Assisted in capture of Spanish, 32 guns, *Forte de Nantz*. 1747 Captured off Finisterre, the French 24 guns *Two Crowns*. 1758 Became Military Hospital Ship at Chatham. 1759 To Sheerness; broken up there; the work completed 13.2.1764.

7. Third rate, 1,770 bm, 74 guns. Built by Pitcher, Northfleet. Launched 27.2.1812. 1812-4 North Sea, Baltic and West Indies. 1822-5 West Indies. 1832 Converted to a fourth rate of 50 guns. 1861 Reduced to Harbour Service. 3.1884 Sold to Castle and Sons, Charlton, for breaking up.

8. "Bristol" class cruiser, 4,800 tons, 2 x 6", 10 x 4" and 4 x 3 pdr guns; 2 x 18" TT. Built by Wm Beardmore, Dalmuir. Launched 28.10.1909. 1910 Home Fleet. 24.6.1911 Coronation Review at Spithead. 1913 Mediterranean. 9 to 11.1914 Dardanelles blockading squadron. 11.1914 Ordered to East Indies to search for *Emden*. 1915 2nd LCS, Grand Fleet. 28.3.1915 Captured German transport *Macedonia*. 31.5.1916 Battle of Jutland. 1916-7 Attached to the Italian Fleet. 1917-8 8th LCS, Adriatic Force. 31.3.1920 Paid off at Devonport. 9.5.1921 Sold to T.W. Ward and broken up at Briton Ferry.

9. Later "Southampton" class cruiser, 9,400 tons, 12 x 6" and 8 x 4" AA guns; 6 x 21" TT. Built in Devonport Dockyard. Launched 19.10.1937. 27.6.1940 In the Mediterranean, with 4 other cruisers, attacked 3 Italian destroyers, sinking the *Espero*. 9.7.1940 South of Crete, struck by a bomb from Italian Air Force; but it failed to explode. 11.1.1941 In Malta Convoy was hit by a bomb which penetrated 5 decks, but failed to explode. 22.5.1941 Hit by 4 bombs during intense air attack, south west of Crete; set on fire; disabled and sank off Island of Antikithera, with very heavy loss of life.

Footnote
a) Brig, 165 bm, 10 guns, was built at Kingston, Ontario, Canada, in 1807. 25.4.1813 Captured by the Americans at York on Lake Erie. 29.5.1813 Destroyed by fire by the British at Sackets Harbour.
b) Frigate, 2,170 tons, ex-*Panther*, was ordered from Portsmouth Dockyard in 1956 but was cancelled before being laid down.

HMS *Gloucester*

GUARDIAN

The former Oil Rig Support Vessel *Seaforth Champion*, 802 tons (gross), 1,030 tons (deadweight). Built by Beverly S.Y. Completed in 1975. Purchased from Seaforth Marine for service as a Falkland Islands Patrol Vessel. 2 x 40mm guns. Commissioned into the RN 21.10.1983.

Description of Badge

Field:- Black.
Badge:- A watchman's halberd and lanthorn gold and silver.

Motto

Vigilante salus — Safe by watching.

Battle Honours

Norway   1940   Sicily   1943

Previous ships of the name

1. Fifth rate, 901 bm, 44 guns. Built by Robert Batson, Limehouse. Launched 23.3.1784. 8.2.1790 Beached in Table Bay after having collided with an iceberg. 8.2.1791 Sold out of the service.

2. Netlayer, 2,860 tons, 2 x 4" HA guns. Built in Chatham Dockyard. Launched 1.9.1932. 13.6.1933 Commissioned for Special Trials as Netlaying and Target Towing Vessel. 1.4.1936 Recommissioned at Devonport for Home Fleet. 1936 Detached to Mediterranean during Abyssinian crisis. 10.1941 East Indies Station. 1942-5 In Mediterranean. 1947-61 In Reserve. 12.1962 Arrived Troon to be broken up.

HMS *Guardian* (May 1937).

GUERNSEY

An "Island" class Offshore Patrol Vessel, 925 tons (standard), 1,260 tons (full load). Built by Hall Russell, Aberdeen. Launched 17.2.1977. 1 x 40mm gun. Able to carry a small RM Detachment.

Description of Badge

Field:- Argent.
Badge:- Issuant from an ancient crown gold, three florets of a Guernsey lily (*nerine samiensis*) proper.

Motto

Battle Honours

Lowestoft	1665	Lagos	1759
Texel	1673		

Previous ships of the name

1. Ship, 255 bm, 22 guns. Built as *Basing* by Shish, Walderswick, in 1654. 1660 Renamed *Guernsey*. 1688 Converted to fireship. 1693 Broken up.

2. Fourth rate, 680 bm, 48 guns. Built by Johnson, Blackwall, in 1696. 1740 Rebuilt at Chatham. 4.1769 Reduced to a hulk. 1786 Sold out of the service.

3. Fifth rate, 704 bm, 32 guns. Built as *Aeolus* by West, Deptford. Launched 29.11.1758. 5.1796 Reduced to Harbour Service. 1800 Renamed *Guernsey*. 5.1801 Broken up.

Footnote
a) "Cormorant" class wood steam sloop, 695 bm, was ordered in 1861 from Pembroke Dock but cancelled 12.12.1863.
b) "G" class destroyer was ordered in 8.1944 from Wm Denny, Dumbarton, but cancelled 28.12.1945.

HMS *Guernsey* (June 1979).

HART

Patrol Craft, former RAF Search and Rescue craft *Stirling*. Built by James and Stone, Brightlingsea, in 1976. Commissioned into the RN in 1985.

Description of Badge
Field:- Blue.
Badge:- A hart statant white.

Motto

Battle Honours

Armada	1583	Atlantic	1944-5
Normandy	1944	Korea	1950-1
English Channel	1944		

Previous ships of the name

1. Galley, of Portsmouth, 300 bm, 4 brass and 52 iron guns. Built in 1546. 1558 Rebuilt. 1562 Engaged in the Suppression of French piracy. Listed to 1568.

2. Ship, 120 bm, 12 guns. Royalist ship captured in 1643 by Parliament. 1652 Captured by the Dutch in the English Channel. Later blown up in Canary Islands.

3. Pink, 6 guns—sometimes *Red Hart*. Captured in 1653; sold in 1654.

4. Pink, 55 bm, 8 guns. Built in Woolwich Dockyard in 1657. 1683 Sold out of the service.

5. Dogger, 8 guns. Captured in 1672. 1673 Captured by the Dutch.

6. Ketch, 96 bm, 10 guns. Built by Rolfe and Castle, Rotherhithe. Launched 23.3.1691. 9.6.1692 Captured by a force under the celebrated French corsair, Du Guay Trouin.

7. Cutter, built in Deptford in 1793. 30.10.1817 Sold to J. Edgar.

8. Brig-sloop, 152 bm, 16 x 12 pdr carriage guns. Ex-French privateer *Empereur*. Captured in 6.1805 by *Eagle*. 1810 Sold in Jamaica.

9. Composite steam gunvessel, 584 tons, 1 x 7", 1 x 64 pdr and 2 x 20 pdr guns. Built by Thomson, Glasgow. Launched 20.8.1868. 1873 Engaged in the blockade of Spanish Mediterranean littoral. 9.1874 With *Charybdis,* in expedition to Indian River in Malay peninsula. 11.1874 In Likut river. 12.1888 Sold out of the service.

10. "A" class destroyer, 295 tons, 1 x 12 pdr and 5 x 6 pdr guns; 2 TT. Built by Fairfield, Govan, Glasgow. Launched 27.3.1895. 1900 Boxer Rebellion. 1912 Sold at Hong Kong.

11. "Heroine" class composite steam corvette, 1,420 tons, 2 x 6" and 10 x 5" guns. Laid down in Devonport Dockyard as *Rapid*. Launched 21.3.1883. 1884 To Cape of Good Hope and West Coast of Africa. 1888-98 Ten years on Australian Station. 1902 Towed to Gibraltar for use as an accommodation ship. 1912 Submarine Depot Ship at Gibraltar. 1916 Renamed *Hart*. 1948 Sold; broken up at Malaga, Spain.

12. Modified "Black Swan" class sloop, 1,350 tons, 6 x 4" and 12 x 20mm AA guns. Built by Alex, Stephen, Linthouse, Glasgow. Launched 7.7.1943. Paid off in 1951. 1958 Sold to West German Navy; renamed *Scheer*. 27.4.1959 Handed over at Palmers, Jarrow. 9.1961 to 11.1962 Converted to Radar Picket Training Ship. 1968 De-commissioned and broken up.

Footnote
a) 80 ton vessel was hired in 1588 for the Armada campaign.
b) Brig, 10 guns, was hired 1800-1.
c) Cutter/Yacht, 80 bm, 2 x 6 pdr guns. Built at Woolwich. Launched 12.6.1822. Employed as Yacht to Navy Board. 1833 On abolition of that office, became Yacht to Admiral at Sheerness; renamed *Sheerness Yard Craft No. 1*. 17.11.1870 Renamed *Drake*. 6.3.1875 Breaking up completed at Chatham.

HECATE

A ''Hecla'' class Ocean Survey Ship, 1,915 tons (standard), 2,733 tons (full load). Built by Yarrow, Scotstoun, Glasgow. Launched 31.3.1965. Designed with combined Oceanographical and Hydrographical role. Hull strengthened for navigation in ice.

Description of Badge

Field:- Blue.
Badge:- In crescent white, over all a cornucopia gold, fructed proper, overflowing to the sinister proper.

Motto

Battle Honours

Java   1811

Previous ships of the name

1. Gunvessel, 168 bm, 12 guns (Gunboat No. 32). Laid down as *Hearty,* but renamed before launch. Built by Wilson, Frindsbury. Launched 2.5.1797. 1809 Sunk as a breakwater at Harwich.

2. ''Cruizer'' class brig-sloop, 384 bm, 16 x 32 pdr and 2 x 6 pdr guns. Built by King, Upnor. Launched 30.5.1809. 1810 Mauritius. 1811 Java. 30.10.1817 Sold to a Mr Parker.

3. Wood paddlewheel sloop, 817 bm, 1 x 10", 1 x 110 pdr and 4 x 32 pdr guns. Built in Chatham Dockyard. Launched 30.3.1839. 1840-3 In the Mediterranean. 1844-7 Coast of Africa. 1848 Again in the Mediterranean. 1852-4 Laid up at Woolwich. 1855-7 West Coast of Africa. 1860s Carried out important survey work around Vancouver Island and British Columbia. c.1865 Sold out of service.

4. Iron Steam turret ship, 3,480 tons, 4 x 10" MLR guns. Built by Dudgeon, Poplar. Launched 30.9.1871. Spent entire life based at Devonport, first as tender to *Indus,* Guardship of the Reserve, then from 1885 as tender to *Cambridge,* Gunnery ship. 12.5.1903 Sold out of the service.

Footnote
Yacht, 471 tons, built in 1903, was hired for auxiliary patrol, with 2 x 6 pdr guns, from 15.10.1914 to 20.3.1919.

HMS *Hecate* (July 1970).

HECLA

Name ship of the class of Ocean Survey ships, 1,915 tons (standard), 2,733 tons (full load). Built by Yarrow, Blythswood. Launched 21.12.1964. Designed with combined Oceanographical and Hydrographical role. Hull strengthened for navigation in ice.

Description of Badge

Field:- Black.
Badge:- Four flames red, one in each quarter.

Motto

De fumo in flammam — From smoke to flame.

Battle Honours

Copenhagen	1801	Alexandria	1882
Algiers	1816	Falkland Islands	1982
Baltic	1854		

Previous ships of the name

1. Bomb, 300 bm, 10 guns. Ex-*Scipio.* 4.1797 Purchased into the RN. 1798 In expedition to destroy the lock gates of Bruges Canal at Ostend. 7.1813 Broken up.

2. Bomb, 375 bm, 1 x 13" mortar and 1 x 10" mortar. Built by Barkworth and Hawkes, North Barton. Launched 22.7.1815. 1819-27 On Parry's four voyages of discovery. 1829 Employed on survey of west coast of Africa. 13.4.1831 Sold to Sir E. Banks.

3. Wood paddlewheel sloop, 817 bm, 2 x 84 pdr and 4 x 32 pdr guns. Built in Chatham Dockyard. Launched 14.1.1839. 1854 In Baltic. Her Mate, C.D. Lucas, was awarded the Victoria Cross for flinging overboard a live shell that fell on board. 1863 Sold to Williams and Co. for breaking up.

4. Torpedo Depot ship, 6,400 tons, 5 x 64 pdr and 1 x 40 pdr guns. Ex-*British Crown* built by Harland and Wolff, Belfast. Purchased for the RN. Launched as *Hecla* 7.3.1878. 1882-4 Egyptian War. 1908 Fitted out as a Destroyer Depot ship. 1912 Rebuilt as 5,600 tons, armed with 4 x 4" guns. During World War 1 served as Depot Ship for 4th Destroyer Flotilla at Scapa, 1914-6; and for 2nd DF at Belfast 1917-8. 13.7.1926 Sold to T.W. Ward, Preston, for breaking up.

5. Depot ship, 10,850 tons, 8 x 4.5" guns. Built by J. Brown, Clydebank. Launched 14.3.1940. 4.1942 Damaged by a mine laid off Agulhas Bank at the Cape. Took part in North African landings. 12.11.1942 Sunk by *U 515* west of Gibraltar.

Footnote

Repair ship, 14,250 tons, was built by Bethlehem, Fairfield, USA. Launched 31.7.1944 for the RN, but actually retained by US Navy as *Xanthus.*

HMS *Hecla,* as a hospital ship during the Falklands conflict.

HELFORD

A ''River'' class Fleet Minesweeper, 890 tons (full load); 1 x 40mm gun. Built by Richards, Great Yarmouth. Launched 16.5.1984. Allocated to Ulster Division, RNR.

Description of Badge

Field:- Argent.
Badge:- In front of a roundel charged with a bend argent between two bendlets wavy also argent three flames in bend proper.

Motto

Battle Honours

None.

Previous ships of the name

1. ''River'' class frigate, 1,370 tons, 2 x 4″ and 10 x 20mm guns. Built by Hall Russell, Aberdeen. Launched 6.2.1943. 1946-50 In Reserve at Devonport. 26.1.1951 Completed refit at Birkenhead. 1952-3 In Reserve at Devonport. 1953-6 In Reserve at Lisahally, Londonderry. 29.6.1956 Arrived Troon to be broken up by West of Scotland Shipbreaking Company.

HMS *Helford*

HELMSDALE

A "River" class Fleet Minesweeper, 890 tons (full load); 1 x 40mm gun. Built by Richards, Lowestoft. Launched 11.1.1985. Allocated to Tay Division, RNR, Dundee.

Description of Badge

Field:- Green.
Badge:- An esquire's close helmet white, garnished gold.
(Helmsdale is said to mean "The valley of the helmet").

Motto

Battle Honours

Atlantic   1943-4

Previous ships of the name

1. "River" class frigate, 1,370 tons, 2 x 4" and 10 x 20mm guns. Built by A. & J. Inglis, Glasgow. Launched 5.6.1943. Operated as convoy escort in North Atlantic. 9.9.1944 With *Portchester Castle* sank *U 743* near convoy 'ONF 252'. 1946-7 Underwater experimental vessel at Portland. Armament removed; and fitted with glass panels in bottom of hull to study effects of water flowing past 'A' brackets and bilge keel, and cavitation of the propellers. 4.1951 Took part in the search for HM Submarine *Affray*. 1953 Paid off. 1954-7 In Reserve at Devonport. 14.11.1957 Arrived Faslane to be broken up.

Footnote
Later "Hunt" class minesweeper was laid down at Eltringham but was renamed *Huntley* before launch 18.1.1919.

HMS *Helmsdale* (February 1952).

HERALD

An improved ''Hecla'' class Ocean Survey ship, 2,000 tons (standard), 2,945 tons (full load). Built by Robb Caledon, Leith. Launched 4.10.1973.

Description of Badge

Field:- Green.
Badge:- A herald in tabard red, emblazoned with the Admiralty anchor gold, bearing a trumpet and staff.

Motto

Famam profero — I proclaim fame.

Battle Honours

China   1841   Falkland Islands   1982

Previous ships of the name

1. Sixth rate, 422 bm, 20 guns. Built by Carver, Littlehampton. Launched 27.12.1806. Saw action in the Adriatic. 9.1817 Broken up.

2. Sixth rate, 500 bm, 28 guns. Built at Cochin. Launched 15.3.1820, as *Termagant*. 5.1824 Renamed *Herald* when converted to a Yacht. On a voyage home from Havana, brought a cargo of a million dollars. 1831 Paid off as a Yacht at Portsmouth. 8.2.1840 Present at Proclamation of New Zealand's accession to the Empire. 1843 Paid off at Chatham. 1845 Duties with the Surveying Service. For 6 years surveyed the Pacific coast of America. 12.1857 Was the first ship docked in Fitzroy Dock, Cockatoo Island, NSW, Australia. 1861 Chapel Ship at Shoreham. 28.4.1862 Sold for breaking up by Castle, Charlton.

3. Paddlewheel river gunboat, 82 tons, 4 x 3 pdr guns. Built by Yarrow, Poplar. Launched 3.5.1890. Shipped to the Zambesi River, in sections, in SS *Buccaneer*; re-erected by artificers from the Fleet. Performed patrol and ceremonial duties on the River. 1.1903 Withdrawn from service. 19.2.1903 Sold to commercial interests; became *Pelopede* of E.C. Sharron's Zambesi S.N. Co. (later B.C. Africa Co.).

4. A ''24'' class, or ''Racehorse'' class, of minesweeping sloops, ex-*Merry Hampton*, 1,320 tons. 2 x 4'' LA guns. Built by Blyth S.B. and D.D. Company. Launched 13.12.1918. 2.1923 Converted at Devonport to a Survey Ship; renamed *Herald*. 1924 to 6.1926 On Australian Station. 6.1926 to 12.1941 On China Station. 2.1942 Scuttled at Seletar, Singapore. Raised by the Japanese and commissioned 10.10.1942 as *Heiryu Maru*; used for survey duties. 1.1944 Renamed *Heiyo*. 14.11.1944 Mined and sunk in the Java Sea.

HMS *Herald*, in grey livery for South Atlantic service.

HERMES

Aircraft Carrier, 22,500 tons. Laid down by Vickers Armstrong, Barrow, as *Elephant*. 5.11.1945 Renamed *Hermes*. Launched 16.2.1953. 1971-3 Converted to Commando Carrier. 1976 Refitted into an Anti-submarine helicopter carrier.

Description of Badge

Field:- Blue.
Badge:- The head of Hermes with winged hat all gold.

Motto

Altiora peto — I seek higher things.

Battle Honours

Burma	1852	Falkland Islands	1982
Atlantic	1940		

Previous ships of the name

1. Dutch brig *Mercurius*, 210 bm, 12 guns. Captured on 12.5.1796 by *Sylph* off the Texel. Purchased by the RN and renamed *Hermes*. 1.1797 Foundered, and lost with all hands.

2. Armed Vessel, 331 bm, 22 guns. Purchased in 1798 for service in the North Sea. 6.1802 Sold out of the service.

3. Sloop ex-*Majestic*, 339 bm, 14 x 24 pdr and 2 x 6 pdr guns. Built at Whitby. Purchased 7.1803 and renamed *Hermes*. Saw service in North Sea, English Channel and North America. Ended her days as a Storeship in the Mediterranean. 24.3.1810 Sold out of the service.

4. Sixth rate, 511 bm, 20 guns. Built in Portsmouth Dockyard. Launched 22.7.1811. 1811-2 North Sea and Channel Stations. Ran down the French privateer *La Mouche*; and captured American privateer *Sword Fish*. 15.9.1814 Grounded, and burnt to avoid falling into enemy hands, at Mobile, Alabama, USA.

5. Wood paddlewheel packet *George IV*, 733 bm. Built at Blackwall in 1824. Purchased for the RN as *Courier* on 20.8.1830. 1831 Renamed *Hermes*. 1835 Converted at Woolwich to a Coal Hulk; renamed *Charger*. 6.1854 Broken up at Deptford.

6. Wood paddlewheel sloop, 716 bm. Built in Portsmouth Dockyard. Launched 26.6.1835. Served on Mediterranean, North American, Cape of Good Hope and East Indies Stations. 1854 Returned home to pay off at Woolwich. Five years further service before being sold and broken up in 1864.

7. Third rate, 1,726 bm, 74 guns. Laid down in Chatham Dockyard as *Minotaur*. Launched 15.4.1816. 11.1842 Reduced to Harbour Service. 27.7.1866 Renamed *Hermes* on conversion to Cholera Hospital Ship at Gravesend. 1869 Broken up at Sheerness.

8. Cruiser, 5,600 tons, 11 x 6" and 9 x 12 pdr guns. Built by Fairfield, Govan, Glasgow. Launched 7.4.1898. 1913 Fitted experimentally with seaplane launching rails on platforms forward and aft. 12.1913 Fittings removed at Devonport. Became Depot Ship for the Naval Wing of Royal Flying Corps. 1914 Again fitted to carry 3 seaplanes. 30.10.1914 Arrived Dunkirk carrying seaplanes from Portsmouth. Left next day for Dover, but when about 8 miles WNW of Calais, was torpedoed by *U 27*. She was hit by 2 torpedoes, but remained afloat for nearly 2 hours.

9. Aircraft Carrier—first vessel specifically designed as such—10,850 tons, 10 x 6" and 4 x 4" guns; 21 aircraft. Built by Armstrong Whitworth, Newcastle-on-Tyne. Launched 11.9.1919. Towed to Devonport Dockyard for completion. 1924 Entered service. 1939 Channel Force at Portland. 7.7.1940 Aircraft carrying torpedoes and the ship's power boat carrying depth charges attacked the French battleship *Richelieu* at Dakar. 1941 On convoy duty, collided with Armed Merchant Cruiser *Corfu*. Bows stove in; limped to Simonstown for repairs. 9.3.1942 Attacked by about 50 Japanese aircraft; hit by some 40 bombs in 10 minutes; sank off Batticaloa, Ceylon.

Footnote
Another aircraft carrier, 18,300 tons, 45 aircraft, was ordered from Cammell Laird, Birkenhead, but cancelled in 10.1945.

HERMIONE

A Batch Three Leander class (broad-beamed) frigate; 2,500 tons (standard). The last warship to be built by Alex Stephen, Glasgow. Launched 26.4.1967. 1979-83 Exocet conversion at Chatham. New Armament:- Exocet SSM and Sea Wolf SAM systems; A/S torpedo tubes; 2 x 20mm guns; 1 helicopter.

Description of Badge

Field:- Blue.

Badge:- In a Ducal coronet, an oak tree fructed gold, penetrated transversely in the main stem by a frame-saw white.

(From the Ducal Arms of Hamilton).

(*Hermione* was the only daughter of Menelaus (brother of Agamemnon) and Helen (of Troy fame). She had been betrothed to Orestes, son of Agamemnon, before the Trojan War, but Menelaus, after his return from the war, gave her to Neoptolemus, son of Achilles. However, Orestes murdered Neoptolemus at Delphi and then married Hermione).

Motto

Battle Honours

Bismarck	1941	Malta Convoys	1941-2
Mediterranean	1941	Diego Suarez	1942

Previous ships of the name

First three ships to bear the name were prizes captured from the French who apparently found *Hermione* a popular name. First was taken 23.11.1757; the second 16.8.1759; and the third 10.1760.

1. The first *Hermione* for the RN was a fifth rate, 716 bm, 32 guns. Built by Teast and Tombe, Bristol. Launched 9.9.1782. Saw service mainly in the West Indies. 22.9.1797 Was the setting for one of the bloodiest mutinies in the Navy; earned her the nickname 'Black Hermione'. Mutineers sailed her into the hands of the Spanish on South American mainland. 25.10.1799 Recaptured by *Surprise*. Renamed *Retaliation*; then in 1800 to *Retribution*. 6.1805 Broken up at Deptford.

2. "Astraea" class second class protected cruiser, 4,360 tons, 2 x 6" and 8 x 4.7" guns. Built in Devonport Dockyard. Launched 7.11.1893. 1898-1901 China Station. Prominent part in Boxer Rebellion. 1904-7 In Reserve. 1910-2 Used in experiments with airships. 1914 Depot Ship in Hamble River, Southampton. 25.10.1921 Purchased by Multilocular Sbkg. Co., Stranraer. 18.12.1921 Purchased by Marine Society for Boys' Training Ship. 1922-39 Replaced *Warspite* in the Thames; adopted her name. 9.1940 Sold to T.W. Ward, Gravesend, for breaking up.

3. Cruiser, 5,450 tons, 10 x 5.25" guns. Built by Alex Stephen, Linthouse, Glasgow. Launched 18.5.1939. 5.1941 In hunt for *Bismarck*. 6.1941 in Force 'H'; acted as escort to *Victorious* delivering aircraft to Malta. 1.8.1941 Rammed and sank Italian submarine *Tambien* off Tunis. Suffered minor damage to her own bows. 4.8.1941 Arrived Gibraltar for 5 days docking. 9 to 11. 1941 Escort to further deliveries of aircraft to Malta. 3.5.1942 Staged pyrotechnic diversion off east coast of Vichy—held Madagascar, while main assault took place on west coast. 7.5.1942 Shelled harbour defences of Diego Suarez. 7.6.1942 Joined 15th CS at Alexandria. 16.6.1942 In operation 'Vigorous', convoy from Alexandria to Malta, was torpedoed by *U 205*. After Boiler Room and Engine Room were flooded; listed to 22° to starboard; lay on her side and sank 21 minutes later.

HUMBER

A ''River'' class Fleet Minesweeper, 890 tons (full load); 1 x 40mm gun. Built by Richards, Lowestoft. Launched 17.5.1984. Allocated to London Division, RNR.

Description of Badge

Field:- Azure.
Badge:- On an escallop reversed argent, a boar's head couped sable.

Motto

Battle Honours

Belgian Coast   1914   Dardanelles   1915

Previous ships of the name

1. Fireship, 254 bm, 8 guns. Built in 1690 but her fate is unknown.

2. Second rate, 1,223 bm, 80 guns. Built by Frame, Hull. Launched 30.3.1693. 1708 Rebuilt at Deptford as 1,294 bm. 1726 Rebuilt at Portsmouth as 1,353 bm. 1727 Renamed *Princess Amelia*. 6.1752 Broken up at Portsmouth.

3. Fifth rate, 829 bm, 44 guns. Built by Smith, Bursledon. Launched 5.3.1747. 16.9.1762 Wrecked on Hazeboro Sand.

4. French sloop, 16 guns. Captured in 1806 and still listed in 1808.

5. Iron steam storeship, ex-*Harar*, 1,640 tons. Built by Earle, Hull. Launched 7.10.1876. Purchased for the RN on 28.5.1878. 1884-5 At Suakim. 1891 Vitu Expedition. 1900 China Station. 1904 Allocated for service with destroyers. 1907 Sold out of the service and renamed *Lucia Victoria*.

6. Brazilian river monitor, *Javary*, 1,260 tons, 2 x 6″ and 2 x 4.7″ howitzers. Built by Vickers, Barrow. Launched 17.6.1913. 8.8.1914 Purchased for the RN and renamed *Humber*. 4.6.1915 At Gallipoli. 1917 Red Sea. 11.1918 In Aegean. 6.1919 In White Sea. 17.9.1920 Sold to F. Rijsdijk and used as a crane ship at Upnor, Kent. Fitted up with German battleship *Rheinland's* turning engines; *Oldenburgh's* gun turret machinery; and sloop *Bend Or's* generator. 1926 Re-sold. Subsequent fate unknown.

Footnote:
a) Sloop, 258 bm, was hired 1804-11.
b) ''Philomel'' class wood steam gun vessel, was laid down at Pembroke Dock on 8.2.1861, but cancelled 12.12.1863.
c) The ''Ton'' class coastal minesweeper *Bronington*, built by Cook, Welton and Gemmell, Beverley; launched 19.3.1953; was for a short time named *Humber*.

HMS *Humber*

HUNTER

An ''Attacker'' class Seamanship and Navigational Training Vessel of 34 tons for the RNR and University RN Units. Built by Fairey Allday Marine, Southampton. Delivered 21.3.1983. Allocated to London University.

Description of Badge

Field:- Green.
Badge:- A crossbow in bend sinister, gold, between two arrows silver.

Motto

Follow on.

Battle Honours

Gabbard	1653	Atlantic	1939-44
Scheveningen	1653	Narvik	1940
Barfleur	1692	Salerno	1943
Vigo	1702	South France	1944
Velez Malaga	1704	Aegean	1944
Louisburg	1758	Burma	1945
Quebec	1759		

Previous ships of the name

1. Dogger Boat. 4.1.1645 First appeared on List of Ships ordered to be fitted out for the Summer Guard. 13.7.1649 Ordered to be sold as unserviceable.

2. French frigate *Chasseur*, 24 guns. Captured 5.9.1652. 1653 Converted to fireship. 31.7.1653 Expended at first Battle of the Texel.

3. Sixth rate, 66 bm, 6 guns. Royalist privateer captured in 1657 on coast of Spain. 1661 Lost at sea.

4. Fireship, 277 bm, 8 guns. Built by Jonas Shish, Rotherhithe. Launched 29.4.1690. 14.1.1709 Ordered to be converted to Fifth rate, 24 guns. 20.9.1710 Captured by Spanish off Cape Sta. Maria and carried into Cadiz.

5. Fireship 253 bm, 8 guns. Purchased 7.9.1739. 12.1739 Renamed *Vulcan*. 10.1743 Hulked in Jamaica.

6. Sloop, 233 bm, 10 guns. Built by Wells and Stanton, Deptford. Launched 28.2.1756. 1759 Campaign of Quebec. 23.11.1775 Taken by 2 American privateers off Boston. Retaken soon afterwards by *Greyhound*. 2.1780 Made Hospital and Prison Ship at New York. 27.12.1780 Sold.

7. Cutter, 72 bm, 8 guns. Purchased in 1.1763. 20.9.1771 sold out of the service.

8. Sloop, 336 bm, 16 guns. Purchased in 1796 while being built by Pender, Bermuda. 27.12.1797 Wrecked on Hog Island, Virginia.

9. Brig-sloop, 309 bm, 16 guns. Ex-mercantile built by King, Dover. 5.1801 Purchased into the RN 1801-2 Channel Service. 1803-8 Jamaica Station. 5.8.1809 Broken up.

10. Brig, 180 bm, 10 guns. 1812 Built on the Great Lakes for service in War with America. 10.9.1813 Captured by the Americans in engagement on Lake Erie.

11. ''Clown'' class wood steam gunboat, 233 bm, 1 x 68 pdr and 1 x 32 pdr guns. Built by Pitcher, Northfleet. Launched 7.6.1856. One of a large class of gunboats built for the Russian War but not completed before the peace. 16.1.1884 Sold.

12. Destroyer, 295 tons, 1 x 12 pdr and 5 x 6 pdr guns; 2 x 18" TT. Built by Fairfield, Govan, Glasgow. Launched 28.12.1895. 10.4.1912 Sold to T.W.Ward, Briton Ferry for breaking up.

13. ''H'' Class destroyer, 1,340 tons, 4 x 4.7" guns; 8 TT. Built by Swan Hunter, Wallsend-on-Tyne. Launched 25.2.1936. 13.5.1937 Seriously damaged by a mine off Almeria during Spanish Civil War. 10.4.1940 Damaged in action at Narvik and lost in collision with *Hotspur*. *Hunter* was set on fire, and was sent out of control. *Hotspur* was in similar trouble and rammed her. When *Hotspur* managed to pull free, *Hunter* sank.

14. Escort Carrier, 11,420 tons, 2 x 4″ AA, 8 x 40mm AA and 15 x 20mm AA guns; 18 aircraft. Built by Ingall's Shipbuilding Corporation, Pascagoula, USA; ex-*Mormacpenn*. Launched as USS *Block Island* 22.5.1942. 11.1942 renamed HMS *Trailer*. 27.11.1942 Renamed *Hunter*. 1942-3 Western Approaches. 1944 to 2.1945 Mediterranean. 1945 East Indies. 12.1945 Returned to USA.

15. LST (3) 3042, 2,256 tons, 10 x 20mm guns. Built by Harland and Wolff, Govan, Glasgow. Launched 31.1.1945. 1947 Renamed *Hunter*. 1956 To Ministry of Transport as *Empire Curlew*. 26.8.1962 Arrived Spezia to be broken up.

Footnote:
Trawler, 185 tons, built in 1903, was hired as Boom Defence Vessel 1914-9.

HMS *Hunter*, 1936

HMS *Hunter*

HURWORTH

A ''Hunt'' class Mine Countermeasures Vessel, 615 tons (standard), 725 tons (full load); 1 x 40mm gun. Built of GRP by Vosper Thornycroft, Woolston, Southampton. Launched 25.9.1984.

Description of Badge

Field:- Red.
Badge:- Within a horseshoe inverted, a whelk shell gold.

Motto

Battle Honours

Atlantic	1941	Malta Convoys	1942
Libya	1942	Sicily	1943
Sirte	1942	Aegean	1943
Mediterranean	1942		

Previous ships of the name

1. ''Hunt'' class, Type 2, ''Blankney'' type, destroyer, 1,050 tons, 6 x 4'' AA guns. Built by Vickers Armstrong, Tyne. Launched 10.4.1941. 1942 Joined 5th Destroyer Flotilla at Alexandria. Escorted convoys to Malta and Tobruk. 28.5.1942 Shared in the destruction of a U-boat. 9.1942 Took part in unsuccessful Commando raid on Tobruk. 10.1942 Assisted in sinking another U-boat off Port Said. 22.10.1943 With a force endeavouring to re-inforce Leros in the Aegean. When east of Kalymnos, the destroyer *Adrias* struck a mine. *Hurworth* went to her assistance but she too, was mined, broke in two, and sank. Six officers and 127 ratings lost their lives. *Adrias* managed to beach herself and finally reached Alexandria under her own steam, but with her bows missing.

HMS *Hurworth*

ILLUSTRIOUS

An "Invincible" class, anti-submarine warfare, aircraft carrier, 20,000 tons. Built by Swan Hunter, Wallsend-on-Tyne. Launched 1.12.1978. Primary role to act as Command Ship of A/S Warfare forces. Armament:- Sea Harriers, Sea King helicopters, Sea Dart missiles, close range weapons.

Description of Badge

Field:- Blue.
Badge:- In front of a trumpet erect, two trumpets in saltire gold.

Motto

Non vox incerta — No uncertain sound.

Battle Honours

Genoa	1795	Diego Suarez	1942
Basque Roads	1809	Salerno	1943
Java	1811	Sabang	1944
Taranto	1940	Palembang	1945
Mediterranean	1940-1	Okinawa	1945
Malta Convoys	1941		

Previous ships of the name

1. Third rate, 1,616 bm, 74 guns. Built by H. Adams, Buckler's Hard. Launched 7.7.1789. 1793 In action against the French off Toulon, and 2 years later at Genoa. There, she captured 2 ships but suffered severe damage. Taken in tow but driven ashore in Valence Bay on 14.3.1795. Crew abandoned her and burned the wreck.

2. Third rate, 1,746 bm, 74 guns. Built by Randall, Rotherhithe. Launched 3.9.1803. After distinguished career became, in 1854, Training Ship for Seamen. 1857 Training Ship for Cadets at Portsmouth. 1861 Attached to *Excellent*. 4.12.1868 Completion of breaking up at Portsmouth.

3. "Majestic" class battleship, 14,900 tons, 4 x 12" and 12 x 6" guns. Built in Chatham Dockyard. Launched 17.9.1896. 1898-1904 In Mediterranean, including operations off Crete. Outbreak of WWI became Guardship at Loch Ewe. 1915 Her 12" guns removed for use in "Lord Clive" class monitors; and converted to Ammunition Storeship based on the Tyne. 1917-9 At Portsmouth. 18.6.1920 Sold for breaking up by T.W. Ward at Barrow.

4. Fleet aircraft carrier, 23,000 tons, 16 x 4.5" guns, 36 aircraft. Built by Vickers Armstrong, Barrow. Launched 5.4.1939. Became one of the most distinguished ships of WW2; one highlight being the successful attack by 20 of her Swordfish aircraft on the Italian naval base at Taranto. 1941 Severely damaged by Stuka dive-bombers off Malta. Refitted in USA. Returned to play a major role in operations off Diego Suarez, Salerno and Sumatra; and to support American landings at Okinawa. Post-war, she became a Trials and Training Ship. 1951 Used to carry troops to Cyprus. 1954 Laid up in the Gareloch. 3.11.1956 Arrived Faslane for breaking up.

HMS *Illustrious* (March 1947).

INTREPID

An Assault Ship (LPD), 11,060 tons (standard), 12,120 tons (full load). Built by John Brown, Clydebank. Launched 25.6.1964. Four Sea Cat SAM systems; 2 x 40mm Bofors AA guns; one flight of Assault helicopters.

Description of Badge

Field:- Red.
Badge:- A lion statant affronté gold.

Motto

Cela va sans dire — That goes without saying.

Battle Honours

Lagos	1759	*Bismarck*	1941
Quiberon Bay	1759	Norway	1941-2
Havana	1762	Arctic	1941-3
St Kitts	1782	Malta Convoys	1942
Martinique	1809	Sicily	1943
Zeebrugge	1918	Salerno	1943
Atlantic	1939-41	Aegean	1943
Dunkirk	1940	Falkland Islands	1982

Previous ships of the name

1. French third rate *Serieux*, 1,300 bm, 64 guns. 3.5.1747 Captured by Lord Anson's forces at Cape Finisterre. Added to RN as *Intrepid*. 20.5.1756 Minorca. 1758 Off Aix. 18.8.1759 Off Gibraltar. 20.11.1759 Quiberon Bay. 1762 Reduction of Havana. 2.8.1765 Her breaking up at Chatham completed.

2. French *Intrépide*, 14 guns. Captured by *Brilliant*, 38 guns on 25.12.1757.

3. Third rate, 1,374 bm, 64 guns. Built in Woolwich Dockyard. Launched 4.12.1770. 17.4.1780 At Martinique. 5.9.1781 Chesapeake Bay. 8.1794 At San Domingo with *Chichester*, captured French *Sirene*, 16 guns. 21.4.1796 Captured French *Percante*, 26 guns. 11.5.1806 At Reduction of Capri. 30.1.1809 Martinique. 5.1810 Reduced to Harbour Service. 26.3.1818 Sold to Beatson.

4. French *Intrepide*, 74 guns. Captured off Newfoundland on 19.11.1809, by *Vestal*, 28 guns.

5. Steamer, ex-*Free Trade* of Southampton, engaged in the Mediterranean trade. Purchased 3.1850. Commissioned as the sloop *Intrepid*. 1850-1 Captain Austin's expedition to the Arctic. 1852-4 Commander F.L. McClintock's expedition to the Arctic. 15.6.1854 Abandoned in the ice in Arctic on Sir E. Belcher's orders.

6. Name ship of class of Wood steam gun vessels, 862 bm, 2 x 68 pdr, and 4 x 32 pdr guns. Built by Wigram, Blackwall. Launched 13.11.1855. Served in the Mediterranean. 7.10.1864 Sold to Marshall, Plymouth, for breaking up.

7. "Apollo" class Second class cruiser, 3,600 tons, 2 x 6" and 6 x 4.7" guns. Built by London and Glasgow Co., Govan, Glasgow. Launched 20.6.1891. 9.1910 Converted to minelayer. 23.4.1918 Sunk as a blockship at Zeebrugge.

8. "I" class destroyer, 1,370 tons, 4 x 4.7" guns; 10 x 21" TT. Built by J.S. White, Cowes. Launched 17.12.1936. 14.10.1939 With other ships, sank *U 45* south west of Ireland. 1939-40 Minelaying operations. 29.5.1940 Damaged by bombing off Dunkirk. 6.1940 Again damaged by bombing. 11.1940 Damaged by mine. 5.1941 *Bismarck* action. 1942-3 Russian convoy escort. 9.1943 Present at surrender of Italian Fleet. 26/27.9.1943 Sunk by German aircraft when in Leros Harbour, Dodecanese.

Footnote:
Another French *Intrepide* was captured, and burnt, at Trafalgar 21.10.1805.

INVINCIBLE

Name ship of her class of anti-submarine warfare aircraft carriers, 20,000 tons. Built by Vickers, Barrow. Launched by HM The Queen. 3.5.1977. Primary role to act as Command Ship of A/S Warfare forces. Armament:- Sea Harriers, Sea King helicopters, Sea Dart missiles, close range weapons.

Description of Badge

Field:- White.
Badge:- A trident or, enfiled through a naval crown.

Motto

Battle Honours

St Vincent	1780	Heligoland	1914
St Kitts	1782	Falkland Islands	1914
First of June	1794	Jutland	1916
Alexandria	1882	Falkland Islands	1982

Previous ships of the name

1. Third rate, 1,793 bm, 74 guns. Captured from the French off Cape Finisterre on 3.5.1747. 19.2.1758 Set out with an expedition to capture Cape Breton Island, but she missed stays and ran ashore on Ower's Shoal, near St Helens. Became a total loss.

2. Third rate, 1,631 bm, 74 guns. Built by Wells, Deptford. Launched 9.3.1765. 4.1780 Serious mutiny on board. Men refused to weigh anchor until paid. 16.3.1801 Grounded on the coast of Norfolk. Ship lightened, drifted into deeper water but flood tide drove her on shore again. About 400 men drowned.

3. Third rate, 1,674 bm, 74 guns. Built in Woolwich Dockyard. Launched 15.3.1808. 1857 Converted to a Coal Hulk at Devonport. 1.1861 Broken up.

4. Iron steam ship, 6,010 tons, 10 x 9" guns. Built by Napier, Dalmuir. Launched 29.5.1869. 1870-1 Guardship at Hull. 1872-6 In Mediterranean. 1878-86 In Mediterranean. 1886-93 Guardship at Southampton. 1901-6 Depot Ship for destroyers at Sheerness. 4.1904 Renamed *Erebus*. 1.1906 Renamed *Fisgard II* for training of boy artificers in Portsmouth. 17.9.1914 Foundered off Portland in a heavy gale, when being towed to Scapa Flow.

5. Name ship of the class of battlecruisers, 17,250 tons, 8 x 12" and 16 x 4" guns; 5 x 18" TT. Built by Armstrong Whitworth on the Tyne. Launched 13.4.1907. 1909 Home Fleet. 1909-10 Refit. 1910—3 Home Fleet. 17.3.1913 Collided with the submarine *C 34* in Stokes Bay. 1913 In Mediterranean. 28.8.1914 Action in Heligoland Bight. 8.12.1914 With *Inflexible*, sank German *Scharnhorst* and *Gneisnau* in Battle of Falklands. 1915 Alterations and Additions at Gibraltar. 31.5.1916 Sunk in the Battle of Jutland, when she blew up after a succession of explosions caused by heavy shell hits. There were only 6 survivors and over 1,000 were lost.

Footnote
Armoured frigate, 9,210 tons, was laid down by Napier, Dalmuir, but was renamed *Black Prince* in 1859 before her launching on 27.2.1861.

ITCHEN

A "River" class Fleet Minesweeper, 890 tons (full load); 1 x 40mm gun. Built by Richards, Lowestoft. Lauched 30.10.1984. Allocated to Solent Division, RNR.

Description of Badge

Field:- Argent.
Badge:- On a rose gules barbed vert, a roundel argent, charged with a fess wavy azure.

Motto

Battle Honours

Atlantic   1943

Previous ships of the name

1. Destroyer, 550 tons, 4 x 12 pdr guns, 2 x 18" TT. Built by Laird Bros., Birkenhead. Launched 17.3.1903. 1905-6 Served on China Station, with *Arun*. 1907 Channel Fleet. 1909-11 2nd DF, Home Fleet. 1911 3rd DF, Home Fleet. 1912 9th Destroyer Patrol Flotilla. 1914-5 In 9th Destroyer Flotilla, North East coast. 1915-16 In 7th DF for similar service. 6.1916 East coast convoy work. 6.7.1917 Sunk by *U 99* in the North Sea.

2. "River" class frigate, 1,370 tons, 2 x 4" and 10 x 20mm guns. Built by Fleming and Ferguson, Paisley. Launched 29.7.1942. 23.9.1943 While escorting a westbound convoy in the Atlantic, was sunk by *U 666*, south of Iceland.

Footnote

A Strath type trawler, *Thomas Haggerty*, 202 GRT, built by Ouse S.B. in 1918, was renamed *Itchen* in 1920. 1926 Sold, renamed *River Endrick*. Served in World War II as *Mary A. Purdy*.

HMS *Itchen*

JERSEY

An "Island" class Offshore Patrol Vessel, 925 tons (standard), 1,260 tons (full load). 1 x 40mm gun. Built by Hall Russell, Aberdeen. Launched 18.3.1976. Able to carry a small RM Detachment.

Description of Badge

Field:- White.
Badge:- Upon water in base barry wavy blue and white, in front of a trident erect, a lion passant guardant or.

Motto

Garde — Guard.

Battle Honours

Santa Cruz	1657	Lagos	1759
Lowestoft	1665	Mediterranean	1941
Orfordness	1666		

Previous ships of the name

1. Fourth rate, 558 bm, 48 guns. Built by Starline, Woodbridge, in 1654. 18.12.1691 Captured by the French in the West Indies.

2. Sixth rate, 262 bm, 24 guns. Built at Deptford. Launched 17.2.1694. 21.10.1698 Renamed *Margate*. 9.12.1707 Wrecked near Cartagena.

3. Fourth rate, 677 bm, 48 guns. Built by Moore and Nye, East Cowes. Launched 24.11.1698. 8.1731 Reduced to a Hulk. 27.5.1763 Sunk.

4. Fourth rate, 1,065 bm, 60 guns. Built in Plymouth Dockyard. Launched 14.6.1736. 1738-9 In the Mediterranean. 1741 In attack on Cartagena. 1756-63 Again in Mediterranean. 20.10.1775 Directed that she be fitted as a Hospital Ship. Ended her days as a Prison Ship at New York. 25.11.1783 Abandoned at New York when that place was evacuated.

5. "J" class destroyer, 1,690 tons, 6 x 4.7" guns; 10 TT. Built by J.S. White, Cowes. Launched 26.9.1938. 22.9.1939 In collision with *Javelin*. 7.12.1939 Hit by torpedo; under repair at Hull until 23.9.1940. 11.10.1940 Damaged by mine off East Knob buoy. 1941 5th Destroyer Flotilla in Mediterranean. 2.5.1941 Sunk by mine at entrance to Malta Harbour when returning from a night sweep. 4.5.1941 Wreck broke in two. 1946-9 The after part, lying in shallow water, was progressively destroyed by explosives.

Footnote
a) Sloop, 7 guns, was built in 1776 on the Canadian Lakes.
b) Cutter, 71 bm, 4 guns. Built by J.S. White, Cowes. Launched 22.3.1860. 8.1873 Sold to E.A.S. Mignon.

HMS *Jersey*, on contractors sea trials.

JUNO

A Batch Two "Leander" class frigate; 2,450 tons (standard). Built by Thornycroft, Woolston, Southampton. Launched 24.11.1965. Limbo A/S weapon; 2 x 4.5" and 2 x 40mm AA guns; 1 helicopter. Exocet conversion halted. Converted to a Training Ship.

Description of Badge

Field:- Blue.
Badge:- The head of Hera (Juno) in profile, couped between two bars wavy white.

Motto

Battle Honours

Louisburg	1758	Mediterranean	1940-41
Atlantic	1939	Matapan	1941
Calabria	1940	Crete	1941
Libya	1940	Malta Convoys	1941

Previous ships of the name

1. Fifth rate, 667 bm, 32 guns. Built by Alexander, Rotherhithe. Launched 29.9.1757. 5.8.1778 Burnt to avoid capture at Rhode Island.

2. Fifth rate, 689 bm, 32 guns. Built by Batson, Limehouse. Launched 30.9.1780. 7.1811 Broken up.

3. French fifth rate, *Junon,* 1,100 bm, 36 guns. Captured by a squadron in the West Indies on 10.2.1809. Retaken by the French ten months later on 13.12.1809.

4. French fifth rate, *Bellone,* 38 guns. Captured at Mauritius on 6.12.1810. Renamed *Junon.* 2.1817 Broken up at Deptford.

5. Sixth rate, 923 bm, 26 guns. Built at Pembroke Dock. Launched 1.7.1844. 10.1.1878 Renamed *Mariner,* a Police Ship. 22.1.1878 Renamed *Atalanta,* a Training Ship. 12.2.1880 Foundered in the Atlantic.

6. Wood steam corvette, 1,462 bm, 8 x 64 pdr guns. Built in Deptford Dockyard. Launched 28.11.1867. 12.1887 Sold out of the service.

7. "Talbot" class cruiser, 5,600 tons, 5 x 6" and 6 x 4.7" guns. Built by Naval Construction and Armament Co., Barrow. Launched 16.11.1895. 1904 Armament changed to 11 x 6" guns. 24.9.1920 Sold to Earle, but re-sold to Petersen and Albeck.

8. "J" class destroyer, 1,690 tons, 6 x 4.7" guns; 10 TT. Laid down as *Jamaica* but renamed *Juno* in 9.1938. Built by Fairfield, Govan, Glasgow. Launched 8.12.1938. 4.1940 Off Norway. 14.5.1940 Detached to the Mediterranean; joined 14th DF. 31.8.1940 Escorted damaged *Cornwall* to Malta. 5.1941 Patrolling in Kaso Strait. 21.5.1941 Sunk by German and Italian aircraft off Crete. Hit in magazine by bomb and sank in 2 minutes.

JUPITER

A Batch Three "Leander" class (broad-beamed) frigate; 2,500 tons (standard). Built by Yarrow, Scotstoun, Glasgow. Launched 4.9.1967. 1980-3 Exocet conversion at Devonport. New armament:- Exocet SSM and Sea Wolf SAM systems; A/S torpedo tubes; 2 x 20mm guns; 1 helicopter.

Description of Badge

Field:- Black.
Badge:- Issuant from clouds in chief proper, rays of lightning gold.

Motto

Battle Honours

Cape of G Hope	1795	Mediterranean	1941
China	1841-2	Malaya	1942

Previous ships of the name

1. Fourth rate, 1,044 bm, 50 guns. Built by Randall, Rotherhithe. Launched 13.5.1778. 4.1795 Brought Princess Caroline of Brunswick to England. 10.12.1808 Wrecked in Vigo Bay.

2. Fourth rate, 1,173 bm, 50 guns. Built in Plymouth Dockyard. Launched 22.11.1813. First few years were spent "In Ordinary" at Plymouth. 6.1822 Conveyed Lord Amherst, new Governor General of India, to Calcutta. 10.1835 Conveyed another Governor General designate, Lord Auckland, to India. 11.1837 Converted to Troopship. 1840-2 In First China War. Took part in expedition up the Yangtse, in capture of Ching-Kiang. 4.1846 Reduced to a Coal Hulk. 28.1.1870 Breaking up completed at Devonport.

3. Fifth rate, 1,215 bm, 44 guns. Built at Pembroke Dock. Launched as *Forth* 1.8.1833. Converted to a steam frigate, 1,228 bm; undocked as such on 21.1.1856. Renamed *Jupiter* when reduced to a Coal Hulk in 12.1869. 1883 Sold.

4. "Majestic" class battleship, 14,900 tons, 4 x 12" and 12 x 6" guns. Built by J. & G. Thomson, Glasgow. Launched 18.11.1895. Served in Home Waters and off Egypt in WW1. 15.1.1920 Sold to Hughes Bolckow, Blyth, for breaking up.

5. "J" class destroyer, 1,690 tons, 6 x 4.7" guns; 10 TT. Built by Yarrow, Scotstoun, Glasgow. Launched 27.10.1938. In Lord Mountbatten's 5th DF. Took part in bombardment of Cherbourg. 1941 In hunt for *Bismarck* but not at sinking. Later in 1941, in Far East. 17.1.1942 Became first HM Ship to sink a Japanese submarine—*I 60.* 27.2.1942 In Java Sea, first thought to have been torpedoed, but later believed to have struck a Dutch mine laid earlier in the day. Five officers and 161 ratings were either captured by the Japanese or posted missing.

Footnote
a) Paddlewheel vessel, 394 tons, built in 1895; armed with 1 x 6 pdr, was hired as *Jupiter II*, minesweeper, from 15.5.1915 to 29.5.1920. Was awarded the Battle Honour "Belgian Coast 1915-6".
b) Dutch coaster, 174 tons, was hired as a Barrage Balloon Vessel 1941-2.

KINGFISHER

A "Bird" class Patrol Boat; 194 tons (full load); 1 x 40mm gun. Built by R. Dunston, Hessle, Humberside. Launched 20.9.1974.

Description of Badge

Field:- White.
Badge:- A kingfisher on a branch, all proper.

Motto

Swift and sure.

Battle Honours

Sardinia	1681	Dunkirk	1940
San Domingo	1806		

Previous ships of the name

1. Ship, 269 bm, was in service 1664-7.

2. Ship, 664 bm, 46 guns. Built by Pett, Woodbridge in 1675. 1699 Rebuilt at Woolwich as 661 bm. 1706 Reduced to a Hulk. 1728 Broken up at Sheerness.

3. Ketch, 61 bm, 4 guns. Purchased in 1684. 3.1690 Captured by the French.

4. Sloop, 275 bm, 14 guns. Built by Darby, Gosport. Launched 12.12.1745. Used as a Bomb Vessel from 9.1758 to 3.1760. 3.5.1763 Sold out of the service.

5. Sloop, 302 bm, 14 guns. Built in Chatham Dockyard. Launched 13.7.1770. 30.7.1778 Burnt to avoid capture at Rhode Island.

6. Brig-sloop, 369 bm, 18 guns. Purchased on the stocks at Rochester in 1782. 3.12.1798 Wrecked on Lisbon Bar.

7. Sloop, 370 bm, 18 guns. Built by King, Dover. Launched 10.3.1804. 10.1816 Broken up at Portsmouth.

8. "Cherokee" class brig-sloop, 237 bm, 10 guns. Built in Woolwich Dockyard. Launched 11.3.1823. 16.8.1838 Sold to Mr Knowland.

9. Brig, 446 bm, 12 guns. Built at Pembroke Dock. Launched 8.4.1845. 1852 Laid up. 1875 Reduced to Harbour Service. 26.4.1890 Sold to W. Tayler.

10. "Osprey" class composite steam sloop, 1,130 tons, 2 x 7" and 4 x 64 pdr guns. Built in Sheerness Dockyard. Launched 16.12.1879. 1880-4 Pacific Station. 1884-91 East Indies. 1891-2 Reserve. 10.11.1892 Renamed *Lark*, training ship. 18.5.1893 Renamed *Cruizer*. Sail training ship for Ordinary Seamen in the Mediterranean. 1903-19 Harbour service at Malta. 1919 Sold out of the service.

11. Brig, 481 bm, 16 guns. Built as *Martin* at Pembroke Dock. Launched 19.9.1850. 2.5.1890 Renamed *Kingfisher,* training brig, attached to *Impregnable* at Devonport. 2.10.1907 Sold to G.H. Collins, Dartmouth.

12. Name ship of class of Patrol Vessels, 510 tons, 1 x 4" gun. Built by Fairfield, Govan, Glasgow. Launched 14.2.1935. 1940 Rescued 640 at evacuation of Dunkirk. Damaged by bomb splinters during raid on Portland Dockyard. 1941-5 A/S experimental ship off west coast of Scotland. 3.1946 Reduced to Reserve at Harwich. 21.4.1947 Sold and broken up by Stockton Ship and Salvage Company.

13. Salvage Vessel, 1,440 tons, ex-*Allegiance*, renamed *King Salvor* in 4.1942. Built by Simons, Renfrew. Launched 18.5.1942. 4.1954 Renamed *Kingfisher*. 1.1961 Sold out of the service.

Footnote

a) Drifter, 76 tons, built in 1882, was hired for a month, 11.1914 to 12.1914.
b) Drifter *Adele,* 100 tons, built in 1915, was hired 1915-9. From 1918-9 was base ship *Kingfisher* and on Harbour Service 1941-6.
c) River gunboat was ordered in 1912 from Yarrow, Scotstoun, Glasgow, but was never built.
d) Trawler, ex-*Alcyon,* 322 tons, built in 1915. Purchased that year and armed with 1 x 12 pdr and 1 x 6 pdr guns. 1918 Renamed *Adele.* 1919 Sold out of the service.

LEANDER

Name ship of the class of improved Type 12 frgates, 2,450 tons (standard); ex-*Weymouth*. Built by Harland and Wolff, Belfast. Launched 28.6.1961. 1970-2 Ikara conversion at Devonport. New armament:- Ikara A/S missiles (forward); Sea Cat SAM system; 2 x 40mm guns; Limbo A/S mortars (aft); 1 helicopter.

Description of Badge

Field:- Blue.

Badge:- An arm in armour holding a lance proper between two lotus flowers silver, over wavelets gold and green.

(Derived from the Crest of Admiral Thompson who commanded *Leander* at the Battle of the Nile).

Motto

Qui patitur vincit — Who suffers conquers.

Battle Honours

Nile	1798	Crimea	1854-5
Algiers	1816	Kula Gulf	1943

Previous ships of the name

1. Fourth rate, 1,044 bm, 52 guns. Built in Chatham Dockyard. Launched 1.7.1780. 18.8.1798 Captured by the French *Genereux*, 80 guns. 3.3.1799 Recaptured by the Russians at Corfu and returned to the RN. 1813 Became Medical Depot; renamed *Hygeia*. 14.4.1817 Sold out of the service.

2. Fourth rate, 1,572 bm, 58 guns. Built (of pitch pine) by Wigham and Green, Blackwall. Launched 10.11.1813. 3.1830 Broken up.

3. Fourth rate, 1,987 bm, 50 guns. Built in Portsmouth Dockyard. Launched 8.3.1848. 16.2.1861 Undocked at Sheerness after being converted to a steam ship, 2,760 tons. 1863-6 Pacific Station. 1867 Sold to Messrs Castle and Beech.

4. Steel Despatch Vessel, classed as a second class cruiser, 4,300 tons, 10 x 6" guns; 4 TT. Built by Napier, Dalmuir. Launched 28.10.1882. 1904 Converted to Destroyer Depot Ship and as such served at Scapa Flow in WW1. 1.7.1920 Sold to S. Castle, Plymouth.

5. Name ship of the class of cruisers, 7,270 tons, 8 x 6" and 4 x 4" AA guns; 8 x 21" TT. Built in Devonport Dockyard. Launched 24.9.1931. She was the first 6" gun cruiser built since 1918 and the first single-funnelled cruiser in the RN. Her launching ceremony was broadcast nationally. 1933-7 Home Fleet. 1937 Joined NZ Division. 1940-1 Red Sea and Indian Ocean. 27.2.1941 Sank Italian raider *Ramb 1* in Indian Ocean. 7.1943 In the Solomons, hit by a torpedo from Japanese destroyer; severely damaged. 1943-5 Repaired in USA, but completed on the Tyne. 10.1946 Corfu Channel incident. 15.12.1947 Left Malta for Chatham to pay off into low category Reserve. 1948 Moved to Devonport; prepared for use as a target; later in the year laid up in River Fal. 15.12.1949 Sold to Hughes, Bolckow. 1.1950 Left Devonport in tow for breaking up at Blyth.

HMS *Leander* (July 1933).

LEDBURY

A ''Hunt'' class Mine Countermeasures Vessel, 615 tons (standard), 725 tons (full load); 1 x 40mm gun. Built of GRP by Vosper Thornycroft, Woolston, Southampton. Launched 5.12.1979.

Description of Badge

Field:- Per fess wavy murrey and red.
Badge:- A seax erect, in front of two hunting horns in saltire white.

Motto

Battle Honours

Malta Convoys	1942	Salerno	1943
Arctic	1942-3	Adriatic	1944
Sicily	1943	Aegean	1944

Previous ships of the name

1. ''Hunt'' class Type 2 ''Blankney'' type, destroyer; 1,050 tons, 6 x 4'' AA guns. Built by Thornycroft, Woolston, Southampton. Construction delayed by bomb damage in the shipyard. Launched 27.9.1941. 1942 Escort to major warships and fleet auxiliaries between Scapa Flow and Iceland. 6.1942 Ocean escort to ill-fated Russian convoy 'PQ 17'. 8.1942 Operation 'Pedestal'. Played major part in assisting damaged tanker *Ohio* to reach Grand Harbour, Malta. Made daring rescue of crew from a petrol-carrying cargo ship; and also searched for survivors from HMS *Manchester*. 1943 Invasions of Sicily and Salerno. 10.1944 Covered return of British troops to Athens. 14.12.1945 Arrived Portsmouth after Gibraltar refit. 3.1946 Reduced to Reserve at Portsmouth. 5.1958 Arrived Charlestown, Fife, to be broken up.

HMS *Ledbury* (1982).

LEEDS CASTLE

An Offshore Patrol Vessel, Mark 2, 1,427 tons. Built by Hall Russell, Aberdeen. Launched 29.10.1980. 1 x 40mm gun. Design includes an ability to lay mines in wartime.

Description of Badge
Field:- Per fess embattled blue and black.
Badge:- A hippocampus white.

Motto

Battle Honours

Atlantic   1945   Falkland Islands   1982

Previous ships of the name

1. "Castle" class corvette, 1,060 tons, 1 x 4" and, 6 x 40mm guns. Built by Wm Pickersgill, Sunderland. Launched 12.10.1943. Later designated a frigate. 1944-5 Atlantic convoy duties. 1946 Anti-Submarine Training Squadron at Portland. 1953 Coronation Review. 11.1956 Paid off at Chatham, after 12½ years continuous service. 5.6.1958 Arrived T.W. Ward, Grays, Essex, to be broken up.

HMS *Leeds Castle* (1981).

LINDISFARNE

An "Island" class Offshore Patrol Vessel, 925 tons (standard), 1,260 tons (full load). Built by Hall Russell, Aberdeen. Launched 1.6.1977. 1 x 40mm gun. Able to carry a small RM Detachment.

Description of Badge

Field:- Azure.
Badge:- In front of an amulet or, a cross quadrant argent.

Motto

Battle Honours

Normandy   1944

Previous ships of the name

1. "Isles" class A/S trawler, 560 tons. Built by Cook, Welton and Gemmell, Beverley. Launched 17.6.1943. 1944 In TF 126 follow-up Force 'B' at Normandy. 1950 Became a Wreck Dispersal Vessel; cleared wrecks in the Bristol Channel. 4.1958 Sold for breaking up at Dover.

HMS *Lindisfarne* (August 1953).

LIVERPOOL

A Batch Two "Town" class Type 42 Guided Missile destroyer; 3,800 tons (standard), 4,250 tons (full load). Built by Cammell Laird, Birkenhead. Launched 25.9.1980. Sea Dart SAM system; 1 x 4.5"; 2 x 20mm Oerlikons; helicopter-launched Sea Skua missiles; 6 TT; 1 helicopter.

Description of Badge

Field:- Silver.
Badge:- A cormorant black, beaked and legged red, holding in its beak a branch of seaweed, called laver, green.
(Derived from the Arms of the City of Liverpool).

Motto

Deus nobis haec otia fecit — God gave us this ease.

Battle Honours

Heligoland	1914	Malta Convoys	1942
Calabria	1940	Arctic	1942
Mediterranean	1940		

Previous ships of the name

1. Fifth rate, 681 bm, 40 guns. Ex-*Enterprise*. 20.2.1741 Renamed *Liverpool*. Built by Okill, Liverpool. Launched 19.7.1741. After service off coast of Spain and in the Mediterranean, she was sold at Woolwich on 14.9.1756.

2. Sixth rate, 590 bm, 28 guns. Built by Gorill and Pownell, Liverpool. Launched 10.2.1758. Joined fleet off North America. 12.1777 Wrecked off Long Island.

3. Fourth rate, 1,240 bm, 50 guns. Built by Wigham and Green, Woolwich. Launched 21.2.1814. 1814-6 Cape of Good Hope Station. 1818-22 East Indies Station. 16.4.1822 Sold at Bombay.

4. Wood steam frigate, 2,656 bm, 51 guns. Built in Devonport Dockyard. Launched 30.10.1860. 1869-70 Wearing the flag of Rear Admiral G.T.P. Hornby led a squadron on a voyage round the world. 15.11.1870 Paid off at Devonport. 23.3.1875 Sold to Castles, Charlton, for breaking up.

5. "Bristol" class cruiser, 4,800 tons, 2 x 6", 10 x 4" and 4 x 3 pdr guns; 2 x 18" TT. Built by Vickers, Son and Maxim, Barrow. Launched 30.10.1909. 1910-4 Home Fleet. 28.8.1914 In Cruiser action off Heligoland. 2.1915 Off African coast searching for German AMC *Kronprinz Wilhelm*. 1915-8 In Adriatic. 1918 Dardanelles. 1918-9 Black Sea. 1919-20 In Reserve. 1921 Sold to Stanlee, Dover. 8.11.1921 Re-sold to Slough T.C. Broken up in Germany.

6. Later "Southampton" class cruiser, 9,400 tons, 12 x 6" and 8 x 4" AA guns; 6 x 21" TT. Built by Fairfield, Govan, Glasgow. Launched 24.3.1937. 9.2.1939 Arrived Colombo to replace *Emerald* in 4th CS, East Indies. 14.11.1939 Transferred to 5th CS. Operated from Hong Kong. 5.1940 7th CS, Mediterranean. 12.6.1940 With *Gloucester*, shelled Tobruk; sank *Giovanni Berta*. 27.6.1940 Suffered minor damage when hit by 4.7" shell from Italian destroyer. 29.7.1940 Hit on bridge by bomb which failed to explode. 14.10.1940 Hit by Italian aerial torpedo. Petrol stowage exploded. Bows blown off. Taken in tow, stern first, by *Orion*. Repaired at Alexandria; then in USA; completed on the Clyde. 2.1942 Joined 18th CS, Home Fleet. 14.6.1942 During Operation 'Harpoon', hit by aerial torpedo; blew hole 24' x 19' in starboard side. Towed by *Antelope* to Gibraltar; then to Rosyth for repairs. 7.1943 Repairs completed, but reduced to C & M at Rosyth until 9.1945. 10.1945 to 5.1952 5th CS, Mediterranean. 5.1952 to 1958 Category 'C' Reserve at Portsmouth. 2.7.1958 Arrived at yard of McLellan, Bo'ness, to be broken up.

Footnote
Fourth rate, 1,487 bm, 58 guns, was ordered from Plymouth Dockyard on 7.1.1826, but was cancelled in 1829.

LONDON

A Batch Two "Broadsword" class Type 22 frigate, ex-*Bloodhound*; 4,100 tons (standard), 4,800 tons (full load). Built by Yarrow, Scotstoun, Glasgow. Launched 27.10.1984. Exocet SSM and Sea Wolf SAM systems; 2 x 40mm and 4 x 20mm guns; 6 TT; 1 helicopter (ability to carry 2); helicopter carried A/S torpedoes.

Description of Badge

Field:- White.
Badge:- A dagger red.
(Part of the Arms of the City of London).

Motto

Domine dirige nos — God guide us.

Battle Honours

Kentish Knock	1652	Chesapeake	1781
Gabbard	1653	Groix Island	1795
Scheveningen	1653	Copenhagen	1801
Lowestoft	1665	*Marengo*	1806
Sole Bay	1672	Crimea	1854-5
Schooneveld	1673	Dardanelles	1915
Texel	1673	Atlantic	1941
Barfleur	1692	Arctic	1941-3

(The Honour "Orfordness 1666" was awarded to *Loyal London*).

Previous ships of the name

1. Ex-East Indiaman, 40 guns. Purchased in 1636. Still listed in 1653.

2. Ship, 1,104 bm, 64 guns. Built in Chatham Dockyard. Launched 7.1656. Escorted Charles II when he returned to England at the Restoration. 7.3.1665 Blown up by accident at the Nore.

HMS *London* (February 1929).

3. Ship, 1,134 bm, 96 guns. Built in Deptford Dockyard. Launched 10.6.1666. Known as *Loyal London* until 1670. 13.6.1667 Partly destroyed by fire. 1670 Rebuilt at Deptford as *London*, 1,348 bm. 1706 Rebuilt at Chatham as 1,685 bm. 1721 Rebuilt again at Chatham as 1,711 bm. 10.1747 Breaking up completed at Chatham.

4. Brigantine, 16 guns. Built at Oswega, Lake Ontario, in 1756. 14.8.1756 Lost to the French on the Canadian Lakes, on fall of Oswego.

5. Second rate, 1,894 bm, 90 guns. Built in Chatham Dockyard. Launched 24.5.1766. 1801 At Copenhagen, from her masthead flew the famous signal that Nelson declined to observe. 4.1811 Broken up.

6. First rate, 4,122 tons, 104 guns. Laid down as *London* in Plymouth Dockyard. When launched 28.7.1828 she was named *Royal Adelaide*. The first and only time she was in a foreign port was when she arrived Dunkirk in 6.1905 to be broken up.

7. Second rate, 4,375 tons, 92 guns. Built in Chatham Dockyard. Launched 28.9.1840. 13.5.1858 Undocked at Devonport as a steam ship, 72 guns. 4.1874 Reduced to Harbour Store Ship. 1884 Sold at Zanzibar to be broken up.

8. Name ship of the class of battleship, 15,000 tons, 4 x 12″, 12 x 6″ and 18 x 12 pdr guns. Built in Portsmouth Dockyard. Launched 21.9.1899. Saw action in Dardanelles. 5.1918 Converted to minelayer, 3 x 6″ and 1 x 4″ guns, 240 mines. 1919 Depot Ship. 4.6.1920 Sold to Stanlee; resold and broken up in Germany.

9. Name ship of the class of cruiser, 9,850 tons, 8 x 8″ and 8 x 4″ guns; 8 TT. Built in Portsmouth Dockyard. Launched 14.9.1927. 3.11.1928 Collided with SS *Runic* off Gourock pier. 1941 *Bismarck* action. Conveyed Allied Mission to Russia for Moscow Conference. 1944 Eastern fleet operations against Japanese. 4.1949 Helped free *Amethyst* from Yangtse. 3.1.1950 Sold for breaking up by T.W. Ward, Barrow.

10. GM Destroyer, 5,440 tons, 4 x 4.5″ guns, Sea Slug GWS. Built by Swan Hunter, Wallsend-on-Tyne. Launched 7.12.1961. 1965 Far East. 1978-80 Extended refit. 12.1981 Returned to Portsmouth to pay off. 1.1982 Sold to Pakistan. 24.3.1982 Transferred after refit; renamed *Babur*. 1986 Still in service.

Footnote
a) Smack, 16 bm, the *Little London*, 1672-97.
b) Busse, 80 bm, 6 guns. Ex-*Holden*. Purchased in 1756. 29.4.1758 Wrecked in East Senegal.
c) Busse, 6 guns, 1759-64.

HMS *London*, at Malta 1970.

MANCHESTER

A Batch Three Type 42 Guided Missile destroyer (stretched version), 4,775 tons (full load). Built by Vickers, Barrow-in-Furness. Launched 24.11.1980. Sea Dart SAM system; 1 x 4.5"; 2 x 20mm Oerlikons; helicopter-launched Sea Skua missiles; 6 TT; 1 helicopter.

Description of Badge

Field:- Blue.
Badge:- A globe proper with five fleur-de-lys issuant white and charged with seven bees volant, gold.
(Derived from the Arms of the City of Manchester).

Motto

Sapere aude — Dare to be wise.
(Motto of Manchester Grammar School).

Battle Honours

Norway	1940	Malta Convoys	1941-2
Spartivento	1940	Arctic	1942

Previous ships of the name

1. Later "Southampton" class cruiser, 9,400 tons, 12 x 6" and 8 x 4" AA guns; 6 x 21" TT. Built by Hawthorn Leslie, Hebburn-on-Tyne. Launched 12.4.1937. 1938-9 4th Cruiser Squadron in East Indies. 1940 Took part in the expedition to, and evacuation from, Norway. 27.11.1940 Was in the van of Vice Admiral Somerville's force when Italian warships were encountered off Cape Spartivento. 23.7.1941 While escorting Malta convoy was hit by aerial torpedo. Emergency repairs were carried out at Gibraltar followed by 7 months at Philadelphia, USA. 7.1942 Was part of the covering force for the ill-fated Russian convoy 'PQ 17'. 13.8.1942 During Operation 'Pedestal'—the relief of Malta—she was ambushed and torpedoed by Italian MAS boats. Both engine rooms, the after boiler room and 4" magazine were flooded. Ship heeled to starboard; and a torpedo from *Pathfinder* helped scuttle *Manchester* four miles off shore. Some of her ship's company were taken off by *Eskimo* and *Pathfinder*. Remainder were interned in Tunisia, until being released during Operation 'Torch' in November.

HMS *Manchester*

MIDDLETON

A "Hunt" class Mine Countermeasures Vessel, 615 tons (standard), 725 tons (full load). 1 x 40mm gun. Built of GRP by Yarrow, Scotstoun, Glasgow. Launched 27.4.1983.

Description of Badge

Field:- White.
Badge:- A fret blue and a hunting horn erect, interlaced, red.

Motto

Battle Honours

Malta Convoys	1942	Normandy	1944
Arctic	1942-3	English Ch	1944
Atlantic	1944	North Sea	1944-5

Previous ships of the name

1. "Hunt" class, Type 2 "Blankney" type destroyer, 1,050 tons, 6 x 4" guns. Built by Vickers Armstrong, Newcastle-on-Tyne. Launched 12.5.1941. 1942 Russian convoys. 6.1942 Operation 'Harpoon'—shipping supplies to Malta. 1943 Further Russian convoys. 6.1944 Normandy landings. 28.8.1944 With MTBs, attacked 8 German TLCs, sank 4 and drove 1 ashore. 9.1944 Joined 21st Destroyer Flotilla at Sheerness. 7.1945 To East Indies fleet. 8. to 12.1945 Refitting at Simonstown. 29.12.1945 Returned to Portsmouth. Paid off into Reserve. 1955 Reduced to a Hulk. 4.10.1957 Arrived Blyth to be broken up by Hughes Bolckow.

HMS *Middleton* (August 1943).

MINERVA

A Batch Two "Leander" class frigate, 2,450 tons (standard). Built by Vickers Armstrong, Newcastle-on-Tyne. Launched 19.12.1964. 1979 Exocet conversion completed at Chatham. New armament:- Exocet SSM and Sea Cat SAM systems; 2 x 40mm guns; 6 TT.; 1 helicopter.

Description of Badge

Field:- Per fess wavy blue and green.
Badge:- An owl affronté white.
(The owl is one of the symbols of Minerva).

Motto

Battle Honours

Quiberon Bay	1759	Dardanelles	1915
*Mutine	1797	Suez Canal	1915
*St Vincent	1797	Falkland Islands	1982
*Egypt	1801		

(*Awarded to *Minerve* for boat service actions).

Previous ships of the name

1. Fifth rate, 664 bm, 32 guns. Built by Quallet, Rotherhithe. Launched 17.1.1759. 28.8.1778 Captured by French *Concorde*. 4.1.1781 Recaptured and renamed *Recovery*. 30.12.1784 Sold out of the service.

2. Sloop, 388 bm, 18 guns. Built at Port Mahon, Minorca, in 1779. Fate unknown.

3. Fifth rate, 941 bm, 38 guns. Built in Woolwich Dockyard. Launched 3.6.1780. 1798 Became a Troopship; renamed *Pallas*. 3.1803 Broken up.

4. French fifth rate, 1,102 bm, 38 guns. Captured in the Mediterranean by *Lowestoft* and *Dido* on 24.6.1795. 3.7.1803 Stranded near Cherbourg and captured by the French. 3.2.1810 Recaptured as *Canonniere* and renamed *Confiance*. 1814 Still on Navy List.

5. French sloop *Minerve*, 246 bm. Captured in 1803. Used as a Prison Hulk. 1811 Broken up.

6. Fifth rate, 661 bm, 32 guns. Built in Deptford Dockyard. Launched 26.10.1805. 2.1815 Broken up.

7. Fifth rate, 1,082 bm, 46 guns. Built in Portsmouth Dockyard. Launched 13.6.1820. 1861 Reduced to Harbour Service; became a Sheer Hulk and Storeship at Portsmouth. 28.2.1895 Sold at Portsmouth.

8. "Eclipse" class cruiser, 5,600 tons, 11 x 6" guns. Built in Chatham Dockyard. Launched 23.9.1895. 1899-1903 In Training Squadron. 1903-11 In the Mediterranean. In WW1 was in Egyptian waters and in 1917, in East Africa. 5.10.1920 Sold to H. Auten Ltd.

9. "M" class Coastal Monitor, *M 33*, 535 tons; 2 x 6" guns. Built by Workman Clark, Belfast. Launched 22.5.1915. 1919 Converted to minelayer. 1.12.1925 Renamed *Minerva*. 1946 Reduced to a Hulk; renamed *C 23* for dockyard use. 1986, still afloat, preservation under discussion.

Footnote

a) Storeship, 689 bm, 26 guns. Purchased in 6.1781. 1782 Sold at Bombay.
b) French submarine *Minerve* was seized at Plymouth on 3.7.1940; manned by a Free French crew. 19.9.1945 Wrecked on Portland Bill.

NAIAD

A Batch One "Leander" class frigate, 2,450 tons (standard). Built by Yarrow, Scotstoun, Glasgow. Launched 4.11.1963. 1972-5 Ikara conversion at Devonport. New armament:- Ikara A/S missiles (forward); Sea Cat SAM system; 2 x 40mm guns; Limbo A/S mortars (aft); 1 helicopter.

Description of Badge

Field:- Green.
Badge:- Upon waves barry wavy white and blue, a sea-nymph gold.

Motto

Battle Honours

Trafalgar	1805	Mediterranean	1941
Crete	1941	Malta Convoys	1941-2

Previous ships of the name

1. French sixth rate, 26 guns. Captured by *Sceptre* on 11.6.1783. Never commissioned into RN. 17.8.1784 Sold out of the service.

2. Fifth rate, 1,020 bm, 38 guns. Built by Hill, Limehouse. Launched 27.2.1797. 1.1847 Became a Coal Depot and Storeship at Callao. 2.2.1866 Sold to the Pacific Steam Navigation Company for similar service. 1901 Still afloat.

3. Danish fifth rate *Nyaden* (also named *Nijaden*) 909 bm, 36 guns. Captured at Copenhagen on 7.9.1807. 5.1812 Broken up.

4. Cruiser, 3,400 tons, 6 x 4.7" guns. Built by Vickers, Barrow. Launched 29.11.1890. 1901-4 In Mediterranean. 1905 Laid up in River Stour. 23.8.1910 Commissioned at Chatham for Home Fleet, Portsmouth. 9.1910 Converted to a minelayer. 1912 2nd Fleet Minelaying Squadron. 9.6.1922 Sold to J.J. King and broken up at Troon.

5. "Dido" class cruiser, 5,574 tons, 10 x 5.25" and 8 x 2 pdr AA guns; 6 x 21" TT. Built by Hawthorn Leslie, Hebburn-on-Tyne. Launched 3.2.1939. 10.4.1940 Received shock damage to her turbines from bombing, while fitting out. 28.1.1941 On Northern patrol. Sighted *Scharnhorst* and *Gneisenau* south of Iceland but lost them in bad weather conditions. 5.1941 Joined 15th CS in Mediterranean. 21/22.5.1941 Attacked by aircraft off Heraklion; suffered splinter damage to fore end which caused some flooding. 7.1941 Shelled Vichy positions on Northern African coast. 9.12.1941 Bombarded Derna. 11.3.1942 When about 50 miles off the North African shore, between Mersa Matruh and Sollum, was torpedoed by *U 565*. Hit on starboard side of forward engine room; lost all power; capsized and sank stern first. She was then flagship of Rear Admiral P.L. Vian, DSO++, who was saved.

NEWCASTLE

A Batch One "Town" class, Type 42, Guided Missile destroyer, 3,500 tons (standard), 4,100 tons (full load). Built by Swan Hunter, Wallsend-on-Tyne. Launched 24.4.1975. Sea Dart SAM system; 1 x 4.5"; 2 x 20mm Oerlikons; helicopter-launched Sea Skua missiles; 1 helicopter.

Description of Badge

Field:- Red.
Badge:- A triple-towered castle silver
(Derived from the City of Newcastle's Arms and Motto).

Motto

Fortitudine vinco — By strength I conquer.

Battle Honours

Porto Farina	1655	Sadras	1758
Santa Cruz	1657	Negapatam	1758
Lowestoft	1665	Porto Novo	1759
Orfordness	1666	Spartivento	1940
Schooneveld	1673	Burma	1944-5
Texel	1673	Korea	1952-3
Marbella	1705		

Previous ships of the name

1. Fourth rate, 641 bm, 54 guns. Built at Ratcliffe in 1653. This ship was responsible for half the Battle Honours. 1692 Rebuilt at Rotherhithe. 27.11.1703 When lying at Spithead, was one of 12 British men-of-war which foundered during a storm.

2. Fourth rate, 676 bm, 54 guns. Built in Sheerness Dockyard. Launched 10.3.1704. 1732 Rebuilt at Woolwich as 759 bm. 1746 Broken up at Portsmouth.

3. Fourth rate, 1,052 bm, 50 guns. Built in Portsmouth Dockyard. Launched 4.12.1750. 1.1.1761 Foundered in a cyclone while engaged in the seizure of Pondicherry.

4. Fourth rate, 1,556 bm, 50 guns. Built by Wigram and Green, Blackwall. Launched 10.11.1813. 1824 Fitted as a Lazaretto at Milford. 1827 Moved to Liverpool for similar service. 6.1850 Sold to J. Brown for breaking up.

5. Wood steam frigate, 4,020 tons, 30 x 8" guns. Built in Deptford Dockyard. Launched 16.10.1860. 1889 Loaned to the War Department for use as a Powder Hulk at Devonport. 1929 Sold for breaking up.

6. "Bristol" class cruiser, 4,800 tons, 2 x 6", 10 x 4" and 4 x 3 pdr guns; 2 x 18" TT. Built by Armstrong Whitworth on the Tyne. Launched 25.11.1909. 1910-4 China Station. 11.8.1914 Sent to Strengthen the forces at Esquimault. 1915-6 Pacific Station. 27.1.1916 Captured the German SS *Mazatlan*. 1916-7 In Mediterranean. 1917 Trade protection off Colombo in the Indian Ocean. 5.1917 Ordered to the Adriatic. 1917-9 South East Coast of America Station. 1920 In Reserve. 9.5.1921 Sold to T.W. Ward. 3.5.1923 Arrived Lelant to be broken up.

7. "Southampton" class cruiser, 9,100 tons, 12 x 6" and 8 x 4" AA guns; 6 x 21" TT. Ex-*Minotaur*; renamed in 1936. Built by Vickers Armstrong on the Tyne. Launched 23.1.1936. 5.3.1937 Commissioned for 2nd CS, Home Fleet. 9.1939 At Scapa Flow with 18th CS. 12.11.1939 In Denmark Strait intercepted German ship *Darana*, which scuttled herself. 23.11.1939 Picked up survivors from *Rawalpindi*. 7.1940 Anti-invasion duty at Plymouth. 11.1940 Force 'H' at Gibraltar. 1.1.1941 South Atlantic Command. 6.1942 Operation 'Vigorous'. 14.6.1942 Torpedoed by *S 56*, north west of Derna; temporary repairs at Bombay; then USA. Refitted at Devonport. 4.1944 Operation 'Cockpit'—carrier raid on Sabang. 5.1944 Operation 'Transom'—carrier raid on Soerabaya. 1.1945 Operation 'Lightning'—assault on Akyab. 1.1945 Operation 'Sankey'—Commando raid on Cheduba Island. 28.4.1945 Left Fremantle for UK. After the war employed on trooping duties. 1947-8 In Mediterranean. 1952-3 In Far East, including Korea. 11.1955 Recommissioned at Singapore— ship's company transported by air—first ship in RN to do so. 8.1958 Arrived Portsmouth after 4 years in Far East. 19.8.1959 Arrived Faslane to be broken up.

NORFOLK

A "Duke" class, Type 23, frigate, 3,000 tons (standard) 3,700 tons (full load). Built by Yarrow, Scotstoun, Glasgow. Laid down 19.12.1985 Harpoon SSM and Sea Wolf SAM systems; 1 x 4.5"; 2 x 30mm. Goalkeeper; 6 TT; 2 helicopters.

Description of Badge

Field:- Red.
Badge:- A feather silver under the Prince of Wales's crown.

Motto

Serviens servo — Serving I preserve.

Battle Honours

Velez Malaga	1704	North Africa	1942
Bismarck	1941	North Cape	1943
Atlantic	1941	Norway	1945
Arctic	1941-3		

Previous ships of the name

1. Third rate, 1,184 bm, 80 guns. Built by Winters, Southampton. Launched 28.3.1693. 1728 Rebuilt in Plymouth Dockyard, as 1,393 bm. Launched 21.9.1728. 9.1731 Returned from the Mediterranean to be Guardship at Plymouth. 1739 in War with Spain. Distinguished herself in attacks on forts at Santiago and San Felipe. 11.2.1744 In action against combined French and Spanish fleets off Toulon. Drove Spanish *Constante*, 70 guns, out of the line, a shattered wreck, but was herself too damaged to pursue. 1747 Surveyed and found to need large repairs. 8.5.1749 Docked, and her breaking up commenced the next day.

2. Third rate, 1,556 bm, 74 guns. Built in Deptford Dockyard. Launched 28.12.1757. 12.1774 Broken up at Portsmouth.

3. Cruiser, 9,925 tons, 8 x 8" and 8 x 4" guns. Built by Fairfield, Govan, Glasgow. Launced 12.12.1928. 11.9.1931 At Invergordon during the Mutiny. 1935 4th CS in East Indies. 1939 Joined 18th CS, Home Fleet. 16.3.1940 At Scapa Flow, hit by a bomb. Repaired on the Clyde. 5.1941 *Bismarck* action, having sighted her in the Denmark Strait. 1942 Russian Convoys, including 'PQ 17'. 26.12.1943 In destruction of *Scharnhorst*. 5.6.1945 Conveyed King Haakon back to Norway. 1945-6 Flagship, East Indies. 11.1947 Docked at Singapore. 9.8.1948 to 22.9.1948 Refit at Simonstown. 3.5.1949 Arrived Devonport for Reserve. 3.11.1949 Towed from Devonport to lay up in River Fal. 3.1.1950 Sold to J. Cashmore. 19.2.1950 Arrived Newport to be broken up.

4. Guided Missile destroyer, 5,440 tons, 4 x 4.5" and Sea Slug GWS. Built by Swan Hunter, Wallsend-on-Tyne. Launched 16.11.1967. Commissioned 1970. 1971-2 HRH the Prince of Wales served on board. 1979 Flagship of 9 ships in tour of Australasia and the Far East. Afterwards served in the Dartmouth Training Squadron. 17.2.1982 Left Portsmouth for Chile, via the Panama Canal. Renamed *Prat* after a 19th century national hero. Officially handed over to the Chilean Navy at Talcahuano, their main naval base. 1985 still in service.

HMS *Norfolk*

NOTTINGHAM

A Batch Two, "Town" class, Type 42, Guided Missile destroyer, 3,800 tons (standard) 4,250 tons (full load). Built by Vosper Thornycroft, Woolston, Southampton. Launched 6.2.1980. Sea Dart SAM system; 1 x 4.5"; 2 x 20mm Oerlikons; helicopter—launched Sea Skua missiles; 6 TT; 1 helicopter.

Description of Badge

Field:- Argent.
Badge:- A cross reguly vert, the lower limb enfiled by a gold ducal coronet.

Motto

Foy pour devoir — My faith is my duty.

Battle Honours

Gibraltar	1704	Louisburg	1758
Velez Malaga	1704	Martinique	1762
Marbella	1705	Havana	1762
Finisterre	1747	Heligoland	1914
Ushant	1747	Dogger Bank	1915
Magnanime	1748	Jutland	1916

Previous ships of the name

1. Fourth rate, 942 bm, 60 guns. Built at Deptford. Launched 10.6.1703. Paid off in 1714 and her timbers used to build another *Nottingham*.

2. Fourth rate, 928 bm, the ship re-built at Deptford in 1719. Saw service in the Baltic and West Indies before again being dismantled to form another *Nottingham*.

3. This ship was re-built at Sheerness as 1,077 bm in 1745. 1746 Captured French *Mars* 64 guns, after 10 hours fight in the Bay of Biscay. 1747 Won distinction at Battle of Finisterre. Later that year, in an action where 6 large, and some small, ships in a convoy were captured. Her Captain, Philip Suamarez, was killed. 1748 In company with *Portland*, captured 74 guns *Magnanime*. 1762 Her last action at the reduction of Havana. 1763 Paid off. 9.1773 Sunk as a breakwater at Sheerness.

4. Birmingham class light cruiser, 5,440 tons, 9 x 6" guns; 2 x 21" TT. Built at Pembroke Dock. Launched 18.4.1913. 1914 1st LCS, Home Fleet. 1914—6 Grand Fleet. 28.8.1914 In action off Heligoland. 24.1.1915 Battle of Dogger Bank. 8/9.8.1915 In the hunt for, and destruction of, the German minelayer *Meteor*. 31.5.1916 Battle of Jutland. 19.8.1916 Whilst engaged on a sweep of the North Sea, she was sunk by the German submarine *U 52*. Three torpedoes struck her, but she took more than an hour to sink so, fortunately, only 38 lives were lost.

Footnote
River barge, 67 bm, was purchased in 3.1794 and used as a gunboat with 3 guns. 1799 Sold out of the service.

OBERON

Name ship of the class of Patrol Submarines; 1,610 tons (surfaced), 2,410 tons (submerged); 8 x 21" TT (6 bow, 2 stern). Built in Chatham Dockyard. Launched 18.7.1959.

Description of Badge

Field:- White.
Badge:- A peacock's head proper, and head plumes centres gold, out of a fairy crown gold.
(Oberon was King of the Fairies).

Motto

Ever shall be fortunate.
(From Midsummer Night's Dream, Act V, Scene 1).

Battle Honours

Crimea   1855

Previous ships of the name

1. Brig-sloop, 283 bm, 16 guns. Built by Shepherd, Hull. Launched 13.8.1805. 5.1816 Broken up.

2. Iron paddlewheel sloop, 649 bm. Built at Deptford. Launched 2.1.1847. 1847-50 In Mediterranean. 1852-3 Laid up at Malta. 1855-6 In service in Mediterranean. 1858-62 South East Coast of America. 1866 West Coast of Africa. 1867 Again on South East Coast of America. From 1873 used by war department for torpedo experiments at Chatham and Portsmouth. 1874 Sunk in mine experiments. 1875 Raised. 1880 Sold out of the service.

3. Coastguard Vessel, *Lady Aline*, 520 tons. Purchased in 1.1888 as *Oberon*. 5.5.1888 Renamed *Hawk*. 1904 Renamed *Undine*. 3.4.1906 Sold at Chatham.

4. "M" class destroyer, 1,025 tons, 3 x 4" guns; 4 TT. Built by Wm. Doxford, Sunderland. Launched 29.9.1916. 3.1917 In collision with *Lightfoot*, whose bows were crushed. 28.11.1919 Reduced to Care and Maintenance Party at the Nore. 9.5.1921 Sold to T.W. Ward, Rainham, for breaking up.

5. Name ship of the class of Patrol Submarines, 1,311 tons (surfaced) 1,805 tons (submerged), 1 x 4" QF gun; 8 x 21" TT. Ex-*O 1*. 19.5.1926 First submarine to be named. Built in Chatham Dockyard. Launched 24.9.1926. 1926-31 5th Submarine Flotilla at Portsmouth. 1931-4 1st S/M Flotilla in Mediterranean. 1937-9 In Reserve at Portsmouth. Early war period in 7th S/M Flotilla in Clyde and Rothesay area. 1942 After refit at Portsmouth, undertook training duties with 7th (Rothesay) S/M Flotilla and 6th (Blyth) S/M Flotilla. 24.8.1945 Sold, to be broken up by Clayton and Davie, Dunston.

HMS *Oberon* (1937).

OCELOT

An "Oberon" class Patrol Submarine, 1,610 tons (surfaced), 2,410 tons (submerged); 8 x 21"
TT (6 bow, 2 stern). Built in Chatham Dockyard. Launched 5.5.1962.

Description of Badge

Field:- Per fess wavy blue and white, two bars
wavy blue.
Badge:- A demi-ocelot guardant proper.

Motto

Battle Honours

None.

Previous ships of the name

None.

HMS *Ocelot*

ODIN

An "Oberon" class Patrol Submarine, 1,610 tons (surfaced), 2,410 tons (submerged); 8 x 21" TT (6 bow, 2 stern). Built by Cammell Laird, Birkenhead. Launched 4.11.1960.

Description of Badge

Field:- Red.
Badge:- Head of an aged man proper with winged helmet silver and gold.
(Odin was the greatest of the Norse gods).

Motto

Attamen video — In spite of my blind eye, I see.
(Odin was blind in one eye).

Battle Honours

Baltic	1854	China	1860
Crimea	1855	Mesopotamia	1914-17

Previous ships of the name

1. Third rate, 1,750 bm, 74 guns. Built in Denmark in 1787. 7.9.1807 Captured at Copenhagen. 2.1811 Reduced to Harbour Service. 20.7.1825 Sold to J. Cristall for breaking up.

2. Wood paddlewheel frigate, 1,326 bm, 5 x 110 pdr and 1 x 68 pdr guns. Built in Deptford Dockyard. Launched 24.7.1846. Served in the Russian and China Wars. 1859-63 East Indies and China. 1865 Sold to Castle and Beech.

3. "Cadmus" class sloop, 1,070 tons, 6 x 4" guns. Built in Sheerness Dockyard. Launched 30.11.1901. 1903-10 Cape of Good Hope and West Coast of Africa Station; from 1905 was utilised as Drill Ship for the Cape Naval Volunteer Corps at Simon's Bay. 1910 East Indies Station. 1914 Persian Gulf. 1914-7 Mesopotamian Campaign. 12.11.1920 Sold at Bombay.

4. "O" class Patrol Submarine, 1,475 tons (surfaced), 2,030 tons (submerged). An improved "Oberon" with much higher speed. Built in Chatham Dockyard. Launched 5.5.1928. 1929-31 In Third Submarine Flotilla, Portsmouth. 1931 Transferred to 4th S/M Flotilla in China. 10.1939 Operating out of Colombo. 5.1940 Transferred to Malta, and joined with 4th (Singapore) Flotilla to form new 1st S/M Flotilla. 6.1940 First patrol out of Malta. 13.6.1940 Sunk by Italian destroyer *Strale* whilst in Gulf of Taranto. She was located on the surface after dark, and attacked with depth charges as she dived; and was straddled with gunfire. There were no survivors.

Footnote
An "Algerine" class Minesweeper was ordered from Redfern, Toronto, but cancelled 8.11.1944 before the ship had been laid down.

HMS *Odin* (1986).

OLYMPUS

An "Oberon" class Patrol Submarine, 1,610 tons (surfaced), 2,410 tons (submerged); 8 x 21" TT (6 bow, 2 stern). Built by Vickers, Barrow-in-Furness. Launched 14.6.1961.

Description of Badge

Field:- Blue.
Badge:- A thunderbolt silver out of a cloud proper.

Motto

Fulmen e sereno — A bolt from the blue.

Battle Honours

Malta Convoys 1941-2

Previous ships of the name

1. "O" class Patrol Submarine, 1,475 tons (surfaced) 2,030 tons (submerged), 1 x 4" QF gun, 8 x 21" TT. Built by Wm. Beardmore, Dalmuir. Launched 11.12.1928. First commissioned in 6.1930. 1931-9 4th Submarine Flotilla in China. Carried out patrols from Singapore. At outbreak of war, she was in the East Indies. 10.1939 to 4.1940 Based at Colombo. 4.1940 to 12.1940 1st Submarine Flotilla in the Mediterranean, based at Malta. 28.7.1941 Torpedoed and sank the Italian SS *Monteponi* off Sardinia. She herself was bombed the next day, but escaped damage. 1941-2 Made several stores trips to Malta from Gibraltar. 8.5.1942 Struck a mine and sank 6 miles from Malta. As she had on board several crews of boats previously sunk in harbour—including *P36* and *P39*—the casualty list was exceptionally heavy. First news of her loss broke when a survivor struggled ashore. Only a handful survived from a total of 98 on board.

Footnote
Drifter, 58 tons, was hired 1915-9.

HMS *Olympus* (July 1930).

ONSLAUGHT

An "Oberon" class Patrol Submarine, 1,610 tons (surfaced), 2,410 tons (submerged); 8 x 21"
TT (6 bow, 2 stern). Built in Chatham Dockyard. Launched 24.9.1960.

Description of Badge

Field:- Blue.
Badge:- Four cutlasses in saltire white, pommels
and hilts gold.

Motto

Fierce in action.

Battle Honours

Jutland	1916	Normandy	1944
Arctic	1942-5	Norway	1945
Atlantic	1943		

Previous ships of the name

1. "M" class destroyer, 1,025 tons, 3 x 4" guns; 4 TT. Built by Fairfield, Govan, Glasgow. Launched 4.12.1915. First went into action against the German battle fleet at Horns Reef, where she torpedoed and sank the *Pommern*, before she herself suffered damage and heavy casualties. 17.10.1919 Reduced to Care and Maintenance Party at Portsmouth. 30.10.1921 Sold to W. and A.T. Burden.

2. River steamer, 102 tons. Purchased in 1925. 26.10.1925 Commissioned into the RN. 1928 Sold at Hong Kong.

3. "Onslow" class destroyer, 1,540 tons, 4 x 4.7" guns; 8 TT. Built by Hawthorn Leslie, Hebburn-on-Tyne. Launched 10.4.1941 as *Onslaught*. 8.1941 Renamed *Pathfinder*. 11.2.1945 Damaged by Japanese aircraft at Ramree Island, East Indies. 1947 Used for target trials. 11.1948 Arrived Milford Haven to be broken up by Howells.

4. "Onslow" class destroyer, 1,540 tons, 4 x 4.7" guns; 8 TT. Laid down by Fairfield, Govan, Glasgow, as *Pathfinder*. 8.1941 Renamed *Onslaught*. Launched 9.10.1941. Convoy duties to Russia. 29.8.1942 With *Martin* and *Marne*, sank German minelayer *Ulm*, south east of Bear Island. 4.3.1944 Sank *U 472* north east of North Cape after submarine had been damaged by Swordfish aircraft from *Chaser*. 1944 Normandy landings. 6.3.1951 Handed over to Royal Pakistan Navy as *Tughril*. Converted into fast anti-submarine frigate by C. & H. Crichton at Liverpool. 1975 Used in Training Duties. 1977 On Disposal List.

HMS *Onslaught* (July 1946).

ONYX

An "Oberon" class Patrol Submarine, 1,610 tons (surfaced), 2,410 tons (submerged); 8 x 21"
TT (6 bow, 2 stern). Built by Cammell Laird, Birkenhead. Launched 18.8.1966.

Description of Badge

Field:- Blue.
Badge:- Upon a lozenge engrailed white, a
lozenge engrailed red, charged with a like
lozenge also white.

Motto

Battle Honours

Manly	1809	Normandy	1944
North Sea	1943	Falkland Islands	1982
Arctic	1944		

Previous ships of the name

1. "Cherokee" class brig-sloop, 237 bm, 10 guns. Built by Bailey, Ipswich. Launched 8.7.1808. 3.2.1819 Sold to T.
Pittman for breaking up.

2. "Cherokee" class brig-sloop, 236 bm, 10 guns. Built in Sheerness Dockyard. Launched 24.1.1822. 1.1837 Sold to J.
Cristall for breaking up.

3. Iron paddlewheel packet, 292 bm. Built by Ditchburn and Mare, Blackwall. Launched 11.1845. Based at Dover. 1854
Sold to Jenkins and Churchward.

4. "Cheerful" class wood steam gunboat, 212 bm, 2 x 32 pdr guns. Built by Young and Magnay, Limehouse. Launched
3.4.1856. 1856 Spithead Review; afterwards to Bermuda as tender to *Terror*, the Guardship. 1865 sent to Jamaica during a
rebellion. 1869 Reduced to a Dockyard Craft. 7.1873 Broken up at Jamaica.

5. Torpedo gunboat, 810 tons, 2 x 4.7" guns; 3 TT. Built by Laird Bros., Birkenhead. Launched 7.9.1892. 1894-1904
Coastguard Ship at Harwich. 1905-6 Laid up. 1907 Converted to Submarine Depot Ship at Devonport. 1.2.1919 Paid off.
6.1919 Renamed *Vulcan II* for Anti-Submarine School at Portland. 1924 Sold to J.J. King, Garston. 9.10.1924 Resold to L.
Basso and broken up at Weymouth.

6. "Algerine" class minesweeper; 850 tons; 1 x 4" gun. Built by Harland and Wolff, Belfast. Launched 27.10.1942. Saw
active minesweeping duties in the North Sea and on Arctic convoys. 1944 Swept Normandy beach approaches prior to
the landings. 1.1946 18th Minesweeping Flotilla, Plymouth Command. 3.1947 3rd M/S Flotilla, Port Edgar. 8.1947
Reserve at Portsmouth. 1956 Reserve at Devonport. 5.4.1967 Arrived Inverkeithing for breaking up by T.W. Ward.

Footnote
An "Oberon" class submarine was laid down as *Onyx* in Chatham Dockyard, but in 2.1964 was renamed *Ojibwa* for the
RCN before launching 29.2.1964. 23.9.1965 Commissioned into RCN at Halifax. 1986 Still in service.

HMS *Onyx* (March 1947).

OPOSSUM

An "Oberon" class Patrol Submarine 1,610 tons (surfaced), 2,410 tons (submerged); 8 x 21″ TT (6 bow, 2 stern). Built by Cammell Laird, Birkenhead. Launched 23.5.1963.

Description of Badge

Field:- white.
Badge:- An opossum suspended by his tail from a tree trunk, all proper.

Motto

Battle Honours

China   1856-60   Korea   1952-3

Previous ships of the name

1. "Cherokee" class brig-sloop, 236 bm, 8 x 18 pdr and 2 x 6 pdr guns. Built by Muddle, Gillingham. Launched 8.7.1808. 3.2.1819 Sold to G. Bailey.

2. Another "Cherokee" class brig-sloop, 236 bm, 8 x 18 pdr and 2 x 6 pdr guns. Built in Sheerness Dockyard. Launched 11.12.1821. 27.5.1841 Sold to Levy, Rochester.

3. "Albacore" class wood steam gunboat, 232 bm, 1 x 68 pdr, 1 x 32 pdr and 2 x 20 pdr guns. Built by Wigram, Northam. Launched 28.2.1856. 1857 East Indies and China. 20.5.1858 In successful first attack on the Taku Forts. 25.6.1859 In second, but unsuccessful attack on same forts. 21.8.1860 In third attack and destruction of these forts. 1865-73 In China. 1876 Converted to a Hospital Hulk. 1891 Used as a Mooring Vessel. 1895 Renamed *Siren*. 1896 Sold at Hong Kong.

4. Destroyer, 320 tons; 1 x 12 pdr and 5 x 6 pdr guns; 2 TT. Built by Hawthorn Leslie, Hebburn-on-Tyne. Launched 9.8.1895. 1897-1903 Based at Devonport. 1904-7 In reserve at Chatham. 1908-9 Home Fleet at the Nore. 1909-10 Attached to Pembroke for the Gunnery School. 1910-4 6th Destroyer Flotilla, Devonport. The first command of Sir Roger Keyes. Limited activities in WWI, mainly on coastal patrols. 29.7.1920 Sold to T.W. Ward, Preston, for breaking up.

5. Modified "Black Swan" class AA sloop, 1,350 tons, 6 x 4″ and 10 x 20mm AA guns. Built by Wm. Denny, Dumbarton. Launched 30.11.1944. 1959 In reserve. 26.4.1960 Arrived Demmelweek and Redding, Plymouth, to be broken up.

HMS *Opossum* (June 1945).

OPPORTUNE

An ''Oberon'' class Patrol Submarine, 1,610 tons (surfaced) 2,410 tons (submerged); 8 x 21″ TT (6 bow, 2 stern). Built by Scotts, Greenock. Launched 14.2.1964.

Description of Badge

Field:- Blue.
Badge:- An hour-glass gold.

Motto

Felix opportunitate pugnae — Happy at the chance of a fight.

Battle Honours

North Africa	1942	North Cape	1943
Arctic	1942-5	Normandy	1944
Atlantic	1943		

Previous ships of the name

1. ''M'' class destroyer, 1,025 tons, 3 x 4″ guns; 4 TT. Built by Wm. Doxford, Sunderland. Launched 20.11.1915. 17.10.1919 Reduced to Care and Maintenance at Portsmouth. 7.12.1923 Sold to J.J. King, Garston, for breaking up.

2. ''Onslow'' class, second group, destroyer, 1,540 tons, 4 x 4″ guns; 8 TT. Built by Thornycroft, Woolston, Southampton. Launched 21.1.1942. Fitted for mine-laying. In 17th Destroyer Flotilla attached to the Home Fleet for Russian convoy duties and operations off Norway. 9.1942 Escort to 'PQ 18'. 25.4.1943 In 5th Escort Group which sank *U 203* south east of Cape Farewell. 26.12.1943 Assisted in sinking of *Scharnhorst* off North Cape. 6. to 8.1944 Normandy operations. 22.4.1945 Minelaying operation in the Arctic Ocean. 1946 Submarine Target ship in Portsmouth Local Flotilla. 1947 Target at Rothesay. 2.1950 Air Training Target ship at Portsmouth. 1951-2 Nore Local Flotilla. 9.1953 Reserve at Portsmouth. 25.11.1955 Arrived Milford Haven to be broken up by T.W. Ward.

HMS *Opportune* (July 1946).

ORACLE

An "Oberon" class Patrol Submarine, 1,610 tons (surfaced), 2,410 tons (submerged); 8 x 21"
TT (6 bow, 2 stern). Built by Cammell Laird, Birkenhead. Launched 26.9.1961.

Description of Badge

Field:- Barry wavy white and blue.
Badge:- A tripod gold, entwined about the legs
with serpents, proper, and supporting a bowl
gold, rising therefrom smoke, also proper.

Motto

Battle Honours

None.

Previous ships of the name

1. "M" class destroyer, 1,025 tons, 3 x 4" guns; 4 TT. Built by Wm. Doxford, Sunderland. Launched 23.12.1915. 8.1917
While on patrol off Norway, rammed and sank *U 44*. Her own bows were damaged. 1.2.1920 Reduced to Care and
Maintenance at Portsmouth. 30.10.1921 Sold to W. and A.T. Burden.

2. Armed anti-submarine Yacht, 625 tons, built 1929. Formerly *Osprey*. 9.1939 Acquired by the RN. 1943 Took part in
radar trials. 29.1.1944 Put out of action by fire off Liverpool. 14.5.1948 Arrived T.W. Ward, Preston, for breaking up.

HMS *Oracle*

ORKNEY

An ''Island'' class Offshore Patrol Vessel, 925 tons (standard), 1,260 tons (full load). Built by Hall Russell, Aberdeen. Launched 29.6.1976. 1 x 40mm gun. Able to carry a small RM Detachment.

Description of Badge

Field:- Argent.
Badge:- In front of an anchor sable, a unicorn's head erased argent, crined and armed or, and collared jules.

Motto

Battle Honours

North Sea   1945

Previous ships of the name

1. ''River'' class frigate, 1,375 tons; 2 x 4" and 10 x 20mm AA guns. Built for the Royal Canadian Navy by Yarrow, Esquimault. Launched 18.9.1943. 1944-5 Anti-submarine patrols in the Atlantic and North Sea. 7.10.1947 Sold, mercantile, as *Violetta*. 1950 To Israeli Navy as *Mivtakh*. 1959 To Sinhalese Navy as *Mahasena*. Sold to British Shipbreakers. 9.1964 Arrived Singapore to be broken up.

HMS *Orkney* (1983).

ORPHEUS

An "Oberon" class Patrol Submarine, 1,610 tons (surfaced). 2,410 tons (submerged). 8 x 21" TT (6 bow, 2 stern). Built by Vickers, Barrow-in-Furness. Launched 17.11.1959.

Description of Badge

Field:- Party per pale black and blue.
Badge:- A Greek lyre gold.
(Colours suggest the descent of Orpheus from the world to Hades).

Motto

Vestigia nulla retrorsum — There is no retreat.

Battle Honours

Guadeloupe   1820

Previous ships of the name

1. Fifth rate, 708 bm, 32 guns. Built by Barnard, Harwich. Launched 7.5.1773. 15.8.1778 Abandoned and burnt at Rhode Island.

2. Fifth rate, 688 bm, 32 guns. Built by Adams and Barnard, Deptford. Launched 3.6.1780. 23.1.1807 Wrecked in the West Indies.

3. Fifth rate, 947 bm, 36 guns. Built in Deptford Dockyard. Launched 12.8.1809. 8.1819 Broken up.

4. Name ship of class of wood steam corvettes, 1,706 tons, 16 x 8" and 1 x 7" guns. Built in Chatham Dockyard. Launched 23.6.1860. She was fitted with a telescopic funnel and hoisting screws. 1861 Commissioned for the Australian Station. 5.12.1862 Left Spithead. 31.1.1863 Left Sydney for New Zealand. 6.2.1863 Struck the Manukau Bar off New Zealand; completely wrecked, with the loss of nearly 200 lives.

5. "M" class destroyer, 1,025 tons, 3 x 4" guns; 4 TT. Built by Wm. Doxford, Sunderland. Launched 17.6.1916. 15.10.1919 Reduced to Care and Maintenance at Chatham. 1.11.1921 Sold to Fryer, Sunderland.

6. "O" class Patrol Submarine, 1,475 tons (surfaced), 2,030 tons (submerged), 1 x 4" gun; 8 TT. Built by Wm. Beardmore, Dalmuir. Launched 26.2.1929. 2.4.1930 Commissioned at Dalmuir. 1931 Joined 3rd Submarine Flotilla in China. 1934-9 4th Submarine Flotilla, also in China. 12.1939 to 1940 8th S/M Flotilla at Colombo. 15.3.1940 Left Colombo for the Mediterranean. 26.4.1940 Arrived Malta. 12.6.1940 On patrol, she sighted 3 Italian cruisers with Destroyer escort, south east of Syracuse. She was unable to attack, but reported the enemy's whereabouts. Mid-June, 1940 may have been sunk by the Italian Destroyer *Tribune* off Tobruk, although mining cannot be ruled out.

Footnote
a) Fifth rate, 1,215 bm, 46 guns, was ordered from Chatham Dockyard in 1825, but cancelled in 1831.
b) Trawler, 228 tons, built in 1905, was hired 1914-9; and again 6.1940 to 1.1946 as a minesweeper.

ORWELL

A "River" class Fleet Minesweeper, 890 tons (full load); 1 x 40mm gun. Built by Richards, Great Yarmouth. Launched 7.2.1985. Allocated to Tyne Division, RNR.

Description of Badge

Field:- White.
Badge:- A sea horse proper, holding between the feet a roundel, barry wavy blue and gold.
(Derived from the Arms of Ipswich, which stands on the banks of the River Orwell).

Motto

Battle Honours

Barents Sea	1942	Normandy	1944
Arctic	1942-5	Norway	1945
Atlantic	1943		

Previous ships of the name

1. "Britomart" class wood steam gunboat, 268 bm, 2 x 64 pdr ML guns. Built in Portsmouth Dockyard. Launched 27.12.1866. 1867-70 At Queenstown. 1872-89 Coastguard Service on coast of Ireland. 1889 Sales List. 1891 Broken up.

2. Destroyer, 360 tons, 1 x 12 pdr and 5 x 6 pdr guns; 2 TT. Built by Laird Bros., Birkenhead. Launched 29.9.1898. 19.4.1900 Commissioned for the Mediterranean. 1900-6 In Mediterranean. 1907-9 Home Fleet at the Nore. 1910 3rd then the 5th DF, Home Fleet. 1912 7th DF, Patrol Flotillas. 1914-7 Patrol and convoy duties. 13.12.1917 Struck rocks in Holland Bay, Orkneys. 30.12.1917 Salvaged and towed into Kirkwall. 1918 Refitted at Aberdeen. 24.9.1920 Sold.

3. "Onslow" class, second group, destroyer, 1,540 tons, 4 x 4" guns; 8 TT. Built by Thornycroft, Woolston, Southampton. Launched 2.4.1942. Fitted for minelaying. Joined 17th Destroyer Flotilla, Home Fleet. 31.12.1942 Battle of Barents Sea. 1943 Third Support Group on North Atlantic convoy duties. 6.1944 Supported Normandy landings. 22.4.1945 Laid minefield in Arctic Ocean. 1946-7 Torpedo training in Portsmouth Local Flotilla. 1947-52 In Reserve. 1952 Converted to Type 16 frigate at Rosyth. 8.1953 Target Ship for 3rd Submarine Flotilla, Rosyth. 1953-8 Devonport Local Flotilla. 1960-3 In Reserve. 28.6.1965 Arrived Newport to be broken up by J. Cashmore.

HMS *Orwell* (June 1947).

OSIRIS

An "Oberon" class Patrol Submarine, 1,610 tons (surfaced), 2,410 tons (submerged); 8 x 21"
TT (6 bow, 2 stern). Built by Vickers, Barrow-in-Furness. Launched 29.11.1962.

Description of Badge

Field:- Black.
Badge:- Within a crook and flail pilewise gold,
the head of Osiris with headdress blue and
gold.
(Osiris was the God of Sun, Moon and Resurrection).

Motto

Resurgam — I shall rise again.

Battle Honours

Mediterranean	1940	Sicily	1943
Malta Convoys	1941		

Previous ships of the name

1. "M" class destroyer, 1,025 tons, 3 x 4" guns; 4 TT. Built by Palmer, Jarrow-on-Tyne. Launched 26.9.1916. 10.1917 With
13th Flotilla in the North Sea. 10.10.1919 Paid off at Chatham. 9.5.1921 Sold to T.W. Ward, Rainham, for breaking up.

2. "O" class Patrol Submarine, 1,475 tons (surfaced), 2,030 tons (submerged), 1 x 4" gun; 8 TT. Built by Vickers
Armstrong, Barrow. Launched 19.5.1928. 13.12.1929 Commissioned. 1930 3rd S/M Flotilla in China. 1933 4th S/M Flotilla
in China. 1937 5th S/M Flotilla at "Dolphin". Survived the European War to go to the Eastern theatre as a Training
Vessel. 9.1946 Sold at Durban to be broken up.

Footnote
a) *Osiris*, 1,728 tons, built in 1898, was hired as an Armed Merchant Cruiser from 5.8.1914. 10.10.1914 Fleet Messenger.
11.4.1915 to 1919 Depot Ship. 1916 Became *Osiris II* and as such was awarded the Battle Honour "Dardanelles 1915-6".
b) Trawler, 173 tons, built in 1898, was hired as *Osiris III* from 1917-9.

HMS *Osiris* (May 1930).

OTTER

An ''Oberon'' class Patrol Submarine, 1,610 tons (surfaced), 2,410 tons (submerged); 8 x 21" TT (6 bow, 2 stern). Built by Scotts, Greenock. Launched 15.5.1961.

Description of Badge

Field:- Blue.
Badge:- an otter passant guardant, holding in the mouth a fish, all proper.

Motto

Hard to catch.

Battle Honours

Copenhagen   1801   Baltic   1854-5

Previous ships of the name

1. Ketch, 83 bm, 4 guns. Built at Deptford in 1700. 28.7.1702 Captured by 2 French frigates when on passage to Barbados, West Indies.

2. Sixth rate, 167 bm, 14 guns. Built by Smith, Rotherhithe. Launched 6.3.1709. 8.1.1713 Sold out of the service.

3. Sloop, 91 bm, 8 guns. Built in Deptford Dockyard. Launched 8.8.1721. 1740 Rebuilt. 13.1.1741 Wrecked in the South Seas.

4. Sloop, 247 bm, 14 guns. Built by Buxton, Rotherhithe. Launched 19.8.1742. 16.6.1763 Sold out of the service.

5. Sloop, 302 bm, 14 guns. Built in Deptford Dockyard. Launched 26.10.1767. 25.8.1778 Wrecked on the coast of Florida.

6. The American sloop *Otter*, 14 guns, was captured in 1778 and commissioned into the RN. 1782 Sold out of the service.

7. Sloop, 202 bm, 14 guns. Built by Hills, Sandwich. Launched in 1782. 1800 Converted to a Fireship. 1801 At Copenhagen. 16.12.1801 Sold out of the service.

8. Sloop, 365 bm, 18 guns. Built by Atkinson, Hull. Launched 2.3.1805. 1809 In the action which resulted in the capture of *Rodriguez*. 1810 Captured *Venus*, 40 guns. 1814 Reduced to Harbour Service. 6.3.1828 Sold to J. Holmes.

9. Wood paddlewheel packet, ex-GPO vessel *Wizard*, 237 bm. Transferred to the Admiralty in 1837. 1854 Commissioned at Woolwich as a gunvessel. 1854-5 Baltic Campaign. 1865 Used as a Tug at Sheerness. 1878 Became a Coal Hulk, still at Sheerness. 1893 Sold out of the service.

10. Destroyer, 385 tons, 1 x 12 pdr and 5 x 6 pdr guns; 2 TT. Built by Naval Armaments and Construction Company, Barrow. Launched 23.11.1896. 1900 To China Station. 1904-5 In Reserve at Hong Kong. 1905 Re-commissioned. 1913 Sales List at Hong Kong. 1914 Again re-commissioned. 1915 Paid off. 25.10.1916 Sold at Hong Kong.

Footnote
a) Tug, 165 tons, built in 1887. Hired into the RN from 10.1914 to 1915.
b) Yacht, 154 tons, built in 1903. Purchased in 1916. Sold 31.7.1919.
c) Yacht, ex-*Conseco*, 416 tons, built in 1921. 4.10.1940 Commissioned into the RCN. 26.3.1941 Lost by fire off Newfoundland.

OTUS

An "Oberon" class Patrol Submarine, 1,610 tons (surfaced), 2,410 tons (submerged); 8 x 21"
TT (6 bow, 2 stern). Built by Scotts, Greenock. Launched 17.10.1962.

Description of Badge

Field:- Blue.
Badge:- In chief blue, beneath a bar wavy silver,
on a field green, a trident.

(The trident is shown underwater because Otus was the son
of Neptune).

Motto

De profundis paratus — Out of the deep I am
ready.

Battle Honours

Malta Convoys   1941

Previous ships of the name

1. Submarine, 1,475 tons (surfaced), 2,030 tons (submerged), 1 x 4" gun; 8 TT. Built by Vickers Armstrong, Barrow.
Launched 31.8.1928. 1931-9 4th Submarine Flotilla in China. 10.1939 to 4.1940 Based at Colombo. 7.5.1940 Arrived Malta.
1941 8th S/M Flotilla at Gibraltar. 2.1941 to 1.3.1941 Repairs at Portsmouth. 7.1941 Made 2 stores trips to Malta and
Alexandria. 1942 A/S Training at Alexandria. 7 and 8.1942 Whilst Operation 'Pedestal' was in progress *Otus, Rorqual* and
Clyde carried urgently needed ammunition, torpedoes and aviation spirit to Malta—deemed too risky to send by surface
ships. 20.8.1942 Collided with breakwater at Gibraltar. 21.9.1942 to 7.5.1943 At Tyneside for repairs. 18.8.1943 Left
Rothesay for South Africa. 1944 A/S Training at Simonstown. 1.1945 At Durban in Reserve. 5.1946 Sold to R. Scott,
Durban. 9.1946 Stripped hull scuttled.

HMS *Otus* (May 1930).

PEACOCK

Name ship of the class designed for Hong Kong patrol duties. 700 tons; 1 x 76mm gun. Built by Hall Russell, Aberdeen. Launched 1.12.1982.

Description of Badge

Field:- White.
Badge:- Upon a pedestal black, a peacock proper.

Motto

Battle Honours

Arctic   1944   Atlantic   1945

Previous ships of the name

1. Frigate *Falcon,* 18 guns, captured in 1651. Renamed after the man who captured her—Captain James Peacock. 1658 Sold out of the service.

2. ''Cruizer'' class brig-sloop, 386 bm, 18 guns. Built by Bailey, Ipswich. Launched 9.12.1806. 24.2.1813 Captured by the American *Hornet,* and sunk.

3. American sloop *Wasp,* 434 bm, 18 guns. Captured 18.10.1812 by *Poictiers* in the Atlantic. 29.8.1814 Foundered with all hands off the south coast of USA.

4. ''Albacore'' class wood steam gunboat, 232 bm, 1 x 68 pdr, 1 x 32 pdr and 2 x 20 pdr guns. Built by Pitcher, Northfleet. Launched 12.4.1856. Never used in service. 3.1869 Broken up at Portsmouth.

5. ''Pigmy'' class composite steam gunboat, 755 tons, 6 x 4" guns. Built at Pembroke Dock. Launched 22.6.1888. 1888-90 Cape of Good Hope and West Coast of Africa Station. 1890-1 China Station; recommissioned at Hong Kong. 1900 Boxer Rebellion. 1901 Returned to UK; laid up at Devonport. 15.5.1906 Sold to Ellis, Chepstow.

6. Sloop, modified ''Black Swan'' class, 1,350 tons, 6 x 4" and 10 x 20mm AA guns. Built by Thornycroft, Woolston, Southampton. Launched 11.12.1943. 1944 Joined 22nd Escort Group, Western Approaches. Involved in several successful actions against U-boats. 24.8.1944 In escort to a Russian convoy, helped destroy *U 354* after it had been attacked by aircraft from *Vindex.* Assisted in sinking *U 394* (2.9.1944) and *U 482* (16.1.1945). Refitted in Liverpool as AA frigate. Spent the remainder of the war in the Mediterranean. 7.5.1958 Arrived Rosyth to be broken up by Shipbreaking Industries.

HMS *Peacock* (June 1953).

PENELOPE

A Batch One "Leander" class frigate (ex-*Coventry*), 2,450 tons (standard). Built by Vickers Armstrong, Newcastle-on-Tyne. Launched 17.8.1962. 1977-81 Exocet conversion at Devonport. New armament:- Exocet SSM and Sea Cat SAM systems; 2 x 40mm; 6 TT; 1 helicopter.

Description of Badge

Field:- Blue.
Badge:- A female head, white.

Motto

Constantia et fide — With constancy and faith.

(The mythological character "Penelope" was pestered by suitors at Ithaca while her husband Ulysses was absent at the siege of Troy).

Battle Honours

Guillaume Tell	1800	Mediterranean	1941-3
Egypt	1801	Sirte	1942
Martinique	1809	Sicily	1943
Baltic	1854	Salerno	1943
Alexandria	1882	Aegean	1943
Norway	1940	Anzio	1944
Malta Convoys	1941-2	Falkland Islands	1982

Previous ships of the name

1. Sixth rate, 524 bm, 24 guns. Built by Baker, Liverpool. Launched 25.6.1778. 10.1780 Foundered in the West Indies with the loss of all her crew.

2. Fifth rate, 721 bm, 32 guns. Built by Barton, Liverpool. Launched 27.10.1783. Saw much action in the West Indies. 11.1797 Broken up at Chatham.

3. Fifth rate, 1,051 bm, 36 guns. Built by Parsons, Bursledon. Launched 26.9.1798. 1800 Employed in the blockade of Malta. 1813 Employed as a Troopship. 1.5.1815 Wrecked off Newfoundland.

4. Fifth rate, 1,091 bm. Was laid down at Portsmouth but the frames were transferred to Chatham Dockyard and re-laid in 11.1827. Launched 13.8.1829. 6.1843 Completed as a paddlewheel frigate, 1,616 bm. 15.7.1864 Sold to Castle and Beech for breaking up.

HMS *Penelope* (June 1939).

5. Armoured corvette, 4,470 tons, 8 x 8″ guns. Built at Pembroke Dock. Launched 18.6.1867. The RN's first large iron-clad to have twin screws and twin rudders. 1869-82 In Coastguard Service at Harwich. 1882 In Mediterranean. 1882-7 Again Guardship at Harwich. 1888-97 Harbour Receiving Ship at Simonstown. 1897 Prison Hulk at Simon's Bay. 12.7.1912 Sold at the Cape. 1914 Broken up at Genoa.

6. ''Arethusa'' class light cruiser, 3,500 tons, 2 x 6″, 6 x 4″ and 1 x 4″ AA guns; 4 x 21″ TT. Built by Vickers, Barrow. Launched 25.8.1914. 1914-8 Harwich Force. 30.9.1915 Captured one and sank three German trawlers. 25.3.1916 In the seaplane raid on Hoyer. 25.4.1916 Torpedoed by submarine *U 29* when returning from an operation against German battlecruisers which had raided Lowestoft. 2.1918 Minelaying in the Kattegat. 1918-9 7th LCS, Grand Fleet. 1919-21 In Reserve. 10.1924 Sold to Stanlee, Dover, for breaking up.

7. ''Arethusa'' class cruiser, 5,270 tons, 6 x 6″ and 8 x 4″ guns; 6 x 21″ TT. Built by Harland and Wolff, Belfast. Launched 15.10.1935. 12.11.1936 Commissioned for 5th Cruiser Squadron. 9.1938 At Alexandria for Munich crisis. 22.3.1939 In collision with *Afridi* whilst transferring mail. Repaired at Malta. 10.4.1940 Off Norway, damaged by a bomb. 11.4.1940 Near Narvik, ran aground, towed to Lofoten Islands; beached for emergency repairs; towed to Greenock, then to the Tyne for permanent repairs. 1941 Actions against Italian convoys in Mediterranean. 1.12.1941 Sank naval auxiliary *Adriatico* during the early hours, and a tanker and her escort that evening. 4.1942 Damaged by near misses in the air raids on Malta. Nicknamed ''Pepperpot''. Fought to survive in dry dock for 5 weeks under constant air attack. Escaped to Gibraltar. Repaired in USA. 1943 In bombardment of Pantalleria. 7.10.1943 Hit by a bomb from a JU 87 which failed to explode; but was damaged by near misses. Repaired at Alexandria. 1.1944 Gun support ship at Anzio. 18.2.1944 Sunk by 3 torpedoes from *U 410*, 35 miles west of Naples, while on passage from the Anzio beaches to Naples.

Footnote
a) Cutter, 18 guns, was hired in 1795. 7.7.1799 Captured in the Mediterranean by Spanish schooner *Del Carmen*.
b) Trawler, 149 tons, built in 1895, was hired in World War 1.

HMS *Penelope* (1981).

PETEREL

A ''Bird'' class Patrol Boat, 194 tons (full load); 1 x 40mm gun. Built by R. Dunston, Hessle, Humberside. Launched 14.5.1976.

Description of Badge

Field:- Silver.
Badge:- A peterel in flight, black.
(The peterel is a harbinger of storm and wreck).

Motto

Reck not — Care not.

Battle Honours

Minorca	1798	*Ligurienne*	1800
Egypt	1801		

Previous ships of the name

1. Survey sloop, 138 bm, 4 guns, ex-*Duchess of Manchester*; purchased in 4.1777. 28.5.1788 Sold out of the service.

2. Sloop, 365 bm, 16 guns. Built by Wilson, Frindsbury. Launched 4.3.1794. Served in the Mediterranean with Admiral Nelson's squadron. Won the ship's only Battle Honours. 8.6.1811 Reduced to Harbour Service as a Receiving Ship at Plymouth. 11.7.1827 Sold out of the service.

3. Brig sloop, 359 bm, 6 guns. Built at Pembroke Dock. Launched 23.5.1838. 1838-50 Employed as a Packet. 1850 Became a workshop for Engineers at Devonport. 11.1.1862 Sold to Marshall, Plymouth.

4. ''Rosario'' class wood steam sloop, 669 bm, 1 x 40 pdr, 6 x 32 pdr and 4 x 20 pdr guns. Built in Devonport Dockyard. Launched 10.11.1860. 1862-5 North America and West Indies Station. 1866-70 Cape of Good Hope. 1872-6 Pacific Station. 1877 Used as a Light Vessel, to mark the wreck of *Vanguard* sunk on 1.9.1875 by *Iron Duke*. 12.1880 Engines removed. 1886-1901 Used as a Coal Depot. 10.1901 On Sales List.

5. Destroyer, 370 tons, 1 x 12 pdr and 5 x 6 pdr guns; 2 x 18'' TT. Built by Palmer, Jarrow-on-Tyne. Launched 30.3.1899. 1900 At Portsmouth. 1904-7 At Portland. 1908 Home Fleet, Portsmouth. 1910 4th DF, Home Fleet. 1912 6th DF, Patrol Flotillas. In WW1 was used for coastal convoy escort. 30.8.1919 Sold to T.R. Sales.

6. River Gunboat, 310 tons, 2 x 3'' guns. Built by Yarrow, Scotstoun, Glasgow. Launched 18.7.1927. Shipped to the Far East in sections and re-assembled. 20.8.1927 Foremast was blown off in a typhoon while ship was under assembly at Taikoo Dockyard, Hong Kong. 4.1930 Wrecked in Upper reaches of River Yangtse; salved to continue to serve on the River. She was the first RN warship in action with Japanese Navy when hostilities commenced in 1941. 8.12.1941 Sunk at Shanghai by Japanese cruiser *Idzumo*. Japanese officers and marines came on board to demand *Peterel's* surrender. The C.O. roared ''Get off my bloody ship''. The enemy cruiser, destroyer and gunboat opened fire at point-blank range. Many died as the ship sank.

Footnote
Schooner, 280 bm, 6 guns, was ordered in 1826 from Woolwich Dockyard but cancelled. in 1831.

PHOEBE

A Batch Two "Leander" class frigate, 2,450 tons (standard). Built by Alex Stephen, Linthouse, Glasgow. Launched 8.7.1964. 1975-7 Exocet conversion at Devonport. New armament:- Exocet SSM and Sea Cat SAM systems; 2 x 40mm guns; 6 TT; 1 helicopter; Towed Array Sonar system.

Description of Badge

Field:- Blue.
Badge:- Over waves in base white and blue, the moon proper.
(Derived from Greek mythology).

Motto

Venatu triumphans — triumphant in the hunt.

Battle Honours

Nereide	1797	Zeebrugge	1918
Africaine	1801	Greece	1941
Trafalgar	1805	Crete	1941
Tamatave	1811	Malta Convoys	1942
Java	1811	Aegean	1943
Essex	1814	Mediterranean	1944
Benin	1897	Sabang	1944
Belgian Coast	1917-8	Burma	1944-5

Previous ships of the name

1. Fifth rate, 926 bm, 36 guns. Built by Dudman, Deptford. Launched 29.9.1795. Served with distinction in many operations. 1805 At Trafalgar. At capture of Isle of France (Mauritius) and Java. 27.5.1841 Sold to J. Cristall for breaking up.

2. Fourth rate, 2,044 bm, 51 guns. Built in Devonport Dockyard. Launched 12.4.1854. For 5 years she lay at Devonport. Taken in to dock to be converted to a steam frigate, 2,896 bm. Undocked as such on 10.4.1860. 1869 Joined Flying Squadron on a cruise around the world. 1871-5 At Devonport. 1875 Sold to Messrs. Castle for breaking up.

3. "Pallas" class cruiser, 2,575 tons, 8 x 4.7" guns. Built in Devonport Dockyard. Launched 1.7.1890. 1894 Operations in Benin River; landed armed parties. 1901-5 In Australian waters. 23.12.1905 Paid off at Portsmouth. 10.7.1906 Sold to A. Anderson of Copenhagen.

4. "M" class destroyer, 1,025 tons, 3 x 4" guns; 4 TT. Built by Fairfield, Govan, Glasgow. Launched 20.11.1916. 1917 In an attack, with Harwich Force, on German destroyers in Flanders Bight. 1918 Blocking of Zeebrugge and Ostend. 15.11.1921 Sold to J. Cashmore and broken up at Newport.

5. "Dido" class cruiser, 5,450 tons, 10 x 5.25" guns; 6 x 21" TT. Built by Fairfield, Govan, Glasgow. Launched 25.3.1939. 1941 In Mediterranean. 25.4.1941 Covered evacuation of troops from Nauplia in Greece. 12.5.1941 Joined 15th CS at Alexandria. 18.5.1941 On patrol off Crete. 8.6.1941 Supported Army in Syria. 27.8.1941 Covered troop run to Tobruk. Hit by aircraft torpedo off Bardia; hole 28' x 18' in starboard side. 11.1941 to 4.1942 Under repair at Brooklyn NY, USA. 8.1942 Operation 'Pedestal'. 23.10.1942 Torpedoed by *U 161*; hole 40' x 30' in port side. 15.1.1943 to 14.6.1943 Under repair at New York. 10.1943 Patrols in the Aegean. 13.11.1943 Bombed in Gulf of Cos. Early 1944, gun support at Anzio. 1944 Operated from Trincomalee. 27.4.1945 Assault on Rangoon. 29.10.1945 Arrived Sheerness; then to Chatham. 1946-7 Flagship of Mediterranean Fleet Destroyers. 4.1948 Flagship of 1st CS. 16.10.1950 In collision with *Gambia* while transferring mail. 14.3.1951 Arrived Chatham to pay off. 5.1952 Nore Reserve, Harwich. 10.1953 to 10.1955 Reserve at Portsmouth. 1.8.1956 Arrived Blyth to be broken up by Hughes Bolckow.

Footnote
a) Cutter, 84 bm, 10 guns, ex-*Betsy*, was hired from 5.1804 to 3.1805.
b) Trawler, 278 tons, built in 1907, was hired as *Phoebe II* 1914-9.
c) Trawler, 178 tons, built in 1906, was hired as *Phoebe III* 1917-9.

PLOVER

A ''Peacock'' class Patrol Vessel—for Hong Kong patrol duties—700 tons; 1 x 76mm gun. Built by Hall Russell, Aberdeen. Launched 12.4.1983.

Description of Badge

Field:- Gold.
Badge:- A plover with wings close proper.

Motto

Noli me tangere — Do not touch me.

Battle Honours

Portland	1653	China	1856-9
China	1842	Normandy	1944

Previous ships of the name

First 2 ships were those captured in 1652 and 1657.

3. Sloop, 422 bm, 18 guns. Built by Betts, Mistleythorn. Launched 23.4.1796. 8.3.1819 Sold to Young, Limehouse.

4. ''Cherokee'' class brig-sloop, 236 bm, 8 x 18 pdr and 2 x 6 pdr guns. Built in Portsmouth Dockyard. Launched 30.6.1821. 27.5.1841 Sold to J. Cristall for breaking up.

5. ''Albacore'' class wood steam gunboat, 232 bm, 1 x 68 pdr, 1 x 32 pdr and 2 x 20 pdr guns. Built by Pitcher, Northfleet. Launched 8.9.1855. 1856 China Station. 1.6.1857 In action in Fatshan Creek. 25.6.1859 Sunk in action with the Pei Ho forts, China.

6. ''Philomel'' class wood steam gunvessel, 428 bm, 1 x 68 pdr, 2 x 24 pdr and 2 x 20 pdr guns. Built by Green, Blackwall. Launched 19.1.1860. 1861-5 North America and West Indies Station. 12.9.1865 Sold out of the service, renamed *Hawk*. 1876 Lost in the ice.

7. Name ship of the class of wood steam gunvessels, 755 tons, 1 x 7" and 2 x 40 pdr guns. Built in Deptford Dockyard. Launched 20.2.1867. Later that year, sailed to West Africa. Bore large share in the destruction of Congo pirate villages. 1869-79 In North America. Employed in chasing Cuban blockade runners out of British West Indian waters. 2.7.1880 Paid off at Portsmouth. 1885 Sold to Castle & Sons for breaking up.

8. ''Pigmy'' class composite steam gunboat, 755 tons, 6 x 4" guns. Built at Pembroke Dock. Launched 18.10.1888. 1889-1902 China Station. 1904 Became a Boom Defence Vessel. 27.4.1927 Sold at Gibraltar.

9. ''M'' class destroyer, 1,025 tons, 3 x 4" guns; 4 TT. Built by Hawthorn Leslie, Hebburn-on-Tyne. Launched 3.3.1916. 9.5.1921 Sold to T.W. Ward, Hayle, for breaking up.

10. Coastal minelayer, 805 tons, 1 x 12 pdr gun. Built by Wm Denny, Dumbarton. Launched 8.6.1937. 11.9.1939 Started laying mines in Dover Straits. 1940-3 Operated from the Nore. 1943-5 Based at Portsmouth. 4. to 6.1944 Laid barrage of mines to protect the Normandy invasion convoy routes. Post-war was attached to *Vernon* until 1955; then *Lochinvar* for experimental work. 12.1967 Paid off; laid up at Rosyth. 4.1969 Broken up at Inverkeithing.

Footnote
Survey cutter, ex-Hon. East India Company's *Bentinck*, 237 bm, was purchased in 2.1842. 24.11.1854 Sold at San Francisco.

PLYMOUTH

A ''Rothesay'' class Type 12 anti-submarine frigate, 2,380 tons (standard), 2,800 tons (full load). Built in Devonport Dockyard. Launched 20.7.1959. One Limbo A/S weapon; 2 x 4.5" and 2 x 40mm guns (later replaced by Sea Cat SAM system); 1 helicopter.

Description of Badge

Field:- Barry wavy of six white and blue.
Badge:- A saltire couped green between four towers black.
(Derived from the Arms of the City of Plymouth).

Motto

Battle Honours

Porto Farina	1655	Orfordness	1666
Santa Cruz	1657	Sole Bay	1672
Lowestoft	1665	Texel	1673
Four Days' Battle	1666	Falkland Islands	1982

Previous ships of the name

1. Sixty guns ship, 752 bm. Built in 1653 by John Taylor at Wapping on the Thames. 6.1697 With *Anglesea* brought in to Kinsale the French privateer *Gaillarde*, 18 guns. 1705 Rebuilt by W. Johnson, Blackwall, as 900 bm, 64 guns. 11.8.1705 Foundered in a gale with all her crew.

2. Sheer hulk, 524 bm, 5 guns. Purchased on 19.5.1689 from Robert Castle, Deptford. 1730 Sold out of the service.

3. Storeship *Plymouth Transport*, 109 bm. Built in Plymouth Dockyard and added to the service on 9.6.1704. A long but undistinguished life. Used mainly for transporting stores from one Yard to another. 8.1742 Rebuilt at Chatham as 160 bm. 22.5.1806 Sold at Plymouth to Thomas Graham.

4. Fourth rate, 922 bm, 64 guns. Built in Plymouth Dockyard. Launched 25.5.1708. 20.9.1709 Distinguished herself when, on her way to Plymouth to make good defects, she came upon the French 44 guns *Adriade*. *Plymouth* was in poor condition for fighting, only half her guns could be manned, but she gave chase and after an hour's engagement forced the French to surrender. 1722 Rebuilt at Chatham as 955 bm. Broken up at Portsmouth. Completed on 3.4.1764.

5. Ketch rigged Yacht, 88 bm, 6 x 2 pdr guns. Built in Plymouth Dockyard. Launched 4.12.1755. 26.8.1793 Admiralty ordered she be broken up. Completed following month.

6. Transport, 8 guns. Built in 1786. 14.12.1815 Sold out of the service.

7. Yacht, 96 bm, 8 guns. Built in Plymouth Dockyard. Launched 2.11.1796. 1814 Rebuilt at Woolwich. 7.1830 Broken up.

8. Lugger, 14 guns. Hired in 1797. Served on the coast of Spain. 13.3.1797 Captured French schooner *Amitie*, 14 guns. 23.3.1797 Off Start Point, captured French privateer *L'Epelvier*, 4 guns. 6.7.1801 In action off Algeciras. Fate unknown.

9. Yacht, 115 bm. Built in Woolwich Dockyard. Launched 21.5.1814. 7.1830 Renamed *Plymouth*. 1866 Reduced to Harbour Service as *YC1*. 10.5.1870 Sold to Lethbridge and Drew.

Footnote
Plymouth Prize, sixth rate, 134 bm, 16 guns, was captured on 19.7.1709, but lost to the French, off the Isles of Scilly, on 21.12.1709.

PROTECTOR

The former Oil Rig Support vessel *Seaforth Saga*, 802 tons (gross) 1,030 tons (deadweight). Built in 1975 by Drypool, Selby. Purchased from Seaforth Marine and converted at Cardiff to a Falkland Islands Patrol Vessel; 2 x 40mm guns. Commissioned into the RN 21.10.1983.

Description of Badge

Field:- Red.
Badge:- A demi-gryphon gold.
(One of the Crests of Edward, Duke of Somerset, Lord Protector of England, 1549).

Motto

Faith for duty.
(Translation of Somerset's motto ''Foy pour devoir'').

Battle Honours

Sadras	1758	Norway	1940
Negapatam	1758	Libya	1940-1
Cape of Good Hope	1806		

Previous ships of the name

1. Indian fifth rate, 44 guns. Listed in 1749. 1.1.1761 Foundered in a cyclone off Pondicherry.

2. Fireship in service in 1758.

3. Gun-brig, 178 bm, 12 guns. Built by Warren, Brightlingsea. Launched 1.2.1805. 4.1817 Converted to a survey vessel. 1818-30 Employed surveying east coast of England. 30.8.1833 Sold to W. Woolcombe, to be broken up.

4. Australian cruiser, 920 tons, 1 x 8" and 5 x 6" guns. Built by Armstrong Whitworth on the Tyne. Launched 27.12.1883. Originally part of the South Australian Navy. 1900 Boxer Rebellon. 1901 At Federation, became unit of Australian Naval Forces. 1910 Gunnery tender to Williamstown Gunnery School. WWI Patrol Vessel in South Tasman Sea. 1.4.1921 Renamed *Cerberus* when hulked as Harbour Training Ship. 1924 Reverted to *Protector*. 10.9.1924 Sold to J. Hill, Melbourne. 1931 Sold to Fenwick Tug Company. Used as Store Hulk. Renamed *Sydney*. WWII Taken over by US Army and used as a barge. 1944 Beached on Heron Island, Barrier Reef, after collision with a US Vessel.

5. Netlayer, 2,900 tons, 2 x 4" guns. Built by Yarrow, Scotstoun, Glasgow. Launched 20.8.1936. 1939 In South Atlantic. 1940 Home Waters. 5.1940 To Mediterranean. 1942-5 At Bombay under repair. In Reserve until 1954. 1954-5 Converted at Devonport to an Ice Patrol Ship. 3.10.1955 Sailed from Portsmouth for her first season in Antarctic. Annual visits until 3.5.1968 when she arrived Portsmouth to pay off for disposal. 1970 Broken up at Inverkeithning.

Footnote
''Britomart'' class wood steam gunboat was laid down in Portsmouth Dockyard in 1861; cancelled 12.12.1863 and taken to pieces.

HMS *Protector* (February 1986).

PUNCHER

A P2000 Coastal Training Craft of 43 tonnes for the RNR. Being built of GRP by Watercraft Ltd, Shoreham-by-Sea. Allocated to Sussex Division, RNR.

Description of Badge

Field:- Blue.
Badge:- A dexter hand clenched, couped at the wrist, proper.

Motto

Battle Honours

Atlantic   1944

Previous ships of the name

1. Escort Carrier, ex-USS *Willapa*, 11,420 tons, 2 x 4", 16 x 40mm AA and 20 x 20mm AA guns; 24 aircraft. Built by Seattle-Tacoma S.B. Corporation, Tacoma, USA Launched 8.11.1943. 5.2.1944 Transferred to RN on Lend-Lease. 16.1.1946 Returned to USN. 1949 Sold mercantile as *Muncaster Castle*. 1954 Renamed *Bardic* and in 1959 *Ben Nevis*.

2. LST(3) 3036, 2,256 tons, 10 x 20mm guns. Built by Ailsa S.B. Company. Launched 20.11.1944. 1947 Renamed *Puncher*. 1957 In Reserve. 12.8.1960 Sold out of the service. 4.6.1961 Arrived Ghent to be broken up.

HMS *Puncher*

PURSUER

A P2000 Coastal Training Craft of 43 tonnes for the RNR, being built of GRP by Watercraft Ltd, Shoreham-by-Sea. Allocated to Solent Division, RNR.

Description of Badge

Field:- White.
Badge:- A greyhound in pursuit, proper.

Motto

Battle Honours

Atlantic	1943-5	South France	1944
Norway	1944	Aegean	1944
Normandy	1944		

Previous ships of the name

1. Escort Carrier, 11,420 tons, 2 x 4" AA, 8 x 40mm AA and 15 x 20mm AA guns; 18 aircraft. ex-*Mormacland* (ii); ex-USS *St George*. Built by Ingalls S.B. Corporation, Pascagoula, USA. Launched 18.7.1942. 14.6.1943 Transferred to RN on Lend-Lease. Employed on convoy escort duties. 3.1944 In Operation 'Tungsten', the Fleet Air Arm attack on *Tirpitz*. 12.2.1946 Returned to the USN and broken up.

2. LST (3) 3504, 2,256 tons, 4 x 40mm and 6 x 20mm guns. Built by Vickers, Montreal. Launched 3.11.1944. 1947 Renamed *Pursuer*. 1956 To Ministry of Transport as *Empire Tern*. 1968 On Sales List.

HMS *Pursuer* (October 1946).

QUORN

A "Hunt" class Mine Countermeasures Vessel, 615 tons (standard), 725 tons (full load); 1 x 40mm gun. Built (of GRP) by Vosper Thornycroft, Woolston, Southampton.

Description of Badge

Field:- Red.
Badge:- A lion's gamb erased holding a hunting horn gold.

Motto

Battle Honours

North Sea	1941-44	Normandy	1944
English Ch	1942-4		

Previous ships of the name

1. Minesweeper, early "Hunt" class, 750 tons, 2 x 12 pdr and 2 x 6 pdr guns. Built by Napier and Miller, Old Kilpatrick, Glasgow. Launched 4.6.1917. Sold J. Smith 18.9.1922.

2. Destroyer, type 1 "Hunt" class, 907 tons, 4 x 4" guns (2 x 2) and 1 x four barrelled pom-pom. Built by J.S. White, Cowes, Isle of Wight. Launched 27.3.1940. 3.8.1940 North Sea and English Channel. 26.7.1941 Operation 'Gideon', English Channel. 6.1944 Normandy Landings. Sunk off Normandy by either human torpedo or mine 3.8.1944.

RANGER

A P2000 Coastal Training Craft of 43 tonnes for the RNR, being built of GRP by Watercraft Ltd, Shoreham-by-Sea. Allocated to Forth Division, RNR.

Description of Badge

Field:- White.
Badge:- Seven blue roundels in orle representing the seven seas, in front of which is set a ship's (steering) wheel.

Motto

Battle Honours

First of June   1794

Previous ships of the name

1. French privateer *Deux Couronnes*, sixth rate, 639 bm, 24 x 9 pdr guns. Captured 5.5.1747 by *Gloucester* in the Channel. 29.5.1749 Sold out of the service.

2. Sloop, 142 bm, 8 guns. Built in Woolwich Dockyard. Launched 7.10.1752. 16.1.1783 Sold out of the service.

3. Cutter, 201 bm. Purchased in 1779. 1781 Renamed *Pigmy* and made a sloop. 21.10.1784 Sold out of the service.

4. Cutter, 195 bm, 14 guns. Purchased on 2.1787. 28.6.1794 Captured by the French off Brest. 14.10.1797 Recaptured and renamed *Venture*. Listed until 1802.

5. Sloop, 361 bm, 16 guns. Built by Hill and Mellish, Limehouse. Launched 19.3.1794. 17.7.1805 Captured by the French and burnt.

6. Brig-sloop, 208 bm. Built on the Thames in 1797 and later purchased by the RN. Fate unknown.

7. Cutter, 217 bm, 16 guns. Built by Avery, Dartmouth. Launched 5.1806, and purchased by the RN. 1807 Renamed *Pigmy*. 6.1814 Lost.

8. Sloop, 428 bm, 18 guns. Built by Thorn, Fremington. Launched 5.9.1807. 2.1814 Broken up.

9. Sixth rate, 502 bm, 28 guns. Built in Portsmouth Dockyard. Launched 7.12.1820. 11.1832 Sold to J. Jackson.

10. Packet brig, 363 bm, 8 guns. Built by Bottomley, Rotherhithe. Launched 25.7.1835. 1860 Reduced to a Hulk. 1867 Sold at Dublin.

11. "Philomel" class wood steam gunvessel, 570 tons, 1 x 68 pdr, 2 x 24 pdr and 2 x 20 pdr guns. Built in Deptford Dockyard. Launched 26.11.1859. 1860-7 West Coast of Africa. 1861 Operations against West African slave trade on the Niger. 1864 Refitted at home. 1867-9 In Reserve. 3.11.1869 Sold to Moss Isaacs.

12. "Algerine" class composite steam gunvessel, 835 tons, 1 x 7" and 2 x 64 pdr guns. Built by John Elder, Govan, Glasgow. Launched 12.2.1880. 1881 To East Indies Station. 1883-5 Employed in the defence of Suakin on the Red Sea during the Sudan War. 1887 In Burmese waters. 24.9.1892 Sold as a Salvage Vessel. 11.1914 to 1919 Hired by the RN. 1954 Broken up.

13. Destroyer, 320 tons, 1 x 12 pdr and 5 x 6 pdr guns; 2 TT. Built by Hawthorn Leslie, Hebburn-on-Tyne. Launched 4.10.1895. 20.5.1920 Sold to Riddle and Co.

Footnote

"C" class destroyer was laid down by J. Brown, Clydebank, but renamed *Caesar* in 11.1942 before her launch on 14.2.1944.

REDPOLE

The RAF "Seal" class long range recovery and support vessel, *Sea Otter*, built by Fairmile Construction, Berwick-on-Tweed in 1967. Transferred to the RN in 3.1985. After refit at Lowestoft emerged as *Redpole*, 159 tons.

Description of Badge

Field:- White.
Badge:- A redpole proper, upon a branch of a tree, also proper.

Motto

Battle Honours

Basque Roads	1809	Normandy	1944
Atlantic	1943-4	Burma	1944-5

Previous ships of the name

1. Cherokee class brig-sloop, 236 bm, 8 x 18 pdr and 2 x 6 pdr guns. Built by Guillaume, Northam. Launched 29.7.1808. 1811 In action, off Boulogne, with 2 French ships of superior armament. 1817-9 St Helena Station. 1819-21 Channel Squadron. 1824-5 Packet Service, based at Falmouth. 10.8.1828 Sailed from Rio de Janeiro. Reported missing. Believed sunk in action with the pirate ship *Congress* off Cape Frio, Brazil.

2. Composite steam gunboat, 805 tons, 6 x 4" guns. Built at Pembroke Dock. Launched 13.6.1889. 20.11.1889 Commissioned at Devonport to relieve *Merlin* in China. Recommissioned at Hong Kong on 17.1.1893; 1.1.1896 and 1.1.1899. 1900 Boxer rising in China. 1902 Returned to Devonport to pay off. 1904 Sales list. 15.5.1906 Sold to Cox, Falmouth, for breaking up.

3. Destroyer, 720 tons, 2 x 4" and 2 x 12 pdr guns; 2 TT. Built by J.S. White, Cowes. Launched 24.6.1910. 1911 2nd DF, Home Fleet. 7.3.1911 In collision with destroyer *Acorn* off Isles of Scilly. Bow of *Redpole* crashed in to stern of *Acorn*. Sent to Portland for repairs. 15.10.1919 Reduced to Care and Maintenance at Devonport. 9.5.1921 Sold to T.W. Ward, Milford, for breaking up.

4. Modified "Black Swan" class sloop, 1,350 tons, 6 x 4" and 12 x 20mm AA guns. Built by Yarrow, Scotstoun, Glasgow. Launched 25.2.1943. 1943-4 In Atlantic as convoy escort. 6.6.1944 Normandy landings. 21.1.1945 Assisted in assault on Ramree Island, Burma. 7.1946 Returned to UK from Far East. 1949 Disarmed and converted to a Tender for the Navigation School. 15.6.1953 Acted as Admiralty Yacht at Coronation Review at Spithead. 7.5.1956 Slightly damaged in collision with Danish Royal Yacht *Dannebrog* at Copenhagen. 12.5.1957 Collided with, and badly damaged, the Gosport ferry *Vadne* at Portsmouth. 20.11.1960 Arrived St David's-on-Forth to be broken up by J.A. White.

Footnote
The paddlewheel tug *Racehorse* was purchased at Constantinople during Crimean War. 1855 Renamed *Redpole*. Employed as a Tender to Flagship of Admiral Superintendent, Gibraltar. 1871 Broken up at Devonport.

RENOWN

A "Resolution" class nuclear powered ballistic missile submarine (SSBN); 7,600 tons (surfaced), 8,500 tons (submerged). Built by Cammell Laird, Birkenhead. Launched 25.2.1967. Sixteen tubes amidship for Polaris ICBMs. 6 x 21" TT.

Description of Badge

Field:- Blue.
Badge:- A torch surrounded by a wreath all gold.

Motto

Antiquae famae custos — Guardian of an ancient renown.

Battle Honours

Gabbard	1653	Bismarck	1941
Scheveningen	1653	Mediterranean	1941
Ushant	1781	Malta Convoys	1941-2
Egypt	1801	Arctic	1942
Atlantic	1940	North Africa	1942
Norway	1940	Sabang	1944
Spartivento	1940		

Previous ships of the name

1. French fireship *Renommee* (English translation *Renown*), 20 guns. Captured off Straits of Gibraltar in 12.1651 by *Nonsuch*. Served in the RN during the Wars with the Dutch. 1654 Sold out of the service.

2. French fifth rate *Renommee*, 669 bm, 30 guns. Captured 13.9.1747 by *Dover* and added to RN as *Fame*. 1748 Renamed *Renown*. 5.1771 Broken up at Woolwich.

3. Fourth rate, 1,050 bm, 50 guns. Built by Fabian, Northam. Named 19.11.1774 but the ship stuck on the ways. Launched 4.12.1774. Saw service on North America and West Indies Station. 1783-94 in Ordinary. 12.1794 Broken up.

4. Third rate, 1,899 bm, 74 guns. Laid down as *Royal Oak* by Dudman, Deptford. 15.2.1796 Renamed *Renown*. Launched 2.5.1798. 1.1814 Reduced to Harbour Service. 5.1835 Broken up.

5. Second rate, steam, 3,319 bm, 91 guns (including 34 x 8"). Built in Chatham Dockyard. Launched 28.3.1857. 1859-61 In the Mediterranean. Following 9 years were spent laid up at Devonport. 24.3.1870 Sold to the North German Confederation Navy.

6. Battleship, 12,350 tons, 4 x 10" and 10 x 6" guns. Built at Pembroke Dock. Launched 8.5.1895. Served as Vice Admiral Sir John Fisher's flagship in the Mediterranean. By 1905 all her 6" guns had been removed to facilitate her employment on Royal Cruises. 2.4.1914 Sold to Hughes Bolckow to be broken up.

7. Name ship of class of battlecruisers, 28,000 tons, 6 x 15", 17 x 4" and 2 x 3" guns; 2 x 21" TT. Built by Fairfield, Govan, Glasgow. Launched 4.3.1916. 1916-9 Grand Fleet. 1919-20 Refit. 1920-1 With the Prince of Wales's tours to USA, Canada and Australasia. 1921-2 Prince of Wales's tour to India and Japan. 1923-6 Modifications. 1926 Atlantic Fleet. 1927 Tour with the Duke of York to Australia. 1928-36 Atlantic and Home Fleets. 1936-9 Reconstruction. 1939-40 Home Fleet. 9.4.1940 In action with *Scharnhorst* and *Gneisnau*. 1940-1 Force H in the Mediterranean. 27.11.1940 In action with the Italian Fleet off Sardinia. 9.2.1941 Bombardment of Genoa. 5.1941 *Bismarck* operations. 11.1942 Covered landings in North Africa. 8.1943 Embarked the Prime Minister for passage from Halifax to Scotland. 11.1943 With Prime Minister to Alexandria. 1944-5 In Eastern Fleet. 7.1944 Bombardment of Sabang. 10.1944 Bombardment of Nicobar Islands. 12.1944 to 3.1945 Refit at Durban. 1945 Home Fleet and Reserve. 19.3.1948 Sold to Metal Industries; broken up at Faslane.

Footnote

a) French Fifth rate, *Renommee*, captured off San Domingo by *Alfred* on 20.7.1796, but remained in service as *Renommee*.
b) Battleship, 10,470 tons, was laid down by Armstrong Mitchell but was renamed *Victoria* before being launched 9.4.1887.
c) Battleship, 14,150 tons, was laid down at Pembroke Dock but renamed *Empress of India* before being launched 7.5.1891.
d) Battleship, 25,750 tons, was laid down by Vickers Armstrong, Barrow, but renamed *Revenge* before being launched 29.5.1915.

REPULSE

A ''Resolution'' class nuclear powered ballistic missile submarine (SSBN), 7,600 tons (surfaced), 8,500 tons (submerged). Built by Vickers, Barrow-in-Furness. Launched 4.11.1967. Sixteen tubes amidships for Polaris ICBM's. 6 x 21" TT.

Description of Badge

Field:- Blue.
Badge:- A castle gold, on which flies the Union Flag, proper, on two wavelets silver.

Motto

Qui tangit frangatur — Who touches me is broken.

Battle Honours

Cadiz	1596	Atlantic	1940
Martinique	1762	Norway	1940
The Saints	1782	Bismarck	1941

Previous ships of the name

1. Galleon, 622 bm, 50 guns. Built at Deptford in 1595. 1596 In attack on Cadiz. 1610 Rebuilt as 764 bm. Listed until 1645.

2. French fifth rate *Bellone*, 676 bm, 32 guns. Captured by *Vestal* on 21.2.1759. 12.1776 Foundered off Bermuda, with the loss of all her crew.

3. Third rate, 1,387 bm, 64 guns. Built by Fabian, East Cowes. Launched 28.11.1780. 9.3.1800 Struck on a sunken rock about 75 miles SW of Ushant. Becoming a total wreck, she had to be abandoned. Ship's company made prisoners, except 4 officers and 8 men who reached Guernsey in a boat.

4. Third rate, 1,727 bm, 74 guns. Built by Barnard, Deptford. Launched 22.7.1803. 1805 Captured Spanish treasure ship. 1809 Fought in capture of Walcheren Island. 1814 Paid off. 9.1820 Broken up.

5. Second rate, steam, 3,087 bm, 91 guns. Built at Pembroke Dock. Launched 27.9.1855. 7.12.1855 Renamed *Victor Emmanuel*. 1873 Became a Receiving Ship. 1899 Sold out of the service.

6. Ironclad, 6,190 tons, 12 x 8" guns. Building began in Woolwich and completed in Sheerness Dockyard. Converted from a 90 guns two-decker to the last wooden-hulled British battleship. Launched 25.4.1868. Only British armoured ship to round Cape Horn under canvas. 1870-2 Guardship at Queensferry. 1872-7 Flagship in the Pacific. 1877-80 Refitting. 1881-5 Guardship at Hull. 1885 In Reserve. 1889 Broken up. The last of the wooden battleships to be so treated.

7. ''Royal Sovereign'' class battleship, 14,150 tons, 4 x 13.5" and 10 x 6" guns; 7 x 18" TT. Built at Pembroke Dock. Launched 27.2.1892. In the Channel and Mediterranean Fleets until 1902, then Home Fleet. 11.7.1911 Sold to T.W. Ward, Morecambe for breaking up.

8. ''Renown'' class battlecruiser, 28,000 tons, 6 x 15", 17 x 4" and 2 x 3" AA guns, 2 x 21" TT. Built by J. Brown, Clydebank. Launched 8.1.1916. 1916-9 Grand Fleet. 17.11.1917 In action with German light forces in the North Sea. 1919-22 Modifications. 1922 Atlantic Fleet. 1923-4 Round the world voyage with *Hood* and the 1st LCS. 1925 Tour with the Prince of Wales to South Africa and South America. 1926-32 Atlantic Fleet. 1934-6 Reconstruction. 1936-8 In Mediterranean. 1938-9 Under refit, then Home Fleet. 1939 Escort to Atlantic convoys. 1940 Norwegian campaign. 10.1941 Transferred to the East Indies, with *Prince of Wales*. 10.12.1941 Sunk by Japanese air attack off east coast of Malaya while en route, with *Prince of Wales*, to attack an enemy force off Kota Bharu.

Footnote
a) Cutter, 136 bm, 10 guns, was purchased in 1779 and listed until 1781.
b) Cutter, 136 bm, 12 guns, was purchased in 3.1780, but was wrecked off Yarmouth in 3.1782.
c) Gunvessel, 54 bm, 4 guns, was purchased in 3.1794 and listed until 1796.

RESOLUTION

Name ship of the class of nuclear powered ballistic missile submarine (SSBN), 7,600 tons (surfaced), 8,500 tons (submerged). Built by Vickers, Barrow-in-Furness. Launched 15.9.1966. Sixteen tubes amidships for Polaris ICBM's. 6 x 21" TT.

Description of Badge

Field:- Red.
Badge:- A mounted knight in tilting armour with lance in rest, all gold.

Motto

Resolute and Vigilant.

Battle Honours

Kentish Knock	1652	Barfleur	1692
Gabbard	1653	Quiberon Bay	1759
Scheveningen	1653	St Vincent	1780
Lowestoft	1665	St Kitts	1782
Orfordness	1666	The Saints	1782
Sole Bay	1672	Basque Roads	1809
Schooneveld	1673	Atlantic	1939-40
Texel	1673	Norway	1940

Previous ships of the name

1. Third rate *Prince Royal*, 890 bm, 64 guns. Built in Woolwich Dockyard. Launched 25.9.1610. 1641 Rebuilt at Woolwich as 1,187 bm. 1650-60 Named *Resolution*. 13.6.1666 Burnt by the Dutch when aground on the Galloper.

2. Third rate *Tredagh* (or *Drogheda*), 771 bm, 60 guns. Built by Ratcliffe in 1654. 1660 Renamed *Resolution*. 25.7.1666 Burnt in action with the Dutch.

3. Third rate, 885 bm, 70 guns. Built by Deane, Harwich. Launched 6.12.1667. 1698 Rebuilt at Chatham. 27.11.1703 Foundered on the Sussex coast.

4. Third rate, 1,103 bm, 70 guns. Built in Woolwich Dockyard. Launched 15.3.1705. 21.3.1707 Ran ashore to avoid capture by the French at Ventiglia.

5. Third rate, 1,118 bm, 70 guns. Built in Deptford Dockyard. Launched 25.3.1708. 10.1.1711 Wrecked near Barcelona.

6. Third rate, 1,569 bm, 74 guns. Built by Bird, Northam. Launched 14.12.1758. Admiral Hawke's flagship at Battle of Quiberon Bay but lost the next day. 20/21.11.1759 Wrecked in Quiberon Bay.

7. Third rate, 1,612 bm, 74 guns. Built in Deptford Dockyard. Launched 12.4.1770. 3.1813 Broken up at Portsmouth.

8. Ex-*Marquis of Granby*, 461 bm, 10 guns. Purchased in 11.1771 for service as a sloop; entered into the RN as *Drake*; renamed *Resolution*. Captain Cook's command on his second voyage (1772-5) and third voyage (1776-9). 12.1780 Fitted as Armed Transport. 9.6.1782 Taken by the French, under Admiral Suffren, off the coast of Coromandel, India.

9. Cutter, 200 bm, 14 guns. Purchased 6.1779. 6.1797 Foundered in the North Sea.

10. "Royal Sovereign" class battleship, 14,150 tons, 4 x 13.5" and 10 x 6" guns; 7 x 18" TT. Built by Palmer, Jarrow-on-Tyne. Launched 28.5.1892. In Channel and Mediterranean Fleets until 1902 then in Home Waters. 2.4.1914 Sold; broken up in Holland.

11. "Revenge" class battleship, 28,000 tons, 8 x 15", 14 x 6" and 2 x 3" guns; 4 x 21" TT. Built by Palmer, Jarrow-on-Tyne. Launched 14.1.1915. 1943 With *Revenge* formed *Imperieuse*, Stokers' Training Establishment. 5.5.1948 Sold; broken up by Metal Industries, Faslane.

Footnote

There were two other *Resolutions*—a lugger hired 1795-1801; and a cutter hired 1807-14.

REVENGE

A "Resolution" class nuclear powered ballistic missile submarine (SSBN); 7,600 tons (surfaced), 8,500 tons (submerged). Built by Cammell Laird, Birkenhead. Launched 15.3.1968. Sixteen tubes amidships for Polaris ICBM's. 6 x 21" TT.

Description of Badge

Field:- Blue.
Badge:- A gryphon gold rising out of three wavelets silver.

(Derived from the Crest of Sir Richard Grenville, (1541-1591), who was killed in an earlier *Revenge*).

Motto

Intaminatis fulget honoribus — Shines with untarnished honour.

Battle Honours

Armada	1588	Quiberon Bay	1759
Azores	1591	Trafalgar	1805
Lowestoft	1665	Basque Roads	1809
Four Days' Battle	1666	Syria	1840
Orfordness	1666	Belgian Coast	1914-5
Bugia	1671	Jutland	1916
Schooneveld	1673	Atlantic	1939-41
Marbella	1705	English Channel	1940
Orphee	1758		

Previous ships of the name

1. Galleon, 580 bm, 46 guns. Built at Deptford. Launched in 10.1577. 1588 Drake's flagship in the action with Spanish Armada. 1591 Off Azores, famous last fight of Sir Richard Grenville's *Revenge*. 5.9.1591 Foundered.

2. Ship, 457 bm, 42 guns. Merchant ship purchased by Royalists in 1650. 1652 Deserted to Parliament and renamed *Marmaduke*. 6.1667 Sunk as a blockship in the Medway.

HMS *Revenge* (May 1934).

3. Ship *Newbury*, 766 bm, 52 guns. Built by Graves, Limehouse. Launched in 4.1654. 1660 Renamed *Revenge*. 1678 Condemned.

4. Third rate, 1,065 bm, 70 guns. Built by Miller, Deptford, in 1699. 16.6.1711 Renamed *Buckingham*. 2.1727 Reduced to a Hulk. 5.1745 Sunk as a foundation.

5. Third rate, *Swiftsure*, 978 bm, 70 guns. Built by Deane, Harwich. Launched 8.4.1673. 1696 Rebuilt at Deptford as 987 bm. 2.1.1716 Renamed *Revenge*, 64 guns. 1742 Rebuilt at Deptford as 1,258 bm. 24.5.1787 Sold out of the service.

6. Brig-sloop, 14 guns, of 1778. 1779 Captured by the Americans.

7. Third rate, 1,954 bm, 74 guns. Built in Chatham Dockyard. Launched 13.4.1805. Fought nobly at Trafalgar. 10.1849 Broken up.

8. Second rate, steam, 5,260 tons, 91 guns. Built at Pembroke Dock. Launched 16.4.1859. 8.1872 Base Ship. 3.1890 Renamed *Empress*, Training Ship. 31.12.1923 Sold; broken up at Appledore.

9. "Royal Sovereign" class battleship, 14,150 tons, 4 x 13.5" and 10 x 6" guns; 7 x 18" TT. Built by Palmer, Jarrow-on-Tyne. Launched 3.11.1892. 1906 Gunnery Training Ship. 2.8.1915 Renamed *Redoubtable*, bombarding ship on Belgian coast. 1918 Tender to *Victory*. 6.11.1919 Sold to T.W. Ward; broken up at Appledore.

10. Name ship of the class of battleships, 28,000 tons, 8 x 15", 14 x 6" and 2 x 3" guns; 4 x 21" TT. Laid down by Vickers Armstrong, Barrow, as *Renown*. 22.10.1913 Renamed *Revenge*. Launched 29.5.1915. 1916 1st BS at Jutland. 1917-8 Served in northern waters. 1939 Convoy duty in Atlantic. 1940 Bombardment of Cherbourg. 1942 Eastern Fleet. 1943 With *Resolution* formed *Imperieuse*, Stokers' Training Establishment. 5.9.1948 Arrived Inverkeithing to be broken up by T.W. Ward.

Footnote

a) Indian sixth rate, 420 bm; 28 guns. Built in Bombay Dockyard. Launched 22.9.1755. 19.4.1782 Foundered in the Indian Ocean.

b) Cutter, 8 guns, was purchased in 1796. Listed until 1798.

HMS *Revenge* (August 1977).

RIBBLE

A "River" class Fleet Minesweeper, 890 tons (full load); 1 x 40mm gun. Built by Richards, Great Yarmouth. Launched 7.5.1985. Allocated to Mersey Division, RNR.

Description of Badge

Field:- Argent.
Badge:- In front of a triangle paly wavy of eight, azure and argent, a pascal lamb couchant or.

Motto

Battle Honours

Dardanelles   1915-6

Previous ships of the name

1. Destroyer, 590 tons, 1 x 12 pdr and 5 x 6 pdr guns; 2 TT. Built by Yarrow, Poplar. Launched 19.3.1904. 1904 Based at Felixstowe. 1905-6 At Portland. 1907 Channel Fleet. 1910 1st DF, Home Fleet; then the 3rd Flotilla. 1911 Went to China to relieve *Handy*. After capture of Tsing-tao, went to the Dardanelles. Remained in the Mediterranean for the rest of the War. 1919 Sales list. 29.7.1920 Sold to T.W. Ward, Preston, for breaking up.

2. "River" class frigate, 1,375 tons, 2 x 4" and 10 x 20mm AA guns. Built by W. Simons, Renfrew. Launched 23.4.1943. 25.6.1943 Transferred to the Dutch Navy as *Johan Maurits van Nassau*. 15.1.1959 Sold to A. Goslar for breaking up.

3. "River" class frigate, 1,375 tons, 2 x 4" and 10 x 20mm AA guns. Laid down by Blyth Shipbuilding Company as *Duddon*. 6.1943 Renamed *Ribble*. Launched 10.11.1943. 24.7.1944 to 11.6.1945 Loaned to the Royal Canadian Navy. Not commissioned after the war. 9.7.1957 Arrived Blyth to be broken up by Hughes Bolckow.

Footnote
a) Trawler, 193 tons, built in 1904, was hired 1917-9.
b) Trawler, 197 tons, built in 1900, was hired as *Ribble II* from 1.1915 to 1919.

HMS *Ribble*

ROEBUCK

A Coastal Survey Vessel , 1,280 tons (full load). Built by Brooke Marine, Lowestoft. Launched 14.11.1985.

Description of Badge

Field:- White.
Badge:- A roebuck guardant proper.

Motto

Battle Honours

Armada	1588	Martinique	1794
Cadiz	1596	Egypt	1801
Gabbard	1653	China	1860
Portland	1653	Sabang	1944
Barfleur	1692	Burma	1944-5
Velez Malaga	1704		

Previous ships of the name

1. Hired ship, 300 bm, fought in the Armada campaign of 1588. In Drake's squadron which joined with Howard at Plymouth.

2. Hired ship, 104 bm. 1596 Was in Raleigh's squadron on Cadiz expedition.

3. Pinnace, 90 bm, 10 guns. Built by Phineas Pett at Woolwich. Launched 28.3.1637. 1648 In Royalist Squadron. 11.1649 Fell into the hands of Parliament at surrender of Kinsale. 1651 Unfit for further service.

4. Dutch prize, 30 guns, captured in 1652. 1653 Battles off Portland, the Gabbard and Texel. 1657 Sold.

HMS *Roebuck* (July 1960).

164

5. Sixth rate, 129 bm, 16 guns. Built at Harwich in 1666. 1666-7 Second Dutch War. 1672-4 Third Dutch War. 1683 Sold.

6. Fireship, 70 bm, 6 guns. Purchased in 1688. 26.8.1692 Sunk to secure a graving place at Portsmouth.

7. Fireship, 276 bm, 8 guns. Built by Ed. Snelgrove, Wapping. Launched 17.4.1690. 1695 Converted at Kinsale to a Fifth rate, 26 guns. 1699-1701 Under Captain William Dampier, made voyage to Australia and New Guinea. 24.2.1701 When homeward bound, sank off Ascension Island.

8. Fifth rate, 494 bm, 42 guns. Built in Portsmouth Dockyard. Launched 5.4.1704. 1705-13 Convoy and cruising duties. 1733 Rebuilt at Woolwich, as 598 bm. 4.1743 Sunk at Sheerness to form a breakwater.

9. Fifth rate, 708 bm, 44 guns. Built (or possibly rebuilt) at Southampton in 1743. 1743-8 In Wars against France and Spain. 1756-9 Service in Seven Years' War. 1761 Out of commission. 3.7.1764 Sold.

10. Fifth rate, 886 bm, 44 guns; Built in Chatham Dockyard. Launched 28.4.1774. 14.4.1781 With *Orpheus*, took USS *Confederancy*, 36 guns. 1798 Became a Storeship. 1806 Guard Ship. 1811 Taken to pieces.

11. ''Intrepid'' class Wood steam gunvessel, 865 tons, 1 x 110 pdr, 1 x 6 pdr and 4 x 20 pdr guns. Built by Scott Russell, Millwall. Launched 22.3.1856. 1860 Service in the Red Sea; Protecting local Christians at Jidda; and quelling a mutinous outbreak in the Andaman Islands. 1864 Sold to Castle, Charlton, for breaking up.

12. Destroyer, 360 tons, 1 x 12 pdr and 5 x 6 pdr guns; 2 TT. Built by Hawthorn Leslie, Hebburn-on-Tyne. Launched 4.1.1901. 1902-4 At Chatham. 1904 In Reserve at Sheerness. 1907 Home Fleet at Devonport. 1909 5th DF, Home Fleet. 1911 4th DF, Home Fleet. 1912 At Dartmouth for instruction of Cadets. 1914-8 Local Defence Flotilla, Devonport. 1919 Broken up at Portsmouth.

13. ''R'' class destroyer, 1,705 tons, 4 x 4.7", 4 x 2 pdr pom-poms, 8 x 20mm AA guns; 8 x 21" TT. Built by Scotts, Greenock. Launched 10.12.1942. Was actually launched by a bomb and lay submerged for 9 months. 1944-5 Far East. 4.1946 to 2.1951 Air Training Target Vessel, Plymouth Command. 1951-3 Converted to Type 15 frigate at Devonport. 1953-6 Fifth FS in the Mediterranean. 11.1957 To Dartmouth Training Squadron. 1962 Reserve at Devonport. 1968 Used at Rosyth in underwater explosion trials. 8.8.1968 Arrived Inverkeithing to be broken up.

Footnote
a) Packet Vessel, 1791-6.
b) Revenue Cutter, 1793-1814.
c) Vessel of 776 tons built in 1925, was hired as a Barrage Balloon Vessel from 22.10.1940 to 10.10.1945. Renamed *Roebuck II* from 1942.

HMS *Roebuck* (1986).

ROTHESAY

Name ship of the class of Type 12 anti-submarine frigates, 2,380 tons (standard), 2,800 tons (full load). Built by Yarrow, Scotstoun, Glasgow. Launched 9.12.1957. One Limbo A/S weapon; 2 x 4.5" and 2 x 40mm AA guns (later replaced by Sea Cat SAM system); 1 helicopter.

Description of Badge

Field:- Blue.
Badge:- A triple towered castle white, upon the dexter tower a crescent, and upon the sinister tower a mullet gold.
(Derived from the Arms of the Corporation of Rothesay).

Motto

Battle Honours

English Channel	1942	Salerno	1943
North Africa	1942-3	Anzio	1944
Sicily	1943	South France	1944

Previous ships of the name

1. ''Bangor'' class turbine minesweeper, 656 tons, 1 x 3" gun. Built by White, Hamilton. Launched 18.3.1941. Her Battle Honours display the extent of her war service in the English Channel and Mediterranean. 4.1950 Broken up by T.W. Ward, Milford Haven.

HMS *Rothesay*

SANDPIPER

A "Bird" class Patrol Boat, 194 tons (full load); 1 x 40mm gun. Built by R. Dunston, Hessle, Humberside. Launched 20.1.1977.

Description of Badge

Field:- White.
Badge:- A sandpiper on a rock, all proper.

Motto

Vivaciter vigilans — Vivaciously watchful.

Battle Honours

None.

Previous ships of the name

1. Shallow draught River Gunboat, 85 tons, 2 x 6 pdr guns. Built by Yarrow, Poplar. Launched 2.7.1897. One of the first real purpose-built river gunboats in the RN as opposed to makeshifts and conversions. Shipped in crates and re-assembled in Hong Kong. Spent all her service on the China Station. 18.10.1920 Sold at Hong Kong.

2. River Gunboat, 185 tons, 1 x 3.7" howitzer. Built by Thornycroft, Woolston, Southampton. Launched in 6.1933. Specially designed to operate on the Si-kiang in Hunan Province, and based at Changsha. Crated and transported to Hong Kong. Also spent all her days on the China Station. 2.1942 Presented to Nationalist China; renamed *Ying Hao* (in English *British Hero*); later taken over by the Republicans.

HMS *Sandpiper*

SCEPTRE

A ''Swiftsure'' class nuclear powered Fleet Submarine, 4,400 tons (surfaced), 4,900 tons (submerged); 5 x 21" TT. Built by Vickers, Barrow-in-Furness. Launched 20.11.1976.

Description of Badge

Field:- Blue.
Badge:- In front of two tridents in saltire gold, a sceptre also gold.

Motto

Honour with authority.

Battle Honours

Trincomalee	1782	Norway	1944
Cape of Good Hope		Atlantic	1944
	1795	Biscay	1944
Guadeloupe	1810		

Previous ships of the name

1. Third rate, 1,398 bm, 64 guns. Built at Deptford. Launched 8.6.1781. Saw much action. 5.12.1799 Wrecked in Table Bay with loss of nearly 300 lives.

2. Third rate, 1,727 bm, 74 guns. Built by Dudman, Deptford. Launched 11.12.1802. 1812-4 Involved in the War against the USA, in a blockade role. 2.1821 Broken up.

3. An Emergency War Programme ''R'' class destroyer, 1,065 tons, 3 x 4" guns; 4 TT. Built by Stephen, Linthouse, Glasgow. Launched 18.4.1917. Used almost exclusively for convoy protection. 15.10.1919 Reduced complement at Devonport. 1924 Reserve Fleet at Devonport. 16.12.1926 Sold to T.W. Ward, Briton Ferry, for breaking up.

4. An ''S'' class submarine, 715 tons (surfaced), 1,000 tons (submerged), 1 x 3" gun; 7 x 21" TT. Built by Scotts, Greenock. Launched 9.1.1943. During her short wartime career, she completed 11 operational patrols. Three were 'special operations' involving midget submarine 'X' craft which were launched against the *Tirpitz*; and other high value targets in Norwegian fjords. Sank a total of 4 merchant ships and 2 escorts, aggregating 15,800 tons. After the war, she was used for training purposes. 8.8.1949 Damaged by an explosion, became partially flooded and filled with chlorine gas. 9.1949 Sold to J.J. King; broken up at Gateshead.

HMS *Sceptre* (January 1981).

SCYLLA

A Batch Three "Leander" class (broad-beamed) frigate; 2,500 tons (standard). Built in Devonport Dockyard. Launched 8.8.1968. 1980-4 Exocet conversion at Devonport. New armament:- Exocet SSM and Sea Wolf SAM systems; A/S torpedo tubes; 2 x 20mm guns; 1 helicopter.

Description of Badge

Field:- Blue.
Badge:- A representation of Scylla, white crined, finned and tailed gold.

Motto

Clara saevitia — Of famous savagery.

Battle Honours

Weser	1813	Atlantic	1943
North Africa	1942	Biscay	1943
Arctic	1942-5	Normandy	1944
Salerno	1943		

Previous ships of the name

1. "Cruizer" class brig-sloop, 385 bm, 18 guns. Built by Davy, Topsham. Launched 29.6.1809. Saw active service off Isle of Batz and, off Ushant in 1813, was engaged in fierce battle with French frigate *Weser*. 1.1846 Broken up.

2. Wood steam corvette, 1,467 bm, 20 x 8" guns. Built in Sheerness Dockyard. Launched 19.6.1856. 1882 Sold out of the service.

3. Cruiser, 3,400 tons, 2 x 6" and 6 x 4.7" guns. Built by Samuda, Poplar. Launched 17.10.1891. 1896 Mediterranean Fleet. Under the command of Captain Percy M. Scott, 'father' of modern gunnery, she acquired the reputation of being the finest gunnery ship in the Mediterranean. 1899 At Sheerness. 5.6.1902 Commissioned to convey a relief crew to *Tribune* on North America and West Indies Station. 23.9.1903 Commissioned at Chatham for special service. Afterwards paid off into Reserve. 24.1.1905 Commissioned for duties with Newfoundland Fisheries. 14.5.1907 Attached to 4th Cruiser Squadron. 1912 Sales list at Chatham. 2.4.1914 Sold out of the service.

4. "Dido' class cruiser, 5,450 tons, 8 x 4.5" HA guns. Built by Scotts, Greenock. Launched 24.7.1940. 8.1942 Flagship of Rear Admiral Burnett for Russian Convoy 'PQ 18'. 16.9.1942 With 'PQ 14'. Flag was transferred when *Scylla* was sent to Iceland to land survivors. 6.11.1942 Operation 'Torch'. 1.12.1942 Joined 12th CS on its formation. 1.1.1943 Sank blockade runner *Rhakotis*, making for Bordeaux. 1943 Russian convoys, then patrols in the Bay of Biscay. 8.1943 Near miss by a bomb which was later to cause severe vibration at speed. 16.10.1943 Sailed from Devonport to Chatham for conversion to Escort Carrier Flagship. 4.1944 10th CS at Scapa Flow. 6.1944 Flagship of Rear Admiral Sir Philip Vian, Commander Eastern Task Force at Normandy landings. 23.6.1944 Set off an acoustic mine. Keel crushed over length of Boiler and Engine Rooms. Lost power. Towed to Chatham and paid off. Three and a half year refit planned but not carried out. 1948 Towed to the Gareloch. Used for ship target trials. 12.4.1950 Sold and broken up by T.W. Ward, Barrow.

SEALION

A ''Porpoise'' class Patrol Submarine, 1,610 tons (surfaced), 2,410 tons (submerged); 8 x 21"
TT. Built by Cammell Laird, Birkenhead. Launched 31.12.1959.

Description of Badge

Field:- Green.
Badge:- A sealion gold.

Motto

Sicut leones — Be like the lions.

Battle Honours

North Sea	1940	Arctic	1941-2
Norway	1940-1		

Previous ships of the name

1. ''S'' class submarine, 670 tons (surfaced) 960 tons (submerged), 1 x 3" and 1 x 20mm AA guns; 6 x 21" TT.; and one external. Built by Cammell Laird, Birkenhead. Launched 16.3.1934. 1939-40 Served with Distinction in the Mediterranean and Norwegian campaigns. 11.4.1940 Penetrated into the Kattegat and sank the German transport *August Leonhardt*. 1941 Service included three months operating from Polyarno in North Russia. 1943 Became Submarine Commanding Officers' training ship until 10.1943 when she was in collision with destroyer *Skate*. 3.3.1945 Sunk off Isle of Arran in Firth of Clyde for use as a sonar target.

Footnote
Trawler, 231 tons, built in 1902, was hired 1914-9.

HMS *Sealion*, in Russian waters.

SENTINEL

The former Oil Rig Support Vessel *Seaforth Warrior*; built in 1975 by Husumwerft, Husum. Purchased from Seaforth Marine for conversion by Tyne Ship Repair Company to a Falkland Islands Patrol Vessel; 1,710 tons (standard); 2 x 40mm guns. Commissioned into the RN 14.1.1984.

Description of Badge

Field:- Black.
Badge:- The heads of Cerberus couped at the neck, gold.
(Cerberus was the watchdog of Hades).

Motto

Battle Honours

None.

Previous ships of the name

1. Gun-brig, ex-*Friendship*, 194 bm; 10 x 18 pdr and 2 x 9 pdr guns. Purchased in 7.1804. 10.10.1812 Wrecked on Rugen Island, Baltic.

2. Name ship of class of Scout Cruisers, ex-*Inchkeith*, 2,895 tons, 10 x 12 pdr and 8 x 3 pdr guns. Built by Vickers, Sons and Maxim, Barrow. 1903 Renamed *Sentinel*. Launched 19.4.1904. 1907-14 Attached to the Home Fleet Destroyer Flotillas. 1914 6th DF at Dover. 1914-5 8th DF in the Forth. 1915 6th LCS guarding the East Coast. 1915-8 In Mediterranean. 18.1.1923 Sold to Young. 20.6.1923 Arrived Sunderland, after stranding en route.

3. ''S'' class submarine, 715 tons (surfaced), 1,000 tons (submerged), 1 x 3'' and 1 x 20mm AA gun; 6 x 21'' TT and one external. Built by Scotts, Greenock. Launched 27.7.1945. 1951 In Mediterranean. 15.6.1953 Coronation Review at Spithead. 1.1959 Recommissioned at Chatham for the Portland Squadron. 1961 Paid off. 28.2.1962 Sold; to be broken up at Gillingham.

Footnote
Destroyer, 1,710 tons, 4 x 4.7'' and 2 x 40mm guns; 8 TT. Laid down by Cammell Laird, Birkenhead as *Sentinel* but renamed *Scorpion* in 1942 before her launch on 26.8.1942. 1.10.1945 Sold to the Netherlands Navy as *Kortenaer*. 1958-9 Converted to a Fast Frigate at Rijkswerf Willemsoord. 15.10.1959 Commissioned after conversion. 12.1962 Disposal List.

HMS *Sentinel* (March 1959).

SHEFFIELD

A Batch Two "Broadsword" class, Type 22, frigate; 4,100 tons (standard), 4,800 tons (full load). Built by Swan Hunter's Neptune Yard on the Tyne. Exocet SSM and Sea Wolf SAM systems; 2 x 40mm and 4 x 20mm guns; 6 TT; 1 helicopter (ability to carry 2); helicopter-carried A/S torpedoes. Launched 26.3.1986.

Description of Badge

Field:- Blue.
Badge:- Eight arrows interlaced, silver feathered and pointed gold.
(Derived from the Arms and Motto of the City of Sheffield).

Motto

Deo adjuvante proficio — With God's help I advance.

Battle Honours

Norway	1940	North Africa	1942
Spartivento	1940	Barents Sea	1942
Bismarck	1941	Biscay	1943
Mediterranean	1941	Salerno	1943
Malta Convoys	1941	North Cape	1943
Atlantic	1941-3	Falkland Islands	1982
Arctic	1941-3		

Previous ships of the name

1. Cruiser from the first group of "Southampton" class, 9,100 tons, 9 x 6" and 8 x 4" AA guns; 6 x 21" TT. Built by Vickers Armstrong, Tyne. Launched 23.7.1936. 8.1937 2nd CS, Home Fleet. 4.1940 Operations off Norway. 8.1940 In Mediterranean; Malta Convoys and operations against the Italian Fleet. 26.5.1941 Intercepted and shadowed German battleship *Bismarck*. 12.6.1941 Forced German tanker *Friedrich Breme* to scuttle herself. 11.1941 Joined Home Fleet. 5.3.1942 Damaged by mine. Escorted convoys to Russia and North Africa. 31.12.1942 Sank German destroyer *Friedrich Eckholdt*. 26.12.1943 Took part in the sinking of German battlecruiser *Scharnhorst* off North Cape. 7.1944 to 5.1946 Refitted in USA; completed at Portsmouth. 8.6.1960 Became Flagship of Reserve Fleet at Portsmouth. 9.1964 Placed on Disposal List. 6.1.1967 Towed from Portsmouth to Rosyth to be de-equipped. 18.9.1967 Towed from Rosyth to Faslane to be broken up.

2. "Town" class Type 42 Guided Missile destroyer, 3,500 tons, 1 x 4.5." and 2 x 20mm Oerlikons; Twin Sea Dart missile launcher. Built by Vickers, Barrow-in-Furness. Launched by HM the Queen 10.6.1971. 16.2.1975 Commissioned for 3 year period of trials. 1977 Silver Jubilee Fleet Review at Spithead. 1978 Attended International Defence Exhibition at Rotterdam. 1979-80 18 months refit. 1981 Five months' Gulf Patrol. 1982 Falklands Task force. 4.5.1982 Hit by Exocet missile fired by Argentine aircraft. It did not explode, but the ensuing fire and smoke spread rapidly throughout the ship. 9.5.1982 Taken in tow by *Yarmouth* to make for a safe anchorage off South Georgia. 10.5.1982 At 7 am, as the wind increased to gale force, she heeled over and sank.

SHETLAND

An ''Island'' class Offshore Patrol Vessel, 925 tons (standard), 1,250 tons (full load). Built by Hall Russell, Aberdeen. Launched 22.10.1976. 1 x 40mm gun. Able to carry a small RM Detachment.

Description of Badge

Field:- Paly of eight argent and gules.
Badge:- A Shetland pony rampant and sable.

Motto

Battle Honours

None.

Previous ships of the name

None.

HMS *Shetland* (1986).

SIRIUS

A Batch Two "Leander" class frigate, 2,450 tons (standard). Built in Portsmouth Dockyard. Launched 22.9.1964. 1975-7 Exocet conversion at Devonport. New armament:- Exocet SSM and Sea Cat SAM systems; 2 x 40mm guns; 6 TT; 1 helicopter; Towed Array sonar system.

Description of Badge

Field:- Blue.

Badge:- In front of a five-pointed estoile white, a mullet gold.

(Derived from the star called Sirius—the dog star—the brightest star in the heavens, which also appears on the City of Portsmouth's Coat of Arms).

Motto

Heaven's light our guide.

Battle Honours

Trafalgar	1805	North Africa	1942-3
Belgian Coast	1914	Sicily	1943
Zeebrugge	1918	Salerno	1943
Arctic	1942	Aegean	1943-4
Malta Convoys	1942	Normandy	1944
Mediterranean	1942	South France	1944

Previous ships of the name

1. Storeship *Berwick*, 512 bm, 22 guns. Purchased in 11.1781. 10.1786 Renamed *Sirius* and converted to a Sixth rate. Conveyed to Botany Bay, Governor Arthur Phillip for the foundation of New South Wales. 15.3.1790 Wrecked on Norfolk Island in the Pacific.

2. Fifth rate, 1,049 bm, 36 guns. Built by Dudman, Deptford. Launched 12.4.1797. 24.10.1798 Captured 2 Dutch frigates off the Texel. 1801 Participated in capture of French ship off Portugal. 1805 One of only 4 frigates to fight at Trafalgar. 1809-10 Involved in capture of Reunion Island. 24.8.1810 In operations against Mauritius, she was destroyed to prevent her falling into French hands.

3. Fifth rate, 1,090 bm, 38 guns. Built by Tyson and Blake, Bursledon—the last ship built there. Launched 11.9.1813. 7.1860 Became Gunnery Target ship. 23.9.1862 Breaking up completed at Portsmouth.

4. "Eclipse" class wood steam sloop, 1,760 tons, 2 x 7" guns. Built in Portsmouth Dockyard. Launched 24.4.1868. 1868-78 Saw service off West Coast of Africa and Cape of Good Hope, North America and the West Indies; and at Blockade of Dahomey. 1885 Sold to Castle, Charlton, for breaking up.

5. Cruiser, 3,600 tons, 2 x 6" and 6 x 4.7" guns. Built by Armstrong Mitchell, Walker-on-Tyne. Launched 27.10.1890. 5.4.1892 Commissioned at Devonport for SO's ship on South East Coast of America. 8.1895 Paid off at Devonport. 9.11.1897 Commissioned at Devonport for Particular Service. 1899-1903 At Devonport. 17.3.1903 Commissioned for China Station. 10.1905 To Reserve at Devonport. 1910-11 At Haulbowline. 1.2.1912 Recommissioned at Devonport for Training Squadron at Chatham. Late 1912 Paid off. 27.1.1913 Commissioned to convey relief crews to *Odin* and *Alert* at Muscat. 17.10.1914 Commissioned for war service. Took part in Rear Admiral Hood's bombardment of the Belgian Coast and saw service in the Cameroons. 23.4.1918 Sunk as blockship at Ostend.

6. "Dido" class cruiser, 5,785 tons, 10 x 5.25" guns. Built in Portsmouth Dockyard. Launched 18.9.1940. 8.1942 'Pedestal' convoy to Malta. 9 to 10.1942 Anti-blockade runner patrols around South Africa. 11.1942 Invasion of North Africa. 2.12.1942 With *Argonaut* and others, sank 4 supply ships and a destroyer off Skerki Bank. Early 1943 operating in area Algiers—Bone. 10.7.1943 Invasion of Sicily. 18.9.1943 Near miss by bombs caused bad shock damage to electrical equipment and loss of power. 17.10.1943 Off Scarpanto, hit by 250kg bomb on the quarter deck. 10.1943 to 2.1944 under repair at Massawa. 6.1944 Off Normandy. Provided AA cover while *Frobisher* bombarded. 15.8.1944 Landings in South France. 13.9.1944 Joined French units for ceremonial re-entry into Toulon. 11.1944 to 4.1946 Operating in Eastern Mediterranean. 11.1947 to 8.1948 Laid up at Portsmouth due to manpower shortage. 5.1949 Reduced to Reserve at Portsmouth. 15.10.1956 Arrived Blyth to be broken up by Hughes Bolckow.

SMITER

A P2000 Coastal Training Craft of 43 tonnes for the RNR being built of GRP by Watercraft Ltd, Shoreham-by-Sea. Allocated to Clyde Division, RNR.

Description of Badge

Field:- Blue.
Badge:- Four swords saltirewise proper, pommels and hilts gold, interlaced by a club, head downwards, white.

Motto

Perentimus crebro — We strike hard and often.

Battle Honours

Atlantic   1944

Previous ships of the name

1. Escort Carrier, 11,420 tons, 2 x 4" AA, 16 x 40mm AA and 20 x 20mm AA guns; 24 aircraft. Ex-USS *Vermillion*. Built by Seattle-Tacoma S.B. Corporation, Tacoma, USA. Launched 27.9.1943. Converted at Willamette Iron and Steel Corporation, Portland, Oregon, USA. 20.1.1944 Transferred to RN on Lend-Lease. 6.4.1946 Returned to USN. 1948 Sold to Emprese Lineas Argentinas of Argentine; renamed *Artillero*. 1955 To Phillipine President Line; renamed *President Garcia*. 7.1967 On passage Manila to Rotterdam, grounded in Saints' Bay, Guernsey. Refloated with great difficulty, and towed to Rotterdam.

2. LST (3) 3514, 2,256 tons, 4 x 40mm and 6 x 20mm guns. Built by Yarrow, Esquimault. Launched 7.10.1944. 1947 Renamed *Smiter*. 3.1949 Sold out of the service. 25.4.1949 Wrecked when in tow off the coast of Portugal.

SOUTHAMPTON

A Batch Two, "Town" class, Type 42, Guided Missile Destroyer, 3,800 tons (standard), 4,250 tons (full load). Built by Vosper Thornycroft, Woolston, Southampton. Launched 29.1.1979. Sea Dart SAM system; 1 x 4.5"; 2 x 20mm Oerlikons; helicopter-launched Sea Skua missiles; 6 TT; 1 helicopter.

Description of Badge

Field:- White.
Badge:- A figure of Justice crowned, holding sword in right hand, scales in left, all proper, arising out of a castle gold.
(Derived from the Arms of the City of Southampton).

Motto

Pro justitia pro rege — For Justice and the King.

Battle Honours

Emeraude	1757	Dogger Bank	1915
Belle Ile	1761	Jutland	1916
First of June	1794	Norway	1940
St Vincent	1797	Spartivento	1940
Heligoland	1914	Malta Convoys	1941

Previous ships of the name

1. Fourth rate, 609 bm, 48 guns. Built by Parker and White, Southampton. Launched 10.6.1693. 1700 Rebuilt at Deptford as 636 bm. 5.1728 Reduced to a Hulk at Jamaica. 1771 Broken up.

2. Fifth rate, 671 bm, 32 guns. Built by Inwood, Rotherhithe. Launched 5.5.1757. Thought to be the first true frigate ever built. 27.11.1812 Wrecked near Concepcion Island in the Bahamas.

3. Fourth rate, 1,476 bm, 60 guns. Built in Deptford Dockyard. Launched 7.11.1820. Reduced to 52 guns before completion. Served throughout the world until 1857. 1857-67 At Sheerness. 18.6.1867 Lent to the Hull Committee as a Training Ship, until the School closed in 5.1912. 26.6.1912 Sold to Hughes Bolckow, Blyth, for breaking up.

4. "Chatham" class light cruiser, 5,400 tons, 8 x 6" and 4 x 3 pdr guns; 2 x 21" TT. Built by J. Brown, Clydebank. Launched 11.5.1912. 1912-3 1st Battle Squadron, Home Fleet. 1914-9 Grand Fleet. 28.8.1914 In action off Heligoland. 24.1.1915 Battle of Dogger Bank. 8/9.8.1915 In the hunt for, and destruction of, the German minelayer *Meteor*. 31.5.1916 Battle of Jutland; in the Battle, 75% of her upper deck personnel became casualties during a brief but fierce night action. Badly hit and on fire, she nonetheless managed to fire a torpedo which sank the leading German light cruiser *Frauenlob*. 10.1917 Scandinavian convoy escort. 1919-20 Flagship 7th LCS, South American Station. 1921-4 Flagship 4th LCS, East Indies Station. 1924-5 In Reserve. 13.7.1926 Sold to T.W. Ward, Pembroke Dock, for breaking up.

5. Name ship of the class of cruisers, 9,100 tons, 12 x 6" and 8 x 4" AA guns; 6 x 21" TT. Laid down as *Polyphemus*. 1936 Renamed *Southampton*. Built by J. Brown, Clydebank. Launched 10.3.1936. 6.3.1937 Flagship, 2nd CS, Home Fleet. 20.5.1937 Coronation Review at Spithead. 9.1938 At Scapa Flow for Munich crisis. 9.1939 With *Glasgow*, formed the Humber Force. 16.10.1939 Attacked by aircraft while at anchor in Firth of Forth. Hit by 1,000lb bomb which passed through 3 decks and out the ship's side. 9.4.1940 Suffered minor damage from aircraft off Norway. 27.5.1940 Supported landings at Narvik. 11.1940 With *Manchester*, conveyed troops to Malta. 27.11.1940 Battle of Cape Spartivento. 10.1.1941 During attacks by Ju 87s in Sicilian Narrows, was hit by 2 delayed action bombs. One burst in the main W/T office and caused extensive fire; 'Y' magazine was flooded. Other bomb hit port hangar and exploded on armoured deck above 'A' Boiler Room, forcing it to be evacuated. Caused loss of power and water supplies. Fires raged uncontrolled. Ship was abandoned and sunk by torpedoes—one from *Gloucester* and 4 from *Orion*.

SOVEREIGN

A "Swiftsure" class nuclear powered Fleet Submarine; 4,400 tons (surfaced), 4,900 tons (submerged); 5 x 21" TT. Built by Vickers, Barrow-in-Furness. Launched 17.2.1973.

Description of Badge

Field:- Red.
Badge:- The Royal Crest of England.

Motto

Battle Honours

Kentish Knock	1652	Texel	1673
Sole Bay	1672	Barfleur	1692
Schooneveld	1673		

Previous ships of the name

1. Ship, 800 bm, built in 1488. One of the first 'Royal' warships, also known as *Trinity Sovereign*. Saw action against the French off Brest. 1510 Rebuilt. Service ended in 1526.

2. First rate, *Sovereign of the Beas*, 1,141 bm, 100 guns. Built in Woolwich Dockyard. Launched 14.10.1637. Probably the first three-decker built in England. 1660 Rebuilt at Chatham as 1,545 bm. 1684 Again rebuilt as 1,683 bm; renamed *Royal Sovereign*. 27.1.1696 Burnt by accident at Chatham while preparing again to being rebuilt. The fire was caused by a candle having been carelessly left alight in the cook's cabin.

Footnote
Later ships were named *Royal Sovereign*:- First rate (1701-1768); First rate (1786-1841); Yacht (1804-1849); First rate (1857-1885); Battleship (1891-1913); and another Battleship (1915-1949).

HMS *Sovereign*

SPARTAN

A ''Swiftsure'' class nuclear powered Fleet Submarine, 4,400 tons (surfaced)' 4,900 tons (submerged); 5 x 21" TT. Built by Vickers, Barrow-in-Furness. Launched 7.4.1978.

Description of Badge

Field:- Blue.
Badge:- Two swan's wings conjoined white, charged with drops of red.

(Derived from the Crest of Admiral Brenton who as the Captain of *Spartan*, 3.5.1810, defeated single-handed a small enemy squadron in the Bay of Naples).

Motto

Courage with great endurance.

Battle Honours

Burma	1852-3	Mediterranean	1944
China	1856-7	Anzio	1944
Atlantic	1943	Falkland Islands	1982

Previous ships of the name

1. Fifth rate, 1,084 bm, 38 guns. Built by Ross, Rochester. Launched 16.8.1806. 3.5.1810 Triumphant in an heroic fight against 4 Neapolitan ships in the Bay of Naples. 4.1822 Broken up.

2. Sixth rate, 911 bm, 26 guns. Built in Devonport Dockyard. Launched 16.8.1841. 1841-5 North America and West Indies Station. 1846-9 During this commission, surveyed the Dead Sea. 1855 Senior Officer's ship in the Canton River. 1857 Returned to Devonport. 4.1862 Admiralty directed that she be used as a hulk by the contractors building the fort in Plymouth Sound. 19.5.1862 Sold to Messrs. Castle and Sons for breaking up.

3. Wood steam sloop, 1,755 tons, 2 x 7" and 4 x 64 pdr guns. Built in Deptford Dockyard. Launched 14.11.1868. 1871-5 North America and West Indies Station. 15.6.1876 Commissioned at Sheerness for East Indies. Mid-1880 Ordered Home to Devonport. Paid off, and afterwards laid up at Chatham. 7.11.1882 Sold to Messrs. Castle and Sons for breaking up.

4. Cruiser, 3,600 tons, 2 x 6" and 6 x 4.7" guns. Built by Armstrong Mitchell, Walker-on-Tyne. Launched 25.2.1891. 16.1.1894 Commissioned at Devonport for China Station. 1897 Paid off at Devonport. 10.6.1903 Commissioned as Drill Ship for RNR *Holyhead*. Harbour Service at Devonport from 1905. 8.1921 Renamed *Defiance*. 26.6.1931 Sold out of the service.

5. Modified ''Dido'' class cruiser, 5,900 tons, 8 x 5.25" guns. Built by Vickers Armstrong, Barrow. Launched 27.8.1942. 3.9.1943 10th CS, Home Fleet. 11.1943 Malta Command. 3.12.1943 At Taranto. 15.1.1944 With *Orion* and 5 destroyers, bombarded Gaeta, as a prelude to the assault on Anzio. 22.1.1944 Provided gunfire support at Anzio. 29.1.1944 At Anzio, hit abaft the after funnel by a glider bomb. Ship set on fire. Abandoned after 1 hour; sank soon afterwards. Survivors taken off by *Laforey* and *Loyal*.

Footnote

a) Fifth rate, 1,215 bm, 46 guns, was ordered from Portsmouth Dockyard in 1825 but cancelled in 1831.
b) Trawler, 120 tons, built in 1893, was hired for Harbour Service from 27.11.1914 to 1919.

SPEY

A "River" class Fleet Minesweeper, 890 tons (full load); 1 x 40mm gun. Built by Richards, Lowestoft. Launched 22.5.1985. Allocated to Forth Division, RNR.

Description of Badge

Field:- Party per fess blue and green, divided by wavelets gold.
Badge:- In chief, six pearls silver, beneath a salmon silver.

(Chief products of the River Spey appear to be salmon and pearls).

Motto

Mack sicker — Make sure

Battle Honours

North Africa	1942-3	Burma	1944-5
Atlantic	1942-4		

Previous ships of the name

1. Sixth rate, 463 bm, 20 guns. Built by Warwick, Eling. Launched 8.1.1814. 18.4.1822 Sold out of the service.

2. "Cherokee" class brig-sloop, 236 bm, 8 x 18 pdr and 2 x 6 pdr guns. Built at Pembroke Dock. Launched 8.10.1827. 1833 Used as a Packet Brig. 28.11.1840 Wrecked on Racoon Key, West Indies.

3. "Albacore" class wood steam gunboat, 232 bm, 1 x 68 pdr, 1 x 32 pdr and 2 x 20 pdr guns. Built by Pitcher, Northfleet. Launched 29.3.1856. Never used in service. 1864 Broken up.

4. "Medina" class Iron steam gunboat, 363 tons, 3 x 64 pdr guns. Built by Palmer, Jarrow-on-Tyne. Launched 5.10.1876. 1878-99 Portsmouth. 1900 At Sheerness. 1905 Became a diving tender. 1923 Sold out of the service.

5. "P" class Patrol Boat, *P 38*, 613 tons, 1 x 4" gun; 2 TT. Built by Wm. Hamilton, Port Glasgow. Launched 10.2.1917. 11.2.1925 Renamed *Spey*. 11.2.1925 Commissioned into the Fishery Protection Flotilla. 1.9.1936 Paid off into Dockyard control. 5.1938 Sold to T.W. Ward, Grays, for breaking up.

6. "River" class frigate, 1,375 tons, 2 x 4" and 10 x 20mm guns. Built at Smith's Dock, Middlesborough. Launched 18.12.1941. 11.7.1942 While escorting a convoy in the Atlantic assisted in the destruction of *U 136*. 18/19.2.1944 In 10th Support Group; sank *U 406* in Bay of Biscay. 1944-5 In East Indies Fleet. 1.1945 In attack on Ramree Island. 11.1948 Sold to Egyptian Navy, renamed *Rasheed*. Still listed in 1984 but believed to be unseaworthy.

SPLENDID

A ''Swiftsure'' class nuclear powered Fleet Submarine, 4,400 tons (surfaced), 4,900 tons (submerged); 5 x 21" TT. Built by Vickers, Barrow-in-Furness. Launched 5.10.1979.

Description of Badge

Field:- Black,
Badge:- A sun in splendour, rising out of wavelets green and silver.

Motto

Splendide audax — Splendidly audacious.

Battle Honours

Mediterranean   1942   Falkland Islands   1982

Previous ships of the name

1. A sloop was listed in 1597, but her fate is unknown.

2. ''S'' class destroyer, 1,075 tons, 3 x 4" guns; 4 x 21" TT. Built by Swan Hunter, Wallsend-on-Tyne. Launched 10.7.1918. 15.5.1920 Commissioned at Chatham. 22.7.1922 Recommissioned at Malta. 29.11.1923 Recommissioned at Chatham with reduced crew for the Mediterranean. 15.5.1926 Recommissioned at Gibraltar. 1928 Cruise to various ports in the Mediterranean was cut short when, on 17.9.1928, she ran aground on a sandbank 16 miles off Malaga. Returned to Gibraltar with twisted propeller blades. 24.11.1928 Recommissioned again at Gibraltar. 18.11.1930 Transferred to Dockyard control at Portsmouth. 8.1.1931 Sold to Metal Industries; broken up at Charlestown, Fife.

3. Improved ''S'' class submarine, ex-*P 228*, 715 tons (surfaced), 1,000 tons (submerged), 1 x 3" guns; 7 x 21" TT. Built in Chatham Dockyard. Launched 19.1.1942. 11.1942 During first patrol in the Mediterranean, she sank the supply ship *Luigi Favorita*. 18.12.1942 Sank Italian destroyer *Aviere*. 1.1943 Landed agents in Corsica. In her 6 mediterranean patrols, destroyed 35,000 tons of enemy shipping. 21.4.1943 Scuttled herself after damage inflicted by the German destroyer *Hermes* off Corsica. Her CO, First Lieutenant and 20 others were rescued.

HMS *Splendid*

STARLING

A "Peacock" class Patrol Vessel—for Hong Kong patrol duties—700 tons; 1 x 76mm gun. Built by Hall Russell, Abrdeen. Was formally named on 6.9.1983, but owing to adverse weather conditions was not floated out until the next day.

Description of Badge

Field:- Green.
Badge:- A starling grasping in its beak a worm, all proper.

Motto

Battle Honours

China	1841-2	Arctic	1944
Baltic	1855	Normandy	1944
China	1856-60	Atlantic	1943-5
Biscay	1943-4		

Previous ships of the name

1. Gun-brig, 184 bm, 16 guns. Built by H. Adams, Buckler's Hard. Launched 4.4.1801. 18.12.1804 Wrecked near Calais.

2. Gun-brig, 181 bm, 12 guns. Built by Rowe, Newcastle. Launched 5.1805. 29.9.1814 Sold out of the service.

3. Schooner, 108 bm, 4 guns. Built at Pembroke Dock. Launched 31.10.1829. 1834 Converted to Survey Vessel. 2.1844 Sold in China.

4. "Dapper" class, wood steam gunboat, 232 bm, 1 x 68 pdr and 2 x 24 pdr guns. Built by Pitcher, Northfleet. Launched 1.2.1855. 1855 In Baltic, including bombardment of Sveaborg. 1857 East Indies and China Stations. 25.6.1859 Damaged in abortive attack on the Taku Forts. 1.12.1871 Sold at Hong Kong.

5. "Banterer" class composite steam gunboat, 465 tons, 2 x 64 pdr and 2 x 20 pdr guns. Built by Samuda, Poplar. Launched 19.4.1882. 1882-4 Cape of Good Hope and West Coast of Africa Station. 1884-90 In the Mediterranean. 1890-1 In Reserve. 7.1.1887 Stranded on Daedalus Reef in the Red Sea, but towed off undamaged. 4.4.1905 Sold out of the service; renamed *Stella Maris*.

6. Tender, ex-war Department vessel *Miner 17*. Transferred in 1905. 26.11.1906 Renamed *Starling*. Attached to *Actaeon*, torpedo school ship at Sheerness. 14.9.1923 Sold to J. Round, Sunderland.

7. Sloop, 1,350 tons, 6 x 4" and 12 x 20mm AA guns. Built by Fairfield, Govan, Glasgow. Launched 14.10.1942. The most successful U-boat destroyer of WW2. Commanded by Captain F.J. Walker, until his death on 9.7.1944. Was Leader of the 2nd Support Group and with other ships was responsible for the following sinkings:- 1.6.1943 *U 202*; 4.6.1943 *U 119*; 6.11.1943 *U226* and *U 842*; 31.1.1944 *U 592*; 9.2.1944 *U 238* and *U 734*; 19.2.1944 *U 264*; 15.3.1944 *U 653*; 29.3.1944 *U 961*; 5.5.1944 *U 473*; 31.7.1944 *U 333*; 6.8.1944 *U 736*; 16.1.1945 *U 482*. 1946 Disarmed for service as a tender to the Navigation School, based at Portsmouth. 6.7.1965 Arrived Lacmotts, Queenborough, to be broken up.

Footnote
Cutter, 151 bm, 10 guns; was built in Chatham Dockyard; launched 3.5.1817; 8.1828 Broken up.

STRIKER

An "Attacker" class Seamanship and Navigational Training Vessel of 34 tons for the RNR and RN University Units. Built by Fairey Allday Marine, Southampton. Allocated to Liverpool University RN Unit.

Description of Badge

Field:- White.
Badge:- A pellet charged with a flash of lightning, white.

Motto

Battle Honours

Atlantic	1943-4	Norway	1944
Arctic	1944	Okinawa	1945

Previous ships of the name

1. Escort Carrier, 11,420 tons, 2 x 4" AA, 8 x 40mm AA and 15 x 20mm AA guns; 18 aircraft. Ex-USS *Prince William*. Built by Western Pipe and Steel Company, San Francisco, California, USA. Launched 7.5.1942. 28.4.1943 Transferred to RN on Lend-Lease. 8.1943 Russian Convoy Escort. 4.1944 Amongst group in planned attack on *Tirpitz* in Altenfiord; cancelled by bad weather. 10.1944 With *Fencer*, left Glasgow for Pacific theatre of war. 2.1946 Returned to the USN.

2. LST (3) 3516, 2,256 tons, 4 x 40mm and 6 x 20mm guns. Built by Yarrow, Esquimault. Launched 15.2.1945. 1947 Renamed *Striker*. 12.12.1952 Arrived Portsmouth from the Mediterranean after service with Amphibious Warfare Squadron. 15.6.1953 Coronation Review at Spithead, representing Portsmouth Home Command. 1960 AWS, East of Suez. 1962 and 1965 Refitted at Gibraltar. 19.6.1966 Arrived Portsmouth to pay off. 15.1.1971 Towed from Portsmouth by German tug *Michel Petersen* bound for Valencia to be broken up.

HMS *Striker* (December 1952).

SUPERB

A "Swiftsure" class nuclear powered Fleet Submarine, 4,400 tons (surfaced), 4,900 tons (submerged); 5 x 21" TT. Built by Vickers, Barrow-in-Furness. Launched 30.11.1974.

Description of Badge

Field:- Blue.
Badge:- A heraldic tiger, statant gold, charged on the shoulder with an anchor, black.
(Derived from the Crest of Admiral Sir Richard Goodwin Keats).

Motto

With sword and courage.

Battle Honours

Passero	1718	Gut of Gibraltar	1801
Sadras	1782	San Domingo	1806
Providien	1782	Algiers	1816
Negapatam	1782	Alexandria	1882
Trincomalee	1782	Jutland	1916

Previous ships of the name

1. French Third rate *Superbe*, 1,029 bm, 64 guns. Captured on 29.7.1710 by *Kent* off the Lizard. 1721 Rebuilt at Woolwich. 1732 Broken up.

2. Fourth rate, 1,068 bm, 60 guns. Built in Woolwich Dockyard in 1736—possibly from the frames of the above ship. 1745 Blockade of Louisburg. 7.1757 Broken up at Sheerness.

3. Third rate, 1,612 bm, 74 guns. Built in Deptford Dockyard. Launched 27.10.1760. 1779 Flagship of East Indies Station. 9.11.1783 Wrecked off Tellicherry, East Indies.

4. French Sixth rate, *Superbe*, 619 bm, 22 guns. Captured 10.10.1795 by *Vanguard* in the West Indies. 1796 Prison Ship at Martinique. 1798 Sold out of the service.

5. Third rate, 1,919 bm, 74 guns. Built by Pitcher, Northfleet. Launched 19.3.1798. 1799 Off Brest. 1803 Off Toulon. 1818-21 South America. 1825 Jamaica Station. 17.4.1826 Her breaking up completed at Portsmouth.

6. Second rate, 2,583 bm, 12 x 8" and 68 x 32 pdr guns. Built at Pembroke Dock. Launched 6.9.1842. 19.6.1845 In Experimental Squadron inspected by HM Queen Victoria at Spithead. 1846-8 In Mediterranean. 1866 Cholera Hospital at Sheerness. 18.2.1869 Her breaking up completed at Portsmouth.

7. Turkish battleship, originally *Memdouhiyeh*, then *Hamidiyeh*, 9,310 tons, 16 x 10" and 6 x 4" guns. Built at Thames Iron Works, Blackwall. Launched 16.11.1875. Completed 1877. 20.2.1878 Before the outbreak of the Russo-Turkish War caused an embargo on new ships, she was purchased for the RN and renamed *Superb*. 1880-7 In the Mediterranean. 1882 Shared in the attack on the forts at Alexandria. 1887-91 Lay idle at Chatham. 14.4.1891 Coastguard Ship at Greenock. 1895 Again idle at Chatham; then to Isle of Bute. 15.5.1906 Sold to Garnham.

8. "Bellerophon" class battleship, 18,800 tons, 10 x 12" and 16 x 4" guns; 3 x 18" TT. Built by Armstrong, Elswick. Launched 7.11.1907. 29.5.1909 Commissioned at Portsmouth for Home Fleet. From 1911, in the 1st Battle Squadron. 1916 At Jutland. 25.3.1920 Paid off at the Nore. 12.12.1922 Sold to Stanlee, Dover.

9. "Minotaur" class cruiser, 8,800 tons (standard), 11,560 tons (full load), 9 x 6" and 10 x 4" AA guns; 6 x 21" TT. Built by Swan Hunter, Wallsend-on-Tyne. Launched 31.8.1943. 1946-7 Flagship, 2nd CS. 18.7.1947 Royal Review in the Clyde. 1949-50 Flagship, 2nd CS. 1951 Flagship of America and West Indies Station. 1952 Home Fleet. Flagship, Flag Officer Flotillas. 15.6.1953 Coronation Review at Spithead. 1955 America and West Indies. 1956-7 East Indies. 8.1957 Arrived Chatham to pay off into Reserve. Laid up in the Gareloch (10.1957). 8.8.1960 Arrived Arnott Young, Dalmuir, for stripping; hull broken up at Troon.

Footnote
a) Central battery ironclad was laid down as *Superb* in Chatham Dockyard but was renamed *Alexandra* before her launch on 7.4.1875.
b) Drifter, 61 tons, built in 1901, was hired for Harbour Service 1916-8.

SWALLOW

A "Peacock" class Patrol Vessel—for Hong Kong patrol duties—700 tons, 1 x 76mm gun. Built by Hall Russell, Aberdeen. Launched 30.3.1984.

Description of Badge

Field:- White.
Badge:- A swallow proper.
(This badge approved in 1984, replaced an earlier design).

Motto

Celeriter adsum — I come quickly.

Battle Honours

Armada	1588	Texel	1673
Lowestoft	1665	Velez Malaga	1704
Four Days' Battle	1666	Marbella	1705
Orfordness	1666	Crimea	1854-5

Previous ships of the name

1. The first King's ship named *Swallow* conveyed Edward III from Sandwich to Sluys in 1345.

2. Ship of 80 bm; built in 1512 as *Rose Henry*, but renamed. 1512-3 Took part in the French war.

3. Ship of 60 bm; listed in 10.1525.

4. Galley, 24 bm; 8 guns; Built in 1544. 1558 Believed rebuilt at Deptford. 1573 Again rebuilt. 1588 In Armada campaign. 1603 Condemned.

5. Ship, 478 bm, 40 guns. Built at Deptford in 1634. 1642 Became part of Parliamentary Fleet. 1648 Carried off in revolt of Downs Squadron. 1654 Condemned and sold to the French.

6. Fourth rate, 559 bm, 48 guns. Built on the Thames in 1653 as *Gainsborough*. 1660 Renamed *Swallow*. 8.2.1693 Ran aground off Kinsale, and sank.

7. Sloop, 66 bm, 6 guns. Built in Chatham Dockyard in 1699. 1702 In Post Office service. 19.4.1703 Captured by the French off the Maas.

8. Fourth rate, 672 bm, 54 guns. Built at Deptford. Launched 10.2.1703. 1706-7 Convoy escort. 1719 Rebuilt at Chatham as 710 bm. 14.5.1728 Paid off. 8.1728 Taken to pieces.

9. Fourth rate, 951 bm, 60 guns. Built in Plymouth Dockyard. Launched 6.10.1732. 16.1.1738 Renamed *Princess Louisa*. 1742-3 Broken up in dock at Woolwich.

10. Sloop, 271 bm, 16 guns. Built by Buxton, Rotherhithe in 1743. 24.12.1744 Wrecked off the Bahamas.

11. Sloop, 278 bm, 14 guns. Built by Bird, Rotherhithe. Launched 14.12.1745. 22.8.1766 With *Dolphin*, left Plymouth under command of Phillip Carteret on voyage of exploration. Discovered Pitcairn Island. 20.3.1769 Returned to England. 6.1769 Sold out of the service.

12. Sloop, 302 bm, 14 guns. Built in Deptford Dockyard. Launched 30.12.1769. 1770-7 In the East Indies. 12.1777 On passage to England, foundered in the Atlantic.

13. Sloop, 300 bm, 18 guns. Built by Ladd, Dover. Launched 2.4.1779. 26.8.1781 Chased by 4 American privateers; driven ashore and lost on Long Island.

14. Sloop, 262 bm, 16 guns. Ex-cutter, built by Fabian, East Cowes. Purchased on the stocks. Launched 10.1781. 1782-91 Cruised mainly in Irish Channel. 20.8.1795 Sold out of the service.

15. Sloop, 365 bm, 18 guns. Built by Perry, Blackwall. Launched 10.9.1795. On West Indies Station. 8.10.1801 Paid off at Portsmouth. 8.1802 Sold out of the service.

16. "Cruizer" class brig-sloop, 387 bm, 18 guns. Built by Tanner, Dartmouth. Launched 24.12.1805. 26.7.1811 Off Sicily, captured privateer *La Belle Geonoise*. 11.1815 Broken up.

17. Steam sloop, 486 bm, 9 x 32 pdr guns. Built at Pembroke Dock. Launched 12.6.1854. 1855 With the Black Seas fleet during Crimean War. 1861-2 Surveying duties in China and Yellow Seas. 12.1866 Sold for breaking up.

18. "Plover" class wood, steam gunvessel, 755 tons, 1 x 7" and 2 x 40 pdr guns. Built in Portsmouth Dockyard. Launched 16.11.1868. 1869-72 In Reserve. 1872-6 North America and West Indies Station. 1877-9 Cape of Good Hope and West Coast of Africa. 1880-2 South America. 18.10.1882 Sold to A. Tobin.

19. "Nymphe" class composite steam sloop, 1,130 tons, 8 x 5" guns. Built in Sheerness Dockyard. Launched 27.10.1885. 1886-96 Spent most of these years off West and East Coasts of Africa. 1897-1900 Around South America and Falkland Islands. 7.12.1900 Paid off at Devonport. 1904 Sold to McCausland and Sons.

20. "S" class destroyer, 1,075 tons, 3 x 4" guns; 4 x 21" TT. Built by Scotts, Greenock. Launched 1.8.1918. 1918-9 10th Destroyer Flotilla, Harwich. 1920-4 Transferred to 6th DF, later 8th DF, at Malta. 1926 To Reserve, first at the Nore, then at Rosyth. 24.9.1936 Handed over to T.W. Ward in part payment for *Majestic*. Broken up at Inverkeithing.

Footnote

a) Several other minor vessels have borne the name *Swallow*. They include a ketch built at Deptford in 1657; sloop built at Deptford in 1672; tender purchased in 1793; two Revenue cutters of 1793 and 1795; sloop taken over for the Admiralty mail packet service in 1818; sloop, built at Falmouth in 1820, purchased by Admiralty in 1824; paddlewheel steamship taken over by the Admiralty in 1838; Dockyard tug 1906; tug hired 6.1917 to 1.1918; trawler hired as a minesweeper 1914-8.

b) *Swallow II* was a trawler hired 1914-9.

c) *Swallow III* hired as net drifter in WWII.

d) Two prizes taken from the French in 1692 and 1704.

e) "C" class destroyer was laid down by Yarrow, Scotstoun, Glasgow, but was renamed *Caprice* in 11.1942 before launching on 16.9.1943.

HMS *Swallow*

HMS *Swallow*

SWIFT

A "Peacock" class Patrol Vessel—for Hong Kong patrol duties—700 tons, 1 x 76mm gun. Built by Hall Russell, Aberdeen. Launched 11.9.1984.

Description of Badge
Field:- White.
Badge:- A swift volant proper.

Motto

Battle Honours

Dover	1917	Normandy	1944
Belgian Coast	1917-8	Arctic	1944
Zeebrugge	1918		

Previous ships of the name

1. Ship, 60 bm, 1549-54.

2. French Sixth rate, 288 bm, 20 guns. Captured in 1689. 1691-2 Off Ireland. 24.4.1695 Moored as a breakwater at Plymouth.

3. Ketch, 78 bm, 6 guns. Built at Chatham. Launched 16.9.1695. 17.8.1696 Foundered.

4. Advice Boat, 154 bm, 10 guns. Built at Arundel in 1697. 24.1.1698 Wrecked on North Carolina coast.

5. Sloop, 65 bm, 4 guns. Built at Portsmouth in 1699. 18.8.1702 Captured off the Isles of Scilly by French privateer *Duc de Bourgogne*.

6. Sloop, 123 bm, 12 guns. Built at Woolwich in 1704. Served on American Station. 8.1719 Sold.

7. Sloop, 93 bm, 12 guns. Built at Woolwich in 1721. 7.7.1741 Sold.

8. Sloop, 203 bm, 10 guns. Built at Limehouse in 1741. 10.1756 Sold.

9. French Cutter *Conde de Valence*, 88 bm, 10 guns. Captured in 1760. 1.1761 Purchased by the Admiralty. Listed in 1762.

10. Sloop, 271 bm, 14 guns. Built at Limehouse. Launched 3.1763. 1766 In Squadron despatched to take possession of Falkland Islands. 13.3.1770 Wrecked at Port Desire on coast of Patagonia.

11. Sloop, 303 bm, 14 guns. Built at Portsmouth in 1.1777. 11.1778 Ran aground and burned on Cape Henry.

12. American Sloop, 16 guns. Captured in 1779. 11.8.1782 Captured by French frigates *Resolue* and *Friponne* in the West Indies.

13. Brig-sloop, 329 bm, 14 guns. Built at Portsmouth. Launched 10.1793. Served in East Indies. 4.1797 Wrecked in South China Sea with loss of all hands.

14. Schooner, 47 bm. Purchased in 1794. Listed until 1796.

15. Cutter, 8 guns. Hired in 1798. 3.4.1804 Captured by French privateer *Esperance*, 10 guns, off Palermo while carrying despatches from the Admiralty to Nelson.

16. Brig *Pacific*, 327 bm, 16 guns. Purchased in 6.1804. 3.11.1814 Sold.

17. Cutter, 80 bm. Built at Deptford. Launched 2.1817. 8.1821 Sold.

18. Packet brig, 361 bm, 8 guns. Built at Deptford. Launched 11.1835. 1836-48 Stationed at Falmouth. 1848-53 Pacific Station. 1853-61 Laid up at Devonport. 1861 To Capetown for use as a Mooring Vessel. Renamed YC3. 1886 Sold.

19. "Linnet" class composite steam gunboat, 756 tons, 1 x 7" and 2 x 64 pdr guns. Built at Blackwall. Launched 29.11.1879. 1881-97 China Station. 1897-8 Guardship at Sandakan. 2.1902 Sold, at Hong Kong, to become mercantile *Hoi Ching*.

20. Destroyer, 1,825 tons, 4 x 4" guns; 2 TT. Built by Cammell Laird, Birkenhead. Launched 7.12.1907. 1914-6 Leader of 4th DF, Grand Fleet. 1916-8 Leader of 6th DF, Dover Patrol. 1917 Re-armed with 1 x 6" and 2 x 4" guns. 21.4.1917 With *Broke*, sank 2 German destroyers in Straits of Dover. 9.11.1921 Sold to Rees, Llanelly, for breaking up.

21. ''S'' class destroyer, 1,710 tons, 4 x 4.7", 2 x 40mm AA and 8 x 20mm AA guns; 8 x 21" TT. Built by J.S. White, Cowes, Launched 15.6.1943. 2.1944 Joined 23rd DF, Home Fleet. Took part in various operations in the Arctic and off Norway. 6.1944 Joined Force 'D' off Sword beach for the Normandy invasion. 24.6.1944 Off Ouistreham, detonated a pressure mine, and sank.

Footnote
Torpedo Gunboat built by J.S. White, Cowes, had been designated *Swift* by the builder, but when purchased in 1.1885 she became ''Torpedo Boat No. 81''.

HMS *Swift* (1916).

HMS *Swift* (1986, off Hong Kong).

SWIFTSURE

Name ship of the class of nuclear powered Fleet Submarines, 4,400 tons (surfaced), 4,900 tons (submerged); 5 x 21" TT. Built by Vickers, Barrow-in-Furness. Launched 7.9.1971.

Description of Badge

Field:- Blue.
Badge:- A heraldic tiger rampant, winged gold, armed and langued red.

(Derived from the figurehead of the first *Swiftsure* built in 1573).

Motto

Battle Honours

Armada	1588	Velez Malaga	1704
Cadiz	1596	Lagos	1759
Santa Cruz	1657	Quiberon Bay	1759
Lowestoft	1665	Belle Ile	1761
Four Days' Battle	1666	Nile	1798
Schooneveld	1673	Egypt	1801
Texel	1673	Trafalgar	1805
Barfleur	1692	Suez Canal	1915
Vigo	1702	Dardanelles	1915-6
Gibraltar	1704	Okinawa	1945

Previous ships of the name

1. Galleon, 360 bm, 41 guns. Built at Deptford in 1573. 1588 Fought against Spanish Armada. 1592 Rebuilt as 416 bm. 1607 Renamed *Speedwell*, 40 guns. 11.1624 Lost near Flushing.

2. Ship, 746 bm, 46 guns. Built at Deptford in 1621. 1653 Rebuilt at Woolwich as 898 bm. 1.6.1666 Captured by the Dutch at the Four Days' Battle.

3. Third rate, 978 bm, 70 guns. Built by Deane, Harwich. Launched 8.4.1673. 1696 Rebuilt at Deptford as 987 bm. 2.1.1716 Renamed *Revenge*, Third rate, 1,104 bm, 64 guns. 1742 Rebuilt at Deptford as 1,258 bm. 24.5.1787 Sold out of the service.

4. Third rate, 1,426 bm, 70 guns. Built in Deptford Dockyard. Launched 25.5.1750. 2.6.1773 Sold out of the service.

5. Third rate, 1,612 bm, 74 guns. Built by Wells, Deptford. Launched 4.4.1787. 24.6.1801 Captured by the French in the Mediterranean. 1805 Recaptured at Trafalgar, renamed *Irresistible*. Used as a Prison Ship. 1.1816 Broken up at Chatham.

6. Third rate, 1,724 bm, 74 guns. Built by H. Adams, Buckler's Hard. Launched 23.7.1804. 1805 Fought at Trafalgar. 5.1819 Used as a Receiving Ship. 18.10.1845 Sold to Barnard.

7. Modified ''Audacious'' class iron armoured ship, 6,910 tons, 10 x 9" and 4 x 6" guns. Built by Palmer, Jarrow-on-Tyne. Launched 15.6.1870. 1872-8 In the Mediterranean; recommissioning at Devonport on 18.4.1875. 1882-90 Flagship in the Pacific. 14.8.1891 Commissioned at Devonport as a Sea-going Guardship. From 1893, lay at Portsmouth. 1903 Used as Fleet Reserve offices. 3.1904 Renamed *Orontes*; continued to be used for Harbour Service including workshops for Artisan ratings. 4.7.1908 Sold to Castle for breaking up.

8. Chilian battleship *Constitucion*, 11,800 tons, 4 x 10" and 14 x 7.5" guns. Built by Armstrong Whitworth, Elswick. Launched 12.1.1903. 3.12.1903 Purchased by the RN to prevent her falling into Russian hands. Renamed *Swiftsure*. 1916 In Reserve. 18.6.1920 Sold to Stanlee, Dover, for breaking up.

9. ''Minotaur'' class cruiser, 8,800 tons (standard), 11,240 tons (full load), 9 x 6" and 10 x 4" AA guns; 6 x 21" TT. Built by Vickers Armstrong, Tyne. Launched 4.2.1943. British Pacific Fleet operations against the Japanese. First British ship to re-enter Hong Kong. A Flagship for most of the post-war years. 9.1953 In Exercise 'Mariner', was damaged in collision with *Diamond* off Iceland. Refitted, then in 9.1954 laid up in the Humber. 12.1955 Reserve Fleet, Gareloch. 8.1956 Towed to Chatham for reconstruction. 9.1959 Reconstruction stopped after £3.3 million had been spent. 6.1960 Disposal List. 17.10.1962 Arrived Inverkeithing to be broken up by T.W. Ward.

TALENT

A ''Trafalgar'' class nuclear powered Fleet Submarine, 4,200 tons (surfaced), 5,208 tons (submerged); 5 x 21" TT; Sub-Harpoon. Built by Vickers, Barrow-in-Furness.

Description of Badge

Field:- Blue.
Badge:- In front of a saltire couped white, a pair of scales gold.

Motto

Battle Honours

None.

Previous ships of the name

1. One of the Third Group ''T'' class submarines, 1,090 tons (surfaced), 1,575 tons (submerged), 1 x 4" and 1 x 20mm AA guns; 11 x 21" TT. Built by Vickers Armstrong, Barrow-in-Furness. Launched 17.7.1943. 6.12.1943 Sold to the Royal Netherlands Navy; renamed *Zwaardvis*. 1.1963 Withdrawn from service. 7.1963 Sold to Antwerp shipbreakers.

2. One of the Third Group ''T'' class submarines, 1,090 tons (surfaced), 1,575 tons (submerged), 1 x 4" and 1 x 20mm AA guns; 11 x 21" TT. Built by Vickers Armstrong, Barrow-in-Furness. Launched as *Tasman* on 13.2.1945. 4.1945 Renamed *Talent*. 15.12.1954 Was swept out of dock in Chatham Dockyard when the caisson collapsed. 8.5.1956 her fin was damaged in collision with an unknown merchant ship when *Talent* was submerged off the Isle of Wight. Made her last dive in the North Sea after a 6 day visit to Sunderland. 12.1966 Paid off. 28.2.1970 Sold to West of Scotland Shipbreaking Company; broken up at Troon.

Footnote
An order for another ''T'' class submarine was placed with Vickers Armstrong, Barrow-in-Furness, in 1944; transferred to Scotts, Greenock; but cancelled in 1945.

HMS *Talent* (October 1956).

TIRELESS

A "Trafalgar" class nuclear powered Fleet Submarine, 4,200 tons (surfaced), 5,208 tons (submerged); 5 x 21" TT; Sub-Harpoon. Built by Vickers, Barrow-in-Furness. Launched 17.3.1984.

Description of Badge

Field:- Blue.
Badge:- An albatross proper, alighting on water barry wavy in base, white and blue.

Motto

Esto perpetua — Be perpetual.

Battle Honours

None.

Previous ships of the name

1. One of the Third Group "T" class submarine, 1,090 tons (surfaced), 1,575 tons (submerged), 1 x 4" and 1 x 20mm AA guns; 11 x 21" TT. Built in Portsmouth Dockyard. Launched 19.3.1943. Completed in 1944 and operated in various areas. After the war, had spells with the Home and Mediterranean Fleets. 1961 Rebuilt at Rosyth. 1967 Laid up to await disposal. 11.1968 Sold to J. Cashmore and broken up at Newport.

HMS *Tireless* (1932).

TORBAY

A "Trafalgar" class nuclear powered Fleet Submarine, 4,200 tons (surfaced), 5,208 tons (submerged); 5 x 21" TT: Sub-Harpoon. Built by Vickers, Barrow-in-Furness. Launched 8.3.1985.

Description of Badge

Field:- Gold
Badge:- A bugle blue, banded red.
(Derived from the Arms of William of Orange (King William III) who landed at Torbay 5.11.1688).

Motto

Je maitiendrai—I will maintain (The Motto of the above).

Battle Honours

Vigo	1702	Mediterranean	1941-3
Velez Malaga	1704	Arctic	1942-3
Quiberon Bay	1759	Sicily	1943
Belle Ile	1761	Aegean	1943
St Kitts	1782	Atlantic	1944
The Saints	1782	English Channel	1944

Previous ships of the name

1. Second rate, 1,202 bm, 80 guns. Built in Deptford Dockyard. Launched 16.12.1693. 1702 Broke the boom at Vigo Harbour. Suffered heavy damage and great loss of life, but laid the foundations of a great victory. 1719 Rebuilt at Woolwich as 1,296 bm. 1.1.1749 Her breaking up at Portsmouth completed.

2. Second rate, 1,377 bm, 90 guns. Built in Deptford Dockyard as *Neptune*. Launched 17.4.1683. 1710 Rebuilt at Blackwall as 1,577 bm. 1730 Rebuilt at Woolwich as 1,573 bm. 1750 Renamed *Torbay*. 17.8.1784 Sold out of the service.

3. "S" class destroyer, 1,087 tons, 3 x 4" guns; 4 x 21" TT. Built by Thornycroft, Woolston, Southampton. Launched 6.3.1919. 16.8.1920 Reduced to Reserve at Portsmouth. 1.3.1928 Renamed *Champlain* in the Royal Canadian Navy. 1937 Sold out of the service.

4. "T" class Patrol Submarine, 1,090 tons (surfaced), 1,575 tons (submerged); 1 x 4" and 1 x 20mm AA guns; 10 x 21" TT. Built in Chatham Dockyard. Launched 9.4.1940. *Torbay* had a particularly varied and distinguished war career. 6.6.1941 Off Cape Helles, torpedoed the Vichy French tanker *Alberta*. 10.6.1941 Torpedoed Italian tanker *Guiseppini Gherardi*. 3.1942 Her CO, Lieutenant Commander ACC Miers, was awarded the Victoria Cross for "One of the most remarkable submarine patrols carried out during the war". Having sighted an enemy troop convoy, but not being able to get within range, Cdr Miers decided to follow the ships into the heavily defended harbour at Corfu. Unfortunately the convoy was no longer there but *Torbay* did sink 2 supply ships. She was hunted for 1½ hours before escaping into open water. 11.1943 Sank a floating dock under tow. Spent later stages of the war in the Pacific. Survived the war, during which she sank 54 ships totalling over 72,000 tons. Suffered a lot of engine troubles in her last commission so on 19.12.1945 was sold to T.W. Ward; broken up at Briton Ferry.

Footnote
Drifter, 83 tons, built in 1910, was hired 1915-9; and again in 11.1939 as *Torbay II*. 1.11.1940 Sunk by air attack off Dover.

HMS *Torbay* (1942).

TRAFALGAR

Name ship of the class of nuclear powered Fleet Submarines, 4,200 tons (surfaced), 5,208 tons (submerged); 5 x 21" TT; Sub-Harpoon. Built by Vickers, Barrow-in-Furness. Launched 1.7.1981.

Description of Badge

Field:- Gold.
Badge:- A cross flory black, within a chaplet of laurel, green.
(Derived from the Arms of Lord Nelson).

Motto

Battle Honours

Crimea   1854

Previous ships of the name

1. First rate, 2,404 bm, 106 guns. Built in Chatham Dockyard. After 7 years on the stocks, was launched 26.7.1820. 22.2.1825 While still fitting out was renamed *Camperdown*. 1854 Reduced to Harbour Service. 1857 Converted to Coal Hulk. 29.8.1882 Renamed *Pitt*. 15.5.1906 Sold to Castle on the Thames for breaking up.

2. First rate, 2,694 bm, 110 guns. Built in Woolwich Dockyard. Even longer on the stocks than her predecessor—16 years. Launched 21.6.1841. At Siege of Sebastopol, took part in first naval battle in which all ships concerned went into action under steam. As *Trafalgar* had no steam propulsion, she earned her only Battle Honour by being towed into the fray by the steam tug *Retribution*. 21.3.1859 Undocked after conversion to steam. 1870 Became a sea-going Training Ship. 1873 Renamed *Boscawen*; moored at Portland. 10.7.1906 Sold to Castle on the Thames for breaking up.

3. Battleship, 11,940 tons, 4 x 13.5" and 6 x 4.7" guns. Built in Portsmouth Dockyard. Launched 20.9.1887. Most of her active life was spent in the Mediterranean. After 1897 was Guardship at Portsmouth. 1905 To Reserve at Devonport. 1907-9 Training Ship for Turret and Torpedo Tube crews at Sheerness. 9.5.1911 Sold to Garnham for breaking up.

4. "Battle" class destroyer, 2,325 tons, 4 x 4.5" and 1 x 4" guns; 8 TT. Built by Swan Hunter, Wallsend-on-Tyne. Launched 12.1.1944. Became operational too late to see action in WW2. 1947 Reduced to Reserve. Not recommissioned until 1958 but did go to sea occasionally as the mobile headquarters of the Admiral Commanding Reserve Ships. 20.5.1958 Recommissioned at Portsmouth as Leader of the 7th DS on Home/Mediterranean cycle. 5.1963 Entered Reserve Fleet for the third and last time. 7.1970 Arrived Dalmuir to be broken up.

HMS *Trafalgar* (June 1953).

TRENCHANT

A ''Trafalgar'' class nuclear powered Fleet Submarine, 4,200 tons (surfaced), 5,208 tons (submerged); 5 x 21" TT; Sub-Harpoon. Built by Vickers, Barrow-in-Furness.

Description of Badge

Field:- Per saltire red and barry wavy of six, white and blue.
Badge:- A sword erect proper, pommel and hilt gold.

Motto

Battle Honours

Malaya   1944-5

Previous ships of the name

1. Modified ''R'' class destroyer, 1,065 tons, 3 x 4" guns; 4 TT. Built by J.S. White, Cowes. Launched 23.12.1916. 4.1917 Commissioned into 15th Flotilla, Grand Fleet. 15.2.1919 Complement reduced. 14.1.1921 Recommissioned at Portsmouth, as a tender to *Colleen*, Receiving Ship at Queenstown. 22.2.1922 Reduced to Reserve at Portsmouth. 15.11.1928 Sold for breaking up.

2. ''T'' class submarine, 1,090 tons (surfaced), 1,575 tons (submerged), 1 x 4" and 1 x 20mm AA guns; 11 x 21" TT. Built in Chatham Dockyard. Launched 24.3.1943. 1944 In the Far East. 23.9.1944 Sank *U 859* off Penang. 28.10.1944 Chariots from *Trenchant* sank *Sumatra Maru* (4,859 tons), in Puket Harbour. 3.1945 With *Terrapin*, sank Japanese submarine chaser *Kusentai 8*. 8.6.1945 Sank Japanese heavy cruiser *Ashigara* in Banka Strait. 8.1945 Sank Japanese special minesweeper No. 105. 1949-50 In Third (Rosyth) Flotilla. 1951-9 In the Mediterranean. 1.7.1963 Sold to Metal Industries. 23.7.1963 Arrived Faslane to be broken up.

HMS *Trenchant*

TRIUMPH

A "Trafalgar" class nuclear powered Fleet Submarine, 4,200 tons (surfaced), ordered to be built by Vickers, Barrow-in-Furness, 3.1.1986.

Description of Badge

Field:- White.
Badge:- A wreath of laurel green.

Motto

We shall triumph.

Battle Honours

Armada	1588	Schooneveld	1673
Dover	1652	Texel	1673
Portland	1653	Cornwallis' Retreat	
Gabbard	1653		1795
Scheveningen	1653	Camperdown	1797
Lowestoft	1665	Dardanelles	1915
Four Days' Battle	1666	Malta Convoys	1941
Orfordness	1666	Mediterranean	1941
Sole Bay	1672	Korea	1950

Previous ships of the name

1. Galleon, 741 bm, 68 guns. Built in 1561. 1588 Among the fleet that left Plymouth to meet the Spanish Armada. 1596 Rebuilt as 928 bm. 1618 Sold out of the service.

2. Ship, 898 bm, 44 guns. Built by Durell, Deptford, in 1623. 1652-3 Flagship of Admiral Blake in his various actions in the Channel with the Dutch Admiral Van Tromp. 3.6.1665 Flagship of Vice Admiral Christopher Myngs in Battle of Texel. 6.1666 Four Days' Battle. 28.5.1672 Battle of Sole Bay in which her CO, W. Hannam, was killed. 1687 Broken up.

3. Second rate, 1,482 bm, 90 guns. Built in Chatham Dockyard in 1698. 12.10.1702 Present at attack on French and Spanish fleets in Vigo Harbour. 27.8.1714 Renamed *Prince*. 1750 Rebuilt at Chatham as 1,677 bm. 18.8.1759 With Admiral Sir Edward Hawke's fleet at Gibraltar. 1775 Broken up at Plymouth.

4. Sloop, 18 guns, ex-Spanish *Triunfo*, captured at Puerto Bello on 23.11.1739. 1.1740 Foundered in the West Indies.

5. Third rate, 1,825 bm, 74 guns. Built in Woolwich Dockyard. Launched 3.3.1764. 11.10.1797 With Admiral Duncan in defeat of the Dutch at Camperdown. 8.1804 Off Toulon. 1807 Off the Chesapeake, coast of America. 10.1813 Reduced to Harbour Service; was Quarantine Ship at Milford for over 30 years. 6.1850 Broken up at Pembroke Dock.

6. Iron armoured ship, steam, 6,640 tons, 10 x 9" and 4 x 64 pdr guns. Built by Palmer, Jarrow-on-Tyne. Launched 27.9.1870. 1873-5 Channel Squadron. 1878 Flagship in the Pacific. 1882-5 In Reserve. 1885-8 Flagship in the Pacific. 1890-2 Guardship at Queenstown. 1893-1900 In Reserve at Devonport. 1900 Depot Ship for Torpedo Boat Destroyers at Devonport. 4.1904 Renamed *Tenedos*. 1905 Tender to *Warrior* at Portsmouth. 1906 Training Ship for Boy Artificers at Chatham. 1910 As *Indus IV*, establishment and workshop for Boy Artificers at Devonport. At outbreak of World War I, was towed to Invergordon for use as a floating store. 1.1915 Renamed *Algiers*. 7.1.1921 Sold to Fryer, Sunderland, for breaking up.

7. Battleship, ex-Chilian *Libertad*, 11,985 tons, 4 x 10", 14 x 7.5" and 14 x 14 pdr guns. Built by Vickers, Barrow-in-Furness. Launched 15.1.1903. Purchased by the RN on 3.12.1903. 6.1904 Home Fleet. 17.9.1904 Ran into by Trinity House steamer *Siren* at Pembroke. 3.6.1905 Collided with *Swiftsure*; bows damaged. 3.1909 to 5.1912 In Mediterranean. 1913 To China. Relieved *Tamar* at Hong Kong. 1914 Commissioned with crews from River Gunboats for operations with Japanese warships at Tsingtau. 1915 Dardanelles Fleet. 25.5.1915 Sunk by *U 21* off Gallipoli.

8. Patrol type "Triton" class submarine, 1,090 tons (surfaced), 1,575 tons (submerged), 1 x 4" gun; 10 x 21" TT. Built by Vickers Armstrong, Barrow-in-Furness. Launched 16.2.1938. 26.12.1939 Hit a mine off Norway; severely damaged. 1940 To Mediterranean. 1941 Close inshore at Mersa Matruh, engaged Italian submarine *Salpa* with gunfire; damaged and stopped her; then sunk her by torpedo. Shore batteries damaged *Triumph* but she remained on station. 14.1.1942 Sunk by unknown cause in the Aegean, whilst conducting special operation.

9. "Colossus" class light fleet carrier, 13,350 tons, 19 x 40mm, 4 x 3 pdr, 24 x 2 pdr pom-poms; 44 aircraft. Built by Hawthorn Leslie, Hebburn-on-Tyne. Launched 2.10.1944. 1945 Pacific Fleet. 1947-8 Flagship of FO (Air) in the Mediterranean. 1953 Accommodation modified for Cadets Training Ship. 1958-65 Converted to Heavy Repair Ship at Portsmouth. Relieved *Hartland Point* in Singapore as Escort Maintenance Ship. 28.2.1972 Returned to UK to pay off. 1975 Reserve at Chatham. 1980 Disposal List. 1981 Sold to Spanish shipbreakers. 9.12.1981 Left Chatham for Spain.

Footnote

a) Second rate, steam, 3,715 bm, 91 guns, was laid down at Pembroke Dock, but renamed *Prince Consort*, 14.2.1862, before launch as an armoured frigate, 4,045 bm, on 26.6.1862.

b) Drifter, *Triumph II*, 90 tons, built in 1907, was hired 1915-9.

c) Drifter, *Triumph III*, 90 tons, built in 1907, was also hired 1915-9.

d) MFV, *Triumph VI*, 46 tons, built in 1903, was hired as a Store Carrier in 1941. Sunk 15.12.1944 in collision in the Rosyth area.

HMS *Triumph*, August 1947, as an aircraft carrier.

HMS *Triumph*, February 1965, as a heavy repair ship.

TRUMPETER

A P2000 Coastal Training Craft of 43 tonnes for the RNR. Being built of GRP by Watercraft Ltd, Shoreham-by-Sea. Allocated to Tyne Division, RNR.

Description of Badge

Field:- Blue.
Badge:- A trumpet gold, suspended therefrom the flag of the Lord High Admiral, proper.

Motto

Battle Honours

Atlantic	1943-4	Norway	1944-5
Arctic	1944		

Previous ships of the name

1. Escort Carrier, 11,420 tons, 2 x 4" AA, 16 x 40mm AA and 20 x 20mm AA guns; 24 aircraft. Ex-USS *Bastian*, ex-*Lucifer*; renamed *Trumpeter* in 1942. Built by Seattle-Tacoma S.B. Corporation, Tacoma, USA. Launched 15.12.1942. Converted by Commercial Iron Works, Portland, Oregon, USA. 4.8.1943 Transferred to RN on Lend-Lease. 6.4.1946 Returned to USN.

2. LST (3) 3524, 2,256 tons, 4 x 40mm and 6 x 20mm guns. Built by Davie Shipbuilders and Repair Company, Levis, Quebec. Launched 25.7.1945. 1947 Renamed *Trumpeter*. 1956 Transferred to the Ministry of Transport as *Empire Fulmar*.

Footnote
Trawler, 192 tons, built in 1913 was hired from 1914-9.

TURBULENT

A "Trafalgar" class nuclear powered Fleet Submarine, 4,200 tons (surfaced), 5,208 tons (submerged); 5 x 21" TT; Sub-Harpoon. Built by Vickers, Barrow-in-Furness. Launched 1.12.1982.

Description of Badge

Field:- Black.
Badge:- A hand grasping a club, all proper, at the head five stars gold.

Motto

Absit nomen — May the name be absent.

Battle Honours

Jutland   1916   Mediterranean   1942

Previous ships of the name

1. Brig, 181 bm, 12 guns. Built by Tanner, Dartmouth. Launched 17.7.1805. 10.6.1808 Captured by the Danes in Malmo Bay.

2. Turkish destroyer *Ogre*—"Talisman" class—renamed *Turbulent* on 15.2.1915. 1,098 tons, 5 x 4" guns; 4 TT. Built by Hawthorn Leslie, Hebburn-on-Tyne. Launched 5.1.1916. 1916 Saw service with the Grand Fleet. With the 10th Flotilla at Jutland. 1.6.1916 At 12.30 in the morning she was last in line of 12 ships, following the light cruiser *Champion*, which met 4 German battleships. The leading battleship rammed *Turbulent* and cut her in two. Only 13 men survived to be prisoners of war.

3. "S" class destroyer, 1,075 tons, 3 x 4" guns; 4 x 21" TT. Built by Hawthorn Leslie, Hebburn-on-Tyne. Launched 29.5.1919. 24.8.1920 Reduced to Reserve at Chatham. 1925 Reserve Fleet, Nore. 29.8.1927 Recommissioned at Chatham for Maintenance Reserve, Rosyth. 25.8.1936 Handed over to T.W. Ward in part payment for *Majestic*. Broken up at Inverkeithing.

4. "T" class submarine, 1,090 tons (surfaced), 1,575 tons (submerged), 1 x 4" and 1 x 20mm AA guns; 11 x 21" TT. Built by Vickers Armstrong, Barrow. Launched 12.5.1941. 1942 Excelled against enemy supply ships in the Mediterranean. Carried out 9 patrols under the command of Commander J.W. Linton. 24.2.1943 Sailed from Algiers. 11.3.1943 Made unsuccessful attack on an Italian ship off Bastia in Corsica. About 23.3.1943 *Turbulent* was sunk by counter-attacking Italian anti-submarine vessels. Cdr. Linton was posthumously awarded the Victoria Cross.

HMS *Turbulent* (1985).

UPHOLDER

A Type 2400 conventional diesel/electric Patrol Submarine, approx 2,400 tons (submerged); 6 x 21" TT. Being built by Vickers, Barrow-in-Furness. Ordered 2.11.1983.

Description of Badge

Field:- Blue.
Badge:- A column white.

Motto

Battle Honours

Mediterranean 1941-2   Malta Convoys 1941-2

Previous ships of the name

1. "U" class submarine, 540 tons (surfaced), 730 tons (submerged), 1 x 12 pdr gun; 4 TT. Buit by Vickers Armstrong, Barrow. Launched 8.7.1940. 10.12.1940 Sailed for the Mediterranean. 10.1.1941 Arrived Malta. In the next 16 months, she carried out 25 patrols from Malta during which she sank 3 U-boats and 1 destroyer; damaged 1 cruiser and 1 destroyer; and sank or damaged 19 supply ships, totalling 119,000 tons. Her Commanding Officer, Lieutenant Commander D. Wanklyn, was awarded the Victoria Cross for an action off Sicily on 24.5.1941, in which she sank four and damaged one enemy ships. One of those sunk was the liner *Conte Rosso*, 18,000 tons, crowded with troops bound for North Africa. 14.4.1942 Sunk by the Italian torpedo boat *Pegaso* while trying to attack a convoy off Tripoli.

HMS *Upholder*, the only known photograph of HMS *Upholder*, at Malta. Inboard is HMS *Urge*.

VALIANT

Name ship of the class of nuclear powered Fleet Submarines, 4,300 tons (surfaced), 4,800 tons (submerged); 6 x 21″ TT. Built by Vickers, Barrow-in Furness. Launched 3.12.1963.

Description of Badge

Field:- Blue.
Badge:- A fighting cock with steel spurs, all proper.

Motto

Valiant for truth.

Battle Honours

Belle Ile	1761	Mediterranean	1940-3
Havana	1762	Malta Convoys	1941
Ushant	1781	Matapan	1941
The Saints	1782	Crete	1941
First of June	1794	Sicily	1943
Groix Island	1795	Salerno	1943
Basque Roads	1809	Sabang	1944
Jutland	1916	Falkland Islands	1982
Norway	1940		

Previous ships of the name

1. Third rate, 1,799 bm, 74 guns. Built in Chatham Dockyard. Launched 10.8.1759. 1775 Rebuilt at Portsmouth. 11.1799 Reduced to Harbour Service. 4.1826 Broken up.

2. Third rate, 1,718 bm, 74 guns. Built by Perry, Wells and Green, Blackwall. Launched 24.1.1807. 1809 Brilliant action against the French at Basque Roads. 11.1823 Broken up before her predecessor.

3. Iron armoured ship, 6,710 tons, 2 x 8″ and 16 x 7″ guns. Built by Westwood and Baillie, Poplar. Launched 14.10.1863. Westwood and Baillie went bankrupt while building *Valiant*. Ship completed by Thames Ironworks in 1868. Never with the active fleet. For 17 years she lay in the south of Ireland, as Guardship of First Reserve. 1885 Paid off. 1888 Harbour Service. 1897 Depot Ship. 1904 Renamed *Indus IV*. 1915 Storeship to Kite Balloon Section. 1919 Renamed *Valiant III*. 1924 Oil Hulk. 1926 Converted to a Floating Oil Pipe Terminal. 9.12.1956 Arrived Zeebrugge to be broken up.

4. Battleship, 27,500 tons, 8 x 15″ and 16 x 6″ guns; 4 x 21″ TT. Built by Fairfield, Govan, Glasgow. Launched 4.11.1914. 1916 Battle of Jutland. 1918 Present at surrender of the German Fleet. Between the Wars, mainly in the Mediterranean and Atlantic Fleets. 3.1941 Battle at Matapan. 5.1941 Whilst operating off Crete, was twice hit by bombs. 12.1941 Was damaged by "human torpedoes" at Alexandria. Ended her career as one of four ships forming *Imperieuse*, Stokers' Training Ship at Devonport. 19.3.1948 Sold. 16.8.1948 Arrived Cairn Ryan to be broken up.

Footnote
a) Lugger, 14 guns, was hired 1794-1801.
b) Third rate, 1,925 bm, 76 guns, was ordered from Plymouth Dockyard in 1826 but cancelled in 1832.
c) Yacht, 184 tons, built in 1893, was hired for auxiliary patrol duties from 18.11.1914 to 6.2.1919.

WAKEFUL

Patrol Vessel, ex-*Dan*, ex-*Herakles*, 900 tons. Built as a Tug for Swedish owners by Cochrane and Sons, Selby, Yorkshire, in 1965. Purchased by the RN in 1974, first for Fishery Protection duties in the North Sea and, in 1976, as a Submarine Support Ship in the Clyde.

Description of Badge

Field:- Black.
Badge:- An eye proper with rays issuing therefrom, gold.

Motto

Si dormiam capiar — Catch a weasel asleep.

Battle Honours

Atlantic	1939-40	North Sea	1944
Dunkirk	1940		

Previous ships of the name

1. ''V/W'' class destroyer, 1,100 tons, 4 x 4'' guns; 6 TT. Built by Willian Beardmore, Clydebank. Launched 6.10.1917. Spent latter part of WW1 on convoy and patrol duties. 1918 Baltic duty. 7.4.1920 Recommissioned at Rosyth. 13.4.1922 Recommissioned as a tender to *Defiance* at Devonport. 1.12.1925 Became a Tender to *Impregnable*, still at Devonport. 11.11.1926 Reduced to reserve at Devonport. 7.10.1930 Commissioned at Sheerness for 1st Destroyer Flotilla, Mediterranean. 18.6.1931 Reduced to Reserve at Chatham. 1931-5 Reserve Fleet, Nore. 1935 20th DF, Home Fleet. 1936-9 In Reserve at Chatham. 1940 Western Approaches. At Dunkirk, transported 600 troops safely back to Dover, but on second trip she met with disaster. On 29.5.1940 she was sunk by German MTBs. About 740 men were lost, only 40 soldiers and 10 naval personnel being picked up.

2. ''W'' class destroyer, 1,710 tons, 4 x 4.7'' and 4 x 40mm AA guns; 8 TT. Laid down by Fairfield, Govan, Glasgow, as *Zebra*. 1.1943 Renamed *Wakeful*. Launched 30.6.1943. Took part in 4 carrier strikes against *Tirpitz*. 1944 Helped beat off midget submarine attack on Scapa Flow. 9.1945 In Tokyo Bay, at the surrender of Japanese forces. 1.1946 At Portsmouth as CW Training Ship. 1948-51 At Rosyth. 1951-3 Converted to Type 15 frigate by Scotts, Greenock. 1953-7 Fifth FS in the Mediterranean. 1957-8 Converted at Portsmouth to a Radar and Navigational Training Ship. 1966-7 Fitted with experimental satellite terminal and stabilisers for trials. 5.5.1971 Arrived Inverkeithing to be broken up.

Footnote
Destroyer was laid down by Wm. Denny, Dumbarton, but was renamed *Zebra* in 1.1943 before being launched 8.3.1944.

HMS *Wakeful* (June 1950).

WALRUS

A ''Porpoise'' class Patrol Submarine, 1,610 tons (surfaced), 2,410 tons (submerged); 8 x 21"
TT. Built by Scotts, Greenock. Launched 22.9.1959.

Description of Badge

Field:- Blue.
Badge:- A walrus head, proper.

Motto

Cave dentes — Beware my tusks.

Battle Honours

None.

Previous ships of the name

1. ''V/W'' class destroyer, 1,100 tons, 4 x 4" guns; 6 TT. Built by Fairfield, Govan, Glasgow. Launched 27.12.1917. Later
fitted to carry mines. 5.2.1918 First Commissioned. 6.6.1924 Recommissioned at Devonport for 5th DF, Mediterranean.
15.11.1926 Paid off into Dockyard control at Sheerness. 5.4.1927 Commissioned at the Nore for the 1st DF in the
Mediterranean. 11.6.1929 Recommissioned at Devonport, again for the Mediterranean. 30.11.1932 Commissioned into
the Reserve at Devonport. 1934 Maintenance Reserve at Rosyth. 12.2.1938 While being towed from Rosyth to
Portsmouth, in a gale, the tow parted. The tug made for shelter but *Walrus*, with only shipkeepers on board, drifted
southwards to Filey Bay. When the tide turned she was driven up the coast to Scarborough where she drifted inshore,
and went aground. She could not be refloated, so the wreck was sold to Round Bros, Sunderland.

HMS *Walrus* (July 1979).

WARSPITE

A "Valiant" class nuclear powered Fleet Submarine, 4,300 tons (surfaced), 4,800 tons (submerged); 6 x 21" TT. Built by Vickers, Barrow-in-Furness. Launched 25.9.1965.

Description of Badge

Field:- Green.
Badge:- A ship's gun, gold.

Motto

Belli dura despicio — I despise the hard knocks of war.

Battle Honours

Cadiz	1596	Norway	1940
Orfordness	1666	Calabria	1940
Sole Bay	1672	Mediterranean	1940-3
Schooneveld	1673	Malta Convoys	1941
Texel	1673	Matapan	1941
Barfleur	1692	Crete	1941
Velez Malaga	1704	Sicily	1943
Marbella	1705	Salerno	1943
Lagos	1759	English Channel	1944
Quiberon Bay	1759	Normandy	1944
Jutland	1916	Walcheren	1944
Atlantic	1939	Biscay	1944
Narvik	1940		

Previous ships of the name

1. Galleon *War Sprite* or *Warspight*, 648 bm, 29 guns. Built in 1596. Flagship of Sir Walter Raleigh. 1635 Condemned but cut down and made into a Lighter for Harbour Service. 1649 Sold out of the service.

2. Third rate, 898 bm, 70 guns. Built by Johnson and Castle, Blackwall. Launched 8.6.1666. 1702 Rebuilt at Rotherhithe as 952 bm. 1706-9 Off Lisbon. 12.1710 With *Breda*, captured French *Maure*, 48 guns. 1712 In Ordinary, at Chatham. 2.1.1716 Renamed *Edinburgh*. 1721 Rebuilt at Chatham as 1,119 bm. 1744 Again rebuilt at Chatham as 1,286 bm, 64 guns. 12.1771 Broken up at Plymouth.

3. Third rate, 1,580 bm, 74 guns. Built at Deptford. Launched 8.4.1758. 1760 Cruising off Brest. 1763 In the Mediterranean. 1763-8 In Ordinary. 1778 Became a Signal Ship at Plymouth. 1800 Renamed *Arundel*. 1802 Broken up.

4. Third rate, 1,890 bm, 76 guns. Built in Chatham Dockyard. Launched 16.11.1807. 1808-12 In the Mediterranean. 1826 First line-of-battleship proper to circumnavigate the world. 1840 Reduced to 50 guns. 1843-6 In the Mediterranean. 27.3.1862 Lent to the Marine Society as a Training Ship. 3.1.1876 Burnt by accident at Woolwich. 2.2.1876 Wreck sold to McArthur and Co.

5. First rate *Waterloo*, 2,694 bm, 120 guns. Built in Chatham Dockyard. Launched 10.6.1833. 12.11.1859 Undocked as a steam ship. 1862 Renamed *Conqueror*. 11.8.1876 Renamed *Warspite* as a Training Ship for the Marine Society. 20.1.1918 Burnt in the Thames.

6. "Imperieuse" class armoured cruiser, 8,400 tons, 4 x 9.2" and 6 x 6" guns; 2 x 14" TT. Built in Chatham Dockyard. Launched 29.1.1884. 1888-90 Reserve. 1890-3 Pacific. 1893-6 Guardship at Queenstown. 1896-9 Refit and Reserve. 1899-1902 Pacific. 1902 Reserve. 4.4.1905 Sold to T.W. Ward, Preston, for breaking up.

7. "Astraea" class cruiser *Hermione*, 4,360 tons, 2 x 6" and 8 x 4.7" guns, 4 x 18" TT. Built in Devonport Dockyard. Launched 7.11.1893. 25.10.1921 Sold to Multilocular Sbkg. Co. 18.12.1922 Re-sold and renamed *Warspite*, Training Ship. 9.1940 Sold to T.W. Ward, for breaking up.

8. "Queen Elizabeth" class battleship, 27,500 tons, 8 x 15" and 16 x 6" guns; 4 x 21" TT. Built in Devonport Dockyard. Launched 26.11.1913. Highlights of her distinguished service in both World Wars included:- 1916 Badly damaged at Jutland; 1940 Battle of Narvik; 1941 Battle of Matapan in which she damaged 2 Italian cruisers; 6.1944 bombarding off the Norway coast. 12.7.1946 Sold to Metal Industries Ltd. 23.4.1947 Driven ashore in Prussia Cove, Cornwall, when being towed to the shipbreakers. Wreck re-sold to R.H. Bennett, Bristol.

WAVENEY

A "River" class Fleet Minesweeper, 890 tons (full load); 1 x 40mm gun. Built by Richards, Lowestoft. Launched 8.9.1983. Allocated to South Wales Division, RNR.

Description of Badge

Field:- Per fess red and black.
Badge:- A fess wavy white, charged with a bar wavy blue, overall on two feathers in saltire white, a leopard's face, gold.

(Derived from the Arms of the County Councils of Norfolk and Suffolk).

Motto

Ab intus jubeo — From within I command.

Battle Honours

Atlantic	1942-3	Normandy	1944
Biscay	1943	Burma	1945

Previous ships of the name

1. "River" or "E" class destroyer, 550 tons, 1 x 12 pdr and 5 x 6 pdr guns; 2 x 18" TT. Built by Hawthorn Leslie, Hebburn-on-Tyne. Launched 16.4.1903. 1905 Attached to *Halcyon* at Devonport. 1906 Attached to *Sapphire*, Flagship at Portland. 1907-12 Home Fleet. 10.2.1920 Sold to T.W. Ward, Grays, for breaking up.

2. "River" class frigate, 1,375 tons, 2 x 4" and 10 x 20mm guns. Built by Smith's Dock, Middlesborough. Launched 30.4.1942. Converted to a Landing Ship Headquarters. 1946-57 In Reserve. 9.11.1957 Sold to West of Scotland Shipbreaking, and arrived Troon to be broken up.

Footnote

a) Drifter, 58 tons, was hired as *Waveney II* in 1915. 27.10.1916 Sank after being damaged in action with German destroyers off Dover.

b) Castle type trawler, *James Connor*, 277 GRT. Built by Wm. Harkess & Son, Middlesborough. Launched 19.7.1917. 1920 Renamed *Waveney*. 1922 Sold to Spanish Navy as *Uad Mulliya*.

HMS *Waveney*

WILTON

A Coastal Minehunter, 450 tons (full load). Built of GRP by Vosper Thornycroft, Woolston, Southampton. The world's first major warship to be constructed of Glass Reinforced Plastic. Launched 18.1.1972. Fitted with the reconditioned machinery and equipment from *Derriton*.

Description of Badge

Field:- White.
Badge:- An eagle's head erased green, gorged with a chain pendant therefrom a bugle horn, gold.

Motto

Battle Honours

Arctic	1942	Aegean	1943
Malta Convoys	1942	Mediterranean	1944
North Africa	1942-3	Adriatic	1944
Sicily	1943	North Sea	1945

Previous ships of the name

1. "Hunt" class, Type 2, "Blankney" type, destroyer, 1,050 tons, 6 x 4" AA guns. Built by Yarrow, Scotstoun, Glasgow. Launched 17.10.1941. 5.1943 In action with German E-boats off North Africa. 1.1944 Engaged in assault on Anzio. 8.1945 to 1.1946 Refitting at Simonstown. 10.2.1946 Arrived Devonport; paid off into Reserve. 12.1949 Recommissioned for Fourth Training Flotilla, Rosyth. 1952 Again reduced to Reserve; then Headquarters Ship Reserve Fleet, South Wales. 30.11.1959 Arrived Faslane to be broken up.

HMS *Wilton*

YORK

A Batch Three, "Town" class, Type 42, Guided Missile Destroyer (stretched version), 4,775 tons (full load). Sea Dart SAM system; 1 x 4.5"; 2 x 20mm Oerlikons; helicopter-launched Sea Skua missiles; 6 TT; 1 helicopter. Built by Swan Hunter, Wallsend-on-Tyne. Launched 21.6.1982.

Description of Badge

Field:- Blue.
Badge:- A white rose with gold rays issuant.
(Derived from the Badge of the Royal House of York (Edward VI)).

Motto

Bon espoir — Good hope.
(The motto used by Edmund Langley, Duke of York, 1391).

Battle Honours

Lowestoft	1665	Louisburg	1758
Orfordness	1666	Martinique	1809
Sole Bay	1672	Atlantic	1939
Schooneveld	1673	Norway	1940
Texel	1673	Mediterranean	1940-1
Barfleur	1692	Malta Convoys	1941

Previous ships of the name

1. *Marston Moor*, 734 bm, 54 guns. Built in 1654 by Johnson, Blackwall. 1660 Renamed *York*. 24.11.1703 Wrecked on the Shipwash Sands, Harwich.

2. Fourth rate, 987 bm, 60 guns. Built in Plymouth Dockyard. Launched 17.4.1706. 1707-9 In the Mediterranean. 1738 Underwent "great repairs" at Plymouth. 18.10.1750 Surveyed in dock at Portsmouth; needed extensive repair. 25.10.1750 Admiralty directed she be used as a breakwater at Sheerness, but was not sunk there until 4.2.1751.

3. Fourth rate, 1,203 bm, 60 guns. Built in Plymouth Dockyard. Launched 10.11.1753. 1759-65 In the East Indies taking part in the abortive expedition against Mauritius (1761) and in the reduction of Manila (1762). 6.1772 Breaking up completed at Plymouth.

4. Brig-sloop *Betsy*, 12 guns. Purchased in North America on 29.3.1777 and renamed *York*. From 10.7.1778 to 23.8.1778 she was in French hands. 7.1779 Finally captured by a French squadron at Grenada, West Indies.

5. East Indiaman *Royal Admiral* purchased whilst being built by Barnard, Deptford. Renamed *York*. Launched 24.3.1796, as a Third rate, 1,433 bm, 64 guns. Missing from 26.12.1803. 1.1804 Believed foundered in the North sea.

6. Third rate, 1,743 bm, 74 guns. Built by Brent, Rotherhithe. Launched 7.7.1807. 11.1819 Became a Convict Hulk at Portsmouth. 3.1854 Broken up at Portsmouth.

7. Name ship of class of cruiser, 8,250 tons, 6 x 8" and 4 x 4" AA guns; 6 x 21" TT. Built by Palmer, Jarrow-on-Tyne. Launched 17.7.1928. 1930 2nd CS, Home Fleet. 1933-4 Refit at Chatham. 1934-7 8th CS, America and West Indies. 4.1940 Conveyed troops to Norway. From 5. to 7.1940 At Rosyth. 8.1940 To the Mediterranean. 10.1940 Among first ships to convoy troops to Crete following German invasion of Greece. Later supported British advance in Libya. 26.3.1941 Hit by an Italian explosive motor boat and had to be beached in Suda Bay to avoid sinking. Suffered further damage by air attack and had to be abandoned on 22.5.1941. 2.1952 Her hulk arrived at Bari to be broken up.

Footnote

a) Storeship, 664 bm, 14 guns. Purchased 24.3.1779. 28.1.1781 Paid off at Bombay and sold out of the service.
b) Ship, 1,132 tons, built in 1907, was hired from 3.1.1915 to 4.4.1919 as an Armed Boarding Steamer with 1 x 4" and 2 x 12 pdr guns.

COASTAL MINESWEEPERS

This badge was worn by the majority of the "Ton" class Coastal Minesweepers.

Description of Badge

Field:- Barry wavy of ten, white and blue.

Badge:- Two keys, wards downwards, gold, surmounted by a naval mine with chain downwards, proper.

(The keys refer to one of the functions of the CMSs, i.e. to "unlock" (by sweeping) channels for shipping).

The 118 vessels of the "Ton" class Coastal Minesweepers, 440 tons (full load), 1 x 40mm and 2 x 20mm guns,—named after villages in the UK—were built between 1953-60, mainly as a result of lessons learned during the Korean War. They replaced the wooden motor minesweepers built during the Second World War, with J.I. Thornycroft, Woolston, Southampton, being the 'lead' yard for their construction. On completion, half of them were placed in Reserve.

Between 1954-72 some two dozen were renamed for RNR Training, and between 1963-9 a number were converted to Minehunters. Furthermore, the following sales or transfers took place:- Argentina (6 in 1968), Australia (6 in 1962), Ghana (1 in 1964), India (4 in 1956), Ireland (3 in 1971), Malaysia (7 in 1960-8), and South Africa (10 in 1958-9).

HMS *Burnaston*

INDEX

HMS *London*, contractors sea trials 1986.